The Pattern Companion:
Knitting

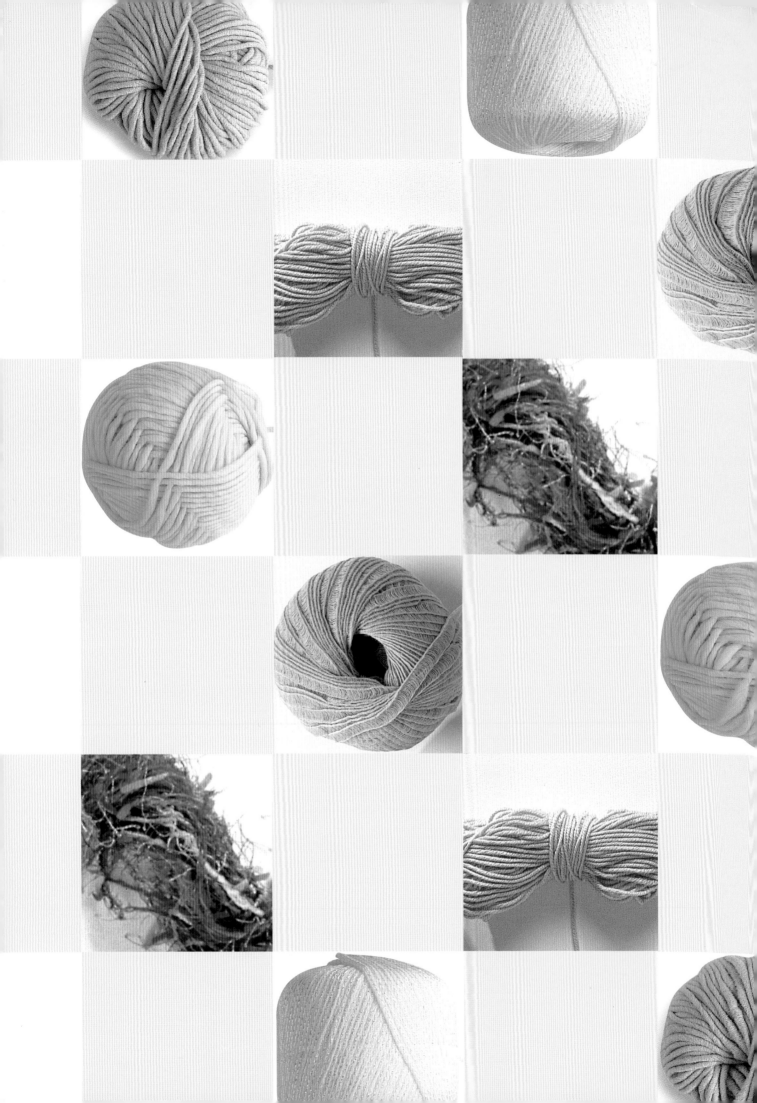

The Pattern Companion: Knitting

Sterling Publishing Co., Inc.
New York

Library of Congress Cataloging-in-Publication Data Available

2   4   6   8   10   9   7   5   3

Material in this collection was adapted from:
 The Weekend Crafter®: Knitting, by Catherine Ham © 2003, Catherine Ham
25 Gorgeous Sweaters for the Brand New Knitter, by Catherine Ham © 2000, Lark Books
Knitting Simple Sweaters from Luxurious Yarns, by Marilyn Saitz Cohen © 2003, Marilyn Saitz Cohen
Knitting Beautiful Classics, by Kristin Nicholas © 1997, Classic Elite Yarns
Knitting Fair Isle Mittens & Gloves, by Carol Rasmussen Noble © 2002, Carol Rasmussen Noble
7-Day Afghans, by Jean Leinhauser & Rita Weiss © 1985, Jean Leinhauser & Rita Weiss
Nursery Rhyme Knits, by Teresa Boyer © 2003, Teresa Boyer
Detailed rights information on page 191.

Edited by Cassia B. Farkas
Book design by Liz Trovato
Cover design by Alan Carr

Published by Sterling Publishing Co., Inc.
387 Park Avenue South, New York, NY 10016
© 2004, Sterling Publishing Co., Inc.
Distributed in Canada by Sterling Publishing
c/o Canadian Manda Group, 165 Dufferin Street
Toronto, Ontario, Canada M6K 3H6
Distributed in Great Britain by Chrysalis Books Group PLC
The Chrysalis Building, Bramley Road, London W10 6SP, England
Distributed in Australia by Capricorn Link (Australia) Pty. Ltd.
P.O. Box 704, Windsor, NSW 2756, Australia

Printed in China

Sterling ISBN 1-4027-1270-7

Contents

Introduction

You already know how to knit. You don't need a book with half of the pages filled with photos or diagrams of fingertips and needles working strands of yarn. You have been knitting since you can remember, or maybe you just learned, and already have a collection of "How-to" knitting books. Now you are looking for projects, inspirations, and challenges—and that is exactly what you will find in the following pages. Here you will find items simple enough for a new knitter, or for a veteran to whip up in a day—or even an hour. You will also find challenging stitch combinations and designs to knit, whether in multiple cable, Fair Isle, or knitted lace.

The materials listed for each project are guidelines. Since brands of yarn change with fashion and season, yarns are listed here generically by weight and/or type, and needle sizes are given accordingly. However, with the measurement templates that are included, those of you feeling venturesome have the ability to adapt any of the patterns to a different yarn and needle size, as long as you are willing and confident enough to make test swatches and figure new stitch counts with the help of a calculator and a sheet of graph paper.

Imperative to the success of any project is to knit test swatches. This can never be stressed enough, whether you follow a pattern exactly or make your own adaptations, have only knitted a few items, or have made so many you lost count years ago. Knit up at least one 4 (10 cm)-square test swatch with your chosen yarn and needles. If a pattern stitch will be involved, make a swatch in the pattern, too, as it will measure differently from a swatch in simple Stockinette stitch. If you have more stitches than the number specified in the pattern, increase the needle size you are using; if you have fewer, decrease the needle size.

For brevity and clarity, the text for all the patterns uses the accepted abbreviations of knitting notation. For your reference, you will find all those in the book listed on p.14 at the end of this introductory section. There are also tables of needle sizes and yarn gauges.

Because of the wide range of techniques represented, some quick refreshers have been included of some of the more complex ones.

Quick Refresher on Working from Charts

Many of the designs in this book include charts, either for colorwork or for textured stitchery, such as knit-and-purl combinations or cables. Charts for knitting can look intimidating, but once you understand how they work, they will become second nature. Keep in mind that charts show the right side of the fabric only. When you are knitting back and forth on straight needles (as for almost all the sweaters in this book), both right and wrong sides of the fabric need to be worked. When working on the right side of the fabric, follow the chart from right to left. When working on the wrong side, read it from left to right.

Near each chart is a key that gives the knitting motion you are to perform for each symbol. On the right side, work the stitches as they appear on the chart. On the wrong side, work the opposite of how the stitch appears on the chart. For instance, if the chart shows a knit stitch on the right side, purl the stitch on the wrong side. You can usually see how a stitch should be worked on the wrong side by how it appears in the photo of the knitted piece. If it looks like a purl stitch, it should be purled; if it looks like a knit stitch, it should be knit. If a difficult, manipulative stitch is done on the wrong side, specific instructions will be stated in the symbol key.

Starting and ending points are noted for each size at the bottom and sides of most charts. Sometimes the rows are numbered, and the instructions may denote the stitch or row with which you should begin. When beginning and ending according to a chart, it's imperative that you start and end at the same stitch on each row for the same side of the fabric. When shaping for armholes and necklines, these points will change as the decreases progress. To make it easier to keep track of where you are on the pattern, you can draw the chart on graph paper and mark the shaping details. After you become familiar with a pattern, you will automatically sense how to continue it while doing the shaping.

Quick Refresher on Fair Isle Knitting

Many of the designs for multicolored garments in this book are knit using the Fair Isle technique, a traditional form of knitting that uses two different colors of yarn in each row to produce a patterned fabric. The color not being used is stranded behind the work and picked up later. This method produces a warm fabric that is thicker than regular knitting because the carried yarn adds extra bulk. Common Fair Isle motifs include geometric shapes, florals, small pattern repeats, and animals. Fair Isle knitting is reminiscent of Scandinavia, the Scottish Shetland Isles, and Iceland, although most cultures with a knitting history practice Fair Isle knitting.

The illustrations here show how to work Fair Isle in either right- or left-handed knitting. If you plan to do a lot of Fair Isle knitting, it's highly recommended that you learn both left- and right-handed knitting. Then you can combine both methods, using each hand for a different color.

To work in Fair Isle successfully, it's necessary not only to work the colors into the row, but you must also obtain the proper tension with the floating yarn. A puckered, uneven fabric usually results from carrying the unused yarn too tightly behind the work. To produce the correct tension, stretch out the stitches on the right-hand needle after they are knit. Then stretch out the next color of yarn behind the knitting so that it will lie flat when the piece is off the needles.

If a pattern skips more than five stitches, the floating color should be caught into the work to avoid long, messy floats. To do this, pull the unused yarn close to the fabric and knit the next stitch around the unused color to hold it flat. Make sure to maintain proper tension.

Some knitters like the back of the fabric to look even and neat, and they weave the floating yarn into the back side of the work. This is done by laying the unused color between the active yarn and the back of the fabric. This catches the yarn and prevents any floats. The resulting fabric is neat on the wrong side but won't drape very well; it's suitable for jackets where a stiff fabric is desired.

Wool yarns are the most forgiving of fibers and are highly recommended for knitters who are attempting Fair Isle for the first time. When Fair Isle work comes off the needles, it often looks lumpy, even when completed by the most experienced of knitters. You can flatten the fabric either by washing and laying it flat to dry or by steaming it. Steaming will not, however, flatten out stitches that don't have the proper amount of float on the wrong side. Many experienced knitters have a sweater or two, made when they were just beginning Fair Isle, that won't fit anyone! The mark of a real expert knitter is a Fair Isle sweater knit in a fine gauge cotton; cotton cannot be steamed to correct unevenness!

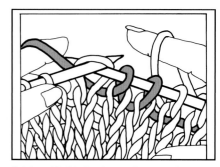
Knitting with right hand, stranding with left

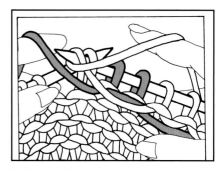
Purling with right hand, stranding with left

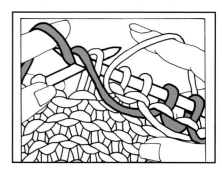
Knitting with left hand, stranding with right

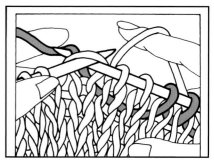
Purling with left hand, stranding with right

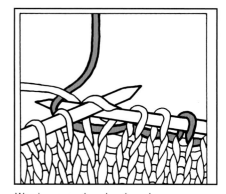
Weaving yarns when changing colors on knit rows

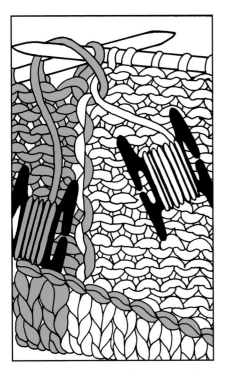

Using bobbins for intarsia knitting

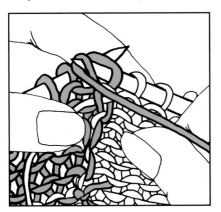

Intarsia knitting with long strands

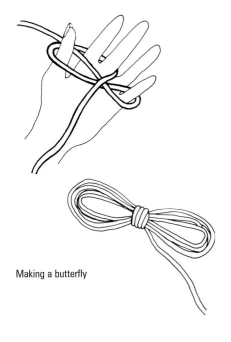

Making a butterfly

Quick Refresher on Intarsia Knitting

Intarsia knitting is sometimes called picture knitting, because blocks of color are worked in one color over a large space to result in an overall motif or shape. Unlike Fair Isle knitting, the yarn not being used is not carried across the back of the fabric. Instead, different colors of yarn are held in bobbins behind the work and picked up when specified on a chart. Intarsia knitting highly resembles the tapestry method of weaving. The most difficult part of intarsia knitting is the joining of the two colors. This makes a fabric that is not bulky or heavy. It also uses less yarn than Fair Isle knitting.

To work intarsia knitting, follow the chart given, and where indicated, change the color. Work the specified number of stitches in the first color; then join the second color by twisting the new color around the stitch just knit and continue with the second color. Continue the piece, twisting the yarns around each other every row to form a join. When the piece is completed, it may be necessary to even out the joins by picking the stitches loose with a tapestry needle. Sometimes holes result where the yarns were not wrapped around each other neatly. To correct them, pull the loose stitch to the wrong side and take a stitch with an extra piece of yarn of the same color.

Bobbins can be purchased to hold the various colors to be worked in intarsia, but a money-saving technique borrowed from tapestry weavers can easily be employed to produce butterflies for intarsia knitting. Leaving a 5- to 6-inch (12.5 to 15 cm) tail of yarn between your ring and middle fingers, wrap the yarn in a figure eight around your thumb and little finger until you have the needed amount. Remove the butterfly from your fingers and wrap the end still connected to the ball of yarn five or six times tightly around the middle of the butterfly. Cut the yarn and end it off by tucking the loose yarn under the tightly wrapped yarn. Begin knitting from the end that was held between your fingers.

In the 1980s Kaffe Fassett, an American artist who lives in London, began working in knitwear. Kaffe made popular the intarsia method of knitting by designing knitwear with many small sections of different colors. His preferred method for holding the yarn behind his knitting is to work with short strands of yarn that are not wound. Colors can be added more freely to result in a painterly fabric, and the yarn can be untangled with relative ease because the strands are short.

As with any technique, each knitter should choose the method that is easiest. Combinations of techniques can be used to develop efficient work methods.

Quick Refresher on Duplicate Stitch

Duplicate stitch, sometimes called Swiss darning, is an embellishing technique that is applied to pieces after knitting is completed. Similar to embroidery, it is primarily used to add colors that aren't easily included while knitting. When applied to plain pieces of Stockinette stitch knitting, duplicate stitch resembles intarsia knitting.

This technique requires a little practice, but its uses are endless. Small flowers, animals, and many other motifs can be done in duplicate stitch, and Fair Isle patterning, which uses only two colors in each row, can also be enhanced with duplicate stitch. Similarly, large blocks of intarsia knitting can be made more complex by adding colors in duplicate stitch.

Working duplicate stitch is actually tracing an existing knit stitch. It is important to cover the entire original stitch with the new color to give a neat

presentation. Work with a large, blunt needle, because sharp needles tend to split the stitch and are more difficult to handle. You can avoid tangles and knots by using a relatively short piece of yarn—about 1 yard (91.5 m)—while you work.

To begin, take one or two small stitches on the wrong side of the fabric, leaving a tail of about 1 inch (2.5 cm). Bring the needle up through the center of the base of the stitch; then, following the stitch, put the needle under the two strands at the top of the stitch and pull the yarn through. Complete the stitch by inserting the needle next to the starting point at the base of the stitch. If only one stitch is to be covered, pull the needle to the wrong side; when covering a large block of stitches, push the needle through the base of the next stitch and pull it to the right side. After making each stitch, it's advisable to smooth it with your fingers to relax the tension and make the added yarn entirely cover the original stitch.

Duplicate stitch works best when applied horizontally or diagonally. If you work it vertically up the center of a series of stitches, it has a tendency to sink into the fabric and disappear.

Quick Refresher on Making Cables

Cables have become an inherent part of the knitwear scene. Although they look complicated, they're actually quite simple, and once the concept of a cable is learned, the variations are endless. A cable is made by crossing one group of specified stitches over another with the help of an extra needle called a cable needle. A cable needle is U-shaped and pointed at both ends. You can also use a short double-pointed needle or a tapestry needle for working cables.

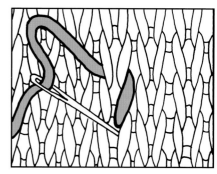

Adding duplicate stitch

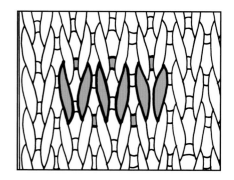

FRONT-CROSS CABLE

KEY

☐ = Knit on RS, purl on WS

☐ = Purl on RS, knit on WS

TWO OVER TWO
FOUR-STITCH CABLE

BACK-CROSS CABLE

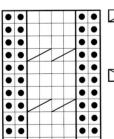

KEY

⬓ = Sl 2 sts on cn and hold in back, k2, k2 from cn

⬓ = Sl 2 sts on cn and hold in front, k2, k2 from cn

TWO OVER TWO
FOUR-STITCH CABLE

To form a cable, you cross a group of stitches either to the right or to the left; to work a four-stitch cable that crosses to the left, slip two stitches to a cable needle and hold them in front of the work, hold the yard firmly and knit the next two stitches on the left-hand needle; then knit the two stitches that are on the cable needle. This is called a front-crossing cable because the stitches are held in front of the work.

To work a four-stitch cable that crosses to the right, slip two stitches to a cable needle and hold them in back of the work, hold the yarn firmly and knit the next two stitches on the left-hand needle; then knit the two stitches that are on the cable needle. This is called a back-crossing cable.

Cables can be worked to form diamonds, ribs, chevrons, diagonal lines and more. Their size can be varied just by the number of stitches worked. In general, the more stitches that are crossed, the more the fabric will compress, producing a denser piece of knitwear. Although many cables are worked on a ground of reverse Stockinette stitch (the purl side of the fabric faces outward), textured stitches, such as seed or garter stitch, can be inserted between them to create more interest.

Many of the instructions for the cabled designs shown in this book are given in chart form. This is a very easy way to describe cables because the charts themselves resemble the cable produced, and each pattern follows a repetition. The charts here show a front- and a back-crossing cable. Keep in mind that the charts show only the right side of the fabric. Follow the chart from right to left for the right side of the fabric and from left to right for the wrong side.

Quick Refresher on Making Bobbles

Adding bobbles is a great way to give texture to your knits. They are easy to make and can be done in many sizes for different effects. In general, bobbles are made by increasing a series of stitches into a designated stitch, working this as a separate piece, then decreasing again.

To make a five-stitch bobble:

■ Make five stitches in one stitch. Without slipping any stitches off the needle, knit into the front loop of the stitch, then into the back loop; repeat this sequence once more, then knit into the front loop one more time. Now slip the stitches from the left needle. The increases can also be made by working a yarn over (yo) instead of knitting into the front and back of the stitch. This increase would be worked as [k1, yo, k1, yo, k1] into one stitch.

■ Turn the work and purl these five stitches; turn the work and knit these five stitches. Repeat this sequence once more.

■ Using the left needle, slip the second, third, fourth, and fifth stitches—one at a time—over the first stitch and off the right needle. This completes the bobble.

The bobble can be made larger by using more stitches to increase the designated one. Because small increases can have noticeable effects, experiment first by increasing the number by two or three stitches instead of four. Similarly, you can increase the number of rows that are worked on the bobble. The more rows that are worked, the larger the bobble will be.

Bobbles can add interest to any knitter's repertoire. They may be worked in reverse Stockinette stitch or inserted into a cable pattern to add extra texture. A textured pattern can be created by placing bobbles in a geometric pattern. Bobbles that are worked in contrasting colors are very intriguing.

Terms and Abbreviations

★	repeat from ★ as many times as indicated	k	knit	ssk	slip 1 st as if to knit, slip next st as if to knit, then insert the tip of the left-hand needle into the fronts of these same 2 sts and k them tog from this position.
()	alternate measurement(s)/ stitch counts	k2tog	knit two sts together		
alt	alternate	kg	kilogram		
approx	approximately	lb	pound		
beg	begin or beginning	m	meter(s)	st(s)	stitch(es)
bet	between	MC	main color	St st	Stockinette stitch: k on RS; p on WS
BO	bind (bound) off	meas	measures		
c4b	cable 4 to the back: sl nxt 2 sts onto cn and hold in back of work, k2 sts from left-hand needle, then k sts from the cn.	mm	millimeter(s)	t2l	twist 2 sts to left: taking needle behind work, k in back loop of 2nd st on left-hand needle, k in front of first st; sl both sts off needle
		nxt	next		
		oz	ounces		
		patt	pattern		
		p	purl		
		PM	place marker		
c4f	cable 4 to the front: sl nxt 2 sts onto cn and hold in front of work, k2 sts from left-hand needle, then k sts from the cn.	psso	pass slipped stitch over		
		pu	pick up	t2r	twist 2 sts to right: k2tog, leaving sts on needle, insert right-hand needle between sts just worked and k first st again; sl both sts from needle
		rem	remain or remaining		
		rep	repeat		
		ret	return		
CC	contrast color	rev	reverse		
cm	centimeter(s)	rnd	round		
cn	cable needle	RS (R)	right side (row)	tbl	through back of loop(s)
CO	cast on	RSS	Reverse Stockinette stitch: p on RS; k on WS		
cont	continued or continuing			tog	together
dec	decrease or decreasing	SC	single crochet	WS(R)	wrong side (row)
dpn	double pointed needle(s)	sl	slip	yds	yards
est	established	slip-stitch	insert crochet hook in st; yo hook from back to front; draw loop through st and through loop on hook	yo	yarn over (UK: yfd—yarn forward; yrn—yarn round needle)
g	gram				
inc	increase or increasing				
incl	include or including				

Yarn Gauges

Yarn	Needles	Stitches per 4"/10 cm
Fine Weight (Baby and Fingering yarns)	0, 1, 2	29–32
Lightweight (Sport, sock, and 4-ply yarns)	2, 3, 4	25–28
Medium Weight (Worsted yarn)	5, 6, 7	21–24
Medium-Heavy Weight (Heavy worsted or Aran)	8, 9, 10	17–20
Bulky Weight (Chunky yarn)	10 1/2, 11, 13	13–16
Extra-Bulky Weight	11, 13, 15	9–12

Knitting Needles

US	Metric	UK	US	Metric	UK
0	2 mm	14	7	4.5 mm	7
1	2.25 mm	13	8	5 mm	6
	2.5 mm		9	5 mm	5
2	2.75 mm	12	10	6 mm	4
	3 mm	11	10 1/2	6.5 mm	3
3	3.25 mm	10		7 mm	2
4	3.5 mm			7.5 mm	1
5	3.75 mm	9	11	8 mm	0
	4 mm	8	13	9 mm	00
6			15	10 mm	000

Women's Sweater Patterns

Crop Top

SIZES

Extra small (small, medium, large)

FINISHED MEASUREMENTS

Bust: 34 (36, 38, 40) inches (86, 91, 96.5, 102 cm)

Length: 17 (17½, 18½, 19) inches (43, 44.5, 47, 48 cm)

MATERIALS

Bulky smooth yarn (1¾ oz [50 g] = 55 yds [50 m]) 6 (6, 7, 8) balls

Note: Choose a smooth yarn, so the eyelet pattern is shown to advantage. A highly textured yarn will obscure the pattern stitch.

14" knitting needles, size 10½ (6.5 mm), or size necessary to achieve correct gauge

One size 11 needle

Crochet hook in size K/10½ (6.5 mm)

GAUGE

13 sts = 4" (10 cm)

PATTERN STITCH

Row 1: (k2, yo, k2tog) to end of row, k2.

Rows 2-6: work in St st.

BACK

CO 54 (58, 62, 66) sts, and work 4 rows in St st. With the RS facing, work the 6-row pattern st a total of 5 times for all sizes; cont in St st until the piece measures 10 (10, 10½, 10½)" (25, 25, 27, 27 cm) from the beg (adjust length here, if needed), ending with a WS row.

ARMHOLE SHAPING

BO 5 (5, 6, 6) sts at the beg of the next 2 rows (44, 48, 50, 54) sts.

Next row: (RS facing) k1, ssk, knit to last 3 sts, k2tog, k1.

Next row: k1, purl to last st, k1. Repeat these 2 rows until 36 (38, 40, 44) sts rem.

Work even in St st, remembering to knit the first and last st of every row, until the work measures 15 (15½, 16, 16½)" (38, 39, 41, 42 cm) from the beg, ending with a WS row.

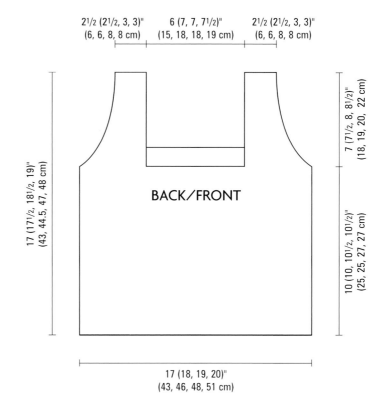

2½ (2½, 3, 3)" (6, 6, 8, 8 cm)   6 (7, 7, 7½)" (15, 18, 18, 19 cm)   2½ (2½, 3, 3)" (6, 6, 8, 8 cm)

7 (7½, 8, 8½)" (18, 19, 20, 22 cm)

17 (17½, 18½, 19)" (43, 44.5, 47, 48 cm)

BACK/FRONT

10 (10, 10½, 10½)" (25, 25, 27, 27 cm)

17 (18, 19, 20)" (43, 46, 48, 51 cm)

BACK NECK AND SHOULDER SHAPING

k1, p6 (6, 7, 8), k22 (24, 24, 26), p6 (6, 7, 8), k1.

Next row: k8 (8, 9, 10), place these sts on a holder, BO the center 20 (22, 22, 24) sts, k8 (8, 9, 10).

Continue working the shoulder on these 8 (8, 9, 10) sts, knitting the first and last st of each row, until the piece measures 17 (18, 19, 20)" (43, 46, 48, 51 cm) from the beg. Place the sts on a holder, and return to the unfinished shoulder sts. Work to match the first shoulder, leaving the sts on a holder when they're completed.

FRONT

Work as given for the back until the piece measures 14 (14½, 15, 15½)" (36, 37, 38, 39 cm) from the beg.

FRONT NECK AND SHOULDER SHAPING

Work shaping as given for the back until the piece matches the back in length from the beg. Place the shoulder sts on holders as before.

FINISHING

Place the right front and back shoulder sts back on the size 10½ needles. Holding RS together, use the size 11 needle to work 3-needle BO: knit through both first sts of front and back shoulder; ★ knit through both second sts, pass first st over second, rep from ★ across shoulder. Rep process for left shoulder.

Sew side seams, and darn in any yarn ends. Crochet one round in sc, RS facing, on neck and armholes, if necessary.

Block by spraying top lightly with water. Pat to measurements on flat surface to dry.

Tailored Vest

SIZES
Small (medium, large, extra large)

FINISHED MEASUREMENTS
Bust: 37 (40, 43, 48) inches (94, 102, 109, 122 cm)

Length: 23½ (24, 25, 25½) inches (60, 61, 63.5, 65 cm)

MATERIALS
Softly brushed or mohair type heavy-weight yarn (1¾ oz [50 g] = 93 yds [84 m]): 4 (5, 5, 6) balls

14" knitting needles, sizes 10 and 11 (6 and 7 mm), or size necessary to achieve correct gauge

5 buttons

GAUGE
11 sts = 4" (10 cm)

2.75 sts = 1" (2.5 cm)

STITCH PATTERNS

Garter stitch: Knit every row.

Reverse Stockinette stitch: Row 1: Purl (RS), Row 2: Knit (WS).

BACK

Using the smaller needles, CO 52 (54, 60, 66) sts, and knit 8 rows (4 Garter st ridges). Change to larger needles, work in rev St st until the piece measures 14½ (14½, 15, 15½)" (37, 37, 38, 39 cm) from beg, ending with a knit row.

★ Next row (RS): k8 (8, 9, 9) sts, p to the last 8 (8, 9, 9) sts, and k to end.

Next row: knit. Rep from ★ once more.

Armhole shaping: With RS facing, BO 5 (5, 6, 6) sts, k3, p to the last 8 (8, 9, 9) sts, k to the end. Next row: BO 5 (5, 6, 6) sts, and k to the end. Continue working 42 (44, 48, 54) sts in rev St st, keeping 3 sts in Garter st at the armhole edges, until the back measures 23½ (24, 25, 25½)" (60, 61, 63.5, 65 cm) from the beg. BO all sts.

LEFT FRONT

With smaller needles, CO 31 (32, 35, 38) sts, and k 8 rows (4 Garter st ridges). Change to larger needles, and k 1 row. Next row, RS facing, p to the last 5 sts, k5. Cont working in rev St st, keeping 5 sts in Garter st at the left front edge until the piece matches the back to the start of underarm shaping.

Armhole shaping: With the RS facing, BO 5 (5, 6, 6) sts, k3, p to the last 5 sts, k5. Next row: knit. Beg dec for the neck shaping: k3, p to the last 7 sts, p2tog, k5. Cont

to dec 1 st at the neck edge every 4 rows until 19 (20, 22, 22) sts rem, remembering to keep 5 sts in Garter st at neck edge and 3 sts at armhole edge for the bands. Work even until the front matches the back in length to the shoulder. Starting at arm edge, BO 14 (15, 17, 17) sts, and cont in Garter st on rem 5 sts until the neckband is long enough to fit to the center back neck. Place sts on a holder.

Mark positions of the buttons on left front band, placing the first ½" (1.5 cm) from bottom and last ½" (1.5 cm) below start of neck shaping. Space rest of markers evenly in between by counting the number of garter st ridges.

RIGHT FRONT

Knit as for left front, reversing all shapings; work buttonholes (k 2 tog, yo) to correspond with button markers.

FINISHING

Join shoulder seams; adjust length of the Garter st borders to meet at center back neck, and join them by weaving them together or with a 3-needle BO (see Finishing on page 17). Sew the border neatly in place along the back neck edge. Sew side seams. Sew on the buttons. Block the vest lightly.

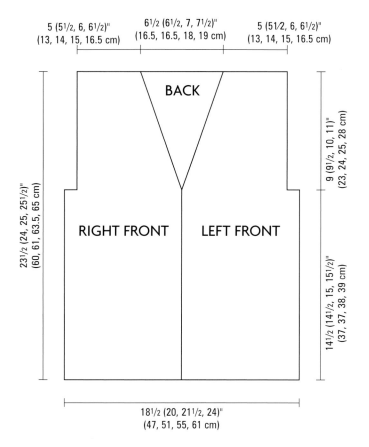

5 (5½, 6, 6½)" (13, 14, 15, 16.5 cm)   6½ (6½, 7, 7½)" (16.5, 16.5, 18, 19 cm)   5 (5½, 6, 6½)" (13, 14, 15, 16.5 cm)

BACK

RIGHT FRONT   LEFT FRONT

9 (9½, 10, 11)" (23, 24, 25, 28 cm)

23½ (24, 25, 25½)" (60, 61, 63.5, 65 cm)

14½ (14½, 15, 15½)" (37, 37, 38, 39 cm)

18½ (20, 21½, 24)" (47, 51, 55, 61 cm)

Weekend Favorite

SIZES
Small (medium, large, extra large)

FINISHED MEASUREMENTS
Bust: 39 (41, 45, 49)" (99, 104, 114, 124.5 cm)

Length: 23½ (24, 25, 26½)" (60, 61, 63.5, 67 cm)

Sleeve length: 16½ (17, 17½, 17½)" (42, 43, 44.5, 44.5 cm)

MATERIALS
Bulky weight yarn, (1¾ oz [50 g] = 60 yds [54 m]) 10 (11, 12, 14) balls

14" knitting needles, sizes 10 and 11 (6 and 8 mm), or size necessary to achieve correct gauge

GAUGE
2.5 sts = 1" (2.5 cm)

BACK
With smaller needles, CO 50 (50, 54, 62) sts, and establish the rib pattern as follows:

Row 1: k4, p1, work (k3, p1) to last st, k1.

Row 2: k2, work (p3, k1) to end of row.

Repeat these two rows for a total of 4 inches (10 cm).

Change to larger needles and work in St st, inc 1 st at each end of the first row for the 2nd and 3rd sizes only for (50, 52, 56, 62) sts, until the piece measures 23 (23½, 24½, 26)" (58, 60, 62, 66 cm).

With RS facing, knit 18 (19, 20, 22) sts. Place rem sts on a holder. Purl 1 row. Dec 1 st at the neck edge on next row (17, 18, 19, 21) sts. Cont in St st until back measures 23½ (24, 25, 26½)" (60, 61, 63.5, 67 cm) from the beg. BO shoulder sts.

Rejoin yarn to sts on holder. Knit across 14 (14, 16, 18) sts, and place on a holder for center back neck. Cont working on the rem sts, and complete as for the first side, reversing shapings.

FRONT
Work as for back until piece meas 20 (21, 22, 23)" (51, 53, 56, 58 cm).

Neck shaping: With RS facing, knit 20 (21, 22, 24), and place the rest of the sts on a holder. Dec 1 st at neck edge every other row until 17 (18, 19, 21) sts remain. Work even until the front matches the back in length. BO shoulder sts. Return to sts on holder, knit across 10 (10, 12, 14) sts, and place these on the holder for the center front neck.

Work on rem sts, and complete shoulder to match first side, reversing shapings.

SLEEVES
Using smaller needles, CO 22 (22, 26, 26) sts, work in rib pattern for 3 inches (8 cm). Change to larger needles and work in St st, inc 1 st

on each side every 4 rows until there are 46 (48, 50, 56) sts on the needle. Cont until sleeve measures 16½ (17, 17½, 17½)" (42, 43, 44.5, 44.5 cm). Adjust length, if necessary. BO all sts loosely.

FINISHING

Block the pieces lightly. Seam front and back together at one shoulder. Place markers 9 (9½, 10, 11)" (23, 24, 25, 28 cm) down from the shoulders for underarms on the back and front.

NECKBAND

Using smaller needles, with RS facing, pu and knit 50 (50, 54, 58) sts evenly around neck, including sts on holders. Work in the rib pattern for 1½ inches (4 cm). BO loosely.

Seam the rem shoulder and neckband sts. Sew sleeves in place between markers. Sew up side and sleeve seams, taking care to match seams at the ribbed bands. Darn in any loose ends.

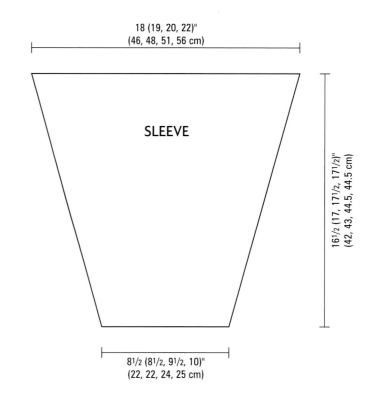

18 (19, 20, 22)"
(46, 48, 51, 56 cm)

SLEEVE

16½ (17, 17½, 17½)"
(42, 43, 44.5, 44.5 cm)

8½ (8½, 9½, 10)"
(22, 22, 24, 25 cm)

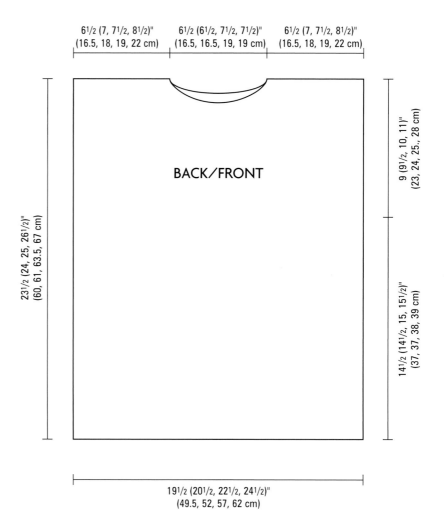

6½ (7, 7½, 8½)"
(16.5, 18, 19, 22 cm)

6½ (6½, 7½, 7½)"
(16.5, 16.5, 19, 19 cm)

6½ (7, 7½, 8½)"
(16.5, 18, 19, 22 cm)

9 (9½, 10, 11)"
(23, 24, 25,, 28 cm)

BACK/FRONT

23½ (24, 25, 26½)"
(60, 61, 63.5, 67 cm)

14½ (14½, 15, 15½)"
(37, 37, 38, 39 cm)

19½ (20½, 22½, 24½)"
(49.5, 52, 57, 62 cm)

Dress-up Tank Top

SIZES

Small (medium, large)

FINISHED MEASUREMENTS

32 (34, 36)" (81.5, 86.5, 91.5 cm)

MATERIALS

Bulky weight polyester ribbon yarn, ¼" (.25 cm) wide, (shown with unfinished edges that fray subtly so tiny threads appear throughout the fabric as part of the design). Approx. 330 (385, 440) yds (302, 352, 402.5 m)

14" knitting needles, size 13 (9 mm), or size needed to obtain gauge.

Crochet hook size H

Tapestry needle for sewing seams

GAUGE

13 sts and 14 rows = 4 inches (10 cm) square

PATTERN STITCH

Stockinette (St st): Row 1: Knit (RS), Row 2: Purl (WS).

BACK

CO 56 (58, 62) sts; work in St st until piece measures 12 (12½, 13)" (30.5, 32, 33 cm).

Armhole shaping: BO 3 (3, 4) sts at beg of next 2 rows; BO 2 sts at beg of following 2 rows; dec 1 st at beg and end of every other row 4 (4, 5) times, leaving 38 (40, 40) sts. Work even until piece measures 3 (3½, 4)" (7.5, 9, 10 cm) from beg of armhole shaping.

Neck shaping: k14 (14, 13), join 2nd ball of yarn, BO 10 (12, 14) sts, k14 (14, 13). At each neck edge, dec 1 st every other row, until back measures 20 (21, 22) inches (51, 53.5, 56 cm); BO all rem sts.

FRONT

Work same as back.

FINISHING

Sew seams. With WS facing and crochet hook H, work slip stitch around neck, armholes, and bottom edges. Steam carefully on WS for softer, flatter finish and to keep edges from rolling.

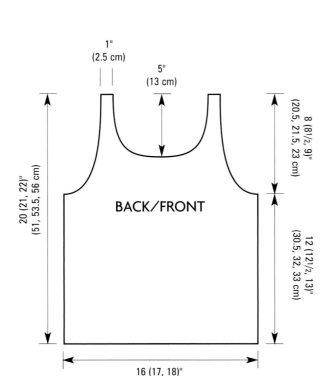

1"
(2.5 cm)

5"
(13 cm)

8 (8½, 9)"
(20.5, 21.5, 23 cm)

20 (21, 22)"
(51, 53.5, 56 cm)

BACK/FRONT

12 (12½, 13)"
(30.5, 32, 33 cm)

16 (17, 18)"
(40.5, 43, 46 cm)

Sparkling Mohair Shell

SIZES

Small (medium, large)

FINISHED MEASUREMENTS

40 (42, 44)" (101.5, 106.5, 112 cm)

MATERIALS

Fingering weight mohair yarn with sequins (or beads or metalic threads):
Approx. 324 (324, 432) yds (296.5, 296.5, 395 m)

14" knitting needles, size 11 (8 mm), or size needed to obtain gauge.

Tapestry needle for sewing seams

GAUGE

12 sts x 14 rows = 4 inches (10 cm) square

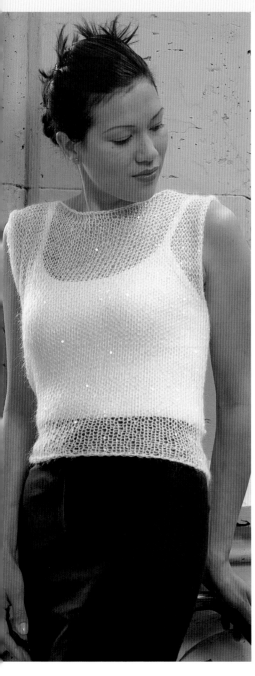

PATTERN STITCH

Stockinette (St st): Row 1: Knit (RS), Row 2: Purl (WS).

BACK

CO 60 (64, 66) sts.

Work in St st until piece measures 19 (20, 21)" (48.5, 51, 53.5 cm).

BO all sts loosely for a soft, slightly rolled finish at the wide neckline

FRONT

Work same as back.

FINISHING

Sew shoulder seams, leaving an 11½-inch (29 cm) neck opening.

Sew side seams, leaving armhole openings of 8 (8, 9) inches (20.5, 20.5, 23 cm).

No finishing is needed on this quick, easy-to-knit sweater.

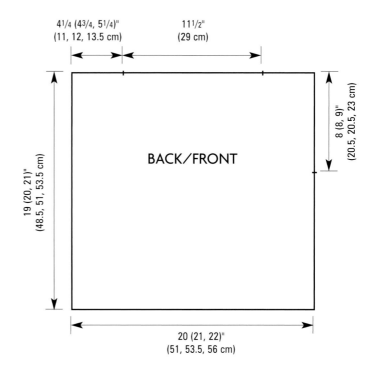

4¼ (4¾, 5¼)" (11, 12, 13.5 cm)

11½" (29 cm)

8 (8, 9)" (20.5, 20.5, 23 cm)

19 (20, 21)" (48.5, 51, 53.5 cm)

BACK/FRONT

20 (21, 22)" (51, 53.5, 56 cm)

Pearly-Shine Sleeveless

SIZES
Small (medium, large)

FINISHED MEASUREMENTS
34 (36, 38)" (86.5, 91.5, 96.5 cm)

MATERIALS
Worsted weight yarn, 70% cotton/20 % viscose/10% polyester: Approx. 891 (990, 1089) yds (814.5, 905, 996 m)

14" knitting needles, size 7 (4.5 mm), or size needed to obtain gauge.

Tapestry needle for sewing seams

GAUGE
20 sts x 26 rows = 4 inches (10 cm) square

PATTERN STITCHES
Stockinette (St st): Row 1: Knit (RS), Row 2: Purl (WS).
Single Rib: k1, p1 every row (even number of sts).

BACK
CO 90 (96, 100) sts; Single rib for ½ inch (1.5 cm).

Work even in St st to 12½ (13½, 14½)" (32, 34.5, 37 cm).

Armhole shaping: BO 3 sts at beg of next 2 rows; then 2 sts at beg of following 2 rows, then dec 1 st each side every other row 6 times.

Work even on 68 (74, 78) sts until armhole measures 7½ (8, 8½)" (19, 20.5, 21.5 cm) and total measurement is 20 (21, 22)" (51, 53.5, 56 cm).

BO 10 sts at beg of next 2 rows for shoulders and continue on 48 (54, 58) sts for 7" (18 cm); BO all sts.

FRONT
Work same as back.

FINISHING
Sew seams. No finishing is needed at the armholes or turtleneck because the material will curl and look perfectly finished when worn.

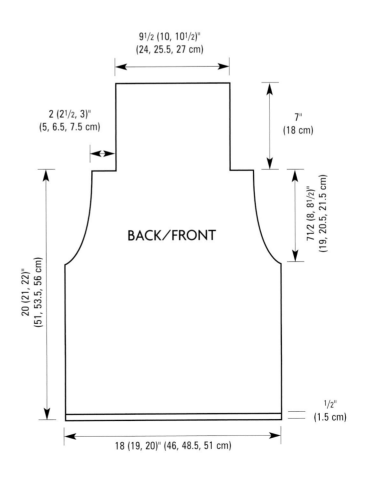

9½ (10, 10½)" (24, 25.5, 27 cm)

2 (2½, 3)" (5, 6.5, 7.5 cm)

7" (18 cm)

7½ (8, 8½)" (19, 20.5, 21.5 cm)

BACK/FRONT

20 (21, 22)" (51, 53.5, 56 cm)

½" (1.5 cm)

18 (19, 20)" (46, 48.5, 51 cm)

Funnel-neck Shell

SIZES

Small (medium, large)

FINISHED MEASUREMENTS

34 (36, 38)" (86.5, 91.5, 96.5 cm)

MATERIALS

Sport weight velvet yarn or chenille yarn: Approx. 480 (600, 720) yds (439, 548.5, 658.5 m)

14" knitting needles, size 5 (3.75 mm), or size needed to obtain gauge.

Crochet hook size F

Tapestry needle for sewing seams

GAUGE

16 sts x 20 rows = 4 inches (10 cm) square

PATTERN STITCHES

Stockinette stitch (St st):
Row 1: Knit (RS), Row 2: Purl (WS).

Garter stitch: Knit every row.

BACK

CO 68 (72, 76) sts; Garter stitch for ¾ inch (2 cm), then work in St st to 12½ (13, 13½)" (32, 33, 34.5 cm).

Armhole shaping: BO 3 sts at beg of next 2 rows; BO 2 sts at beg of following 2 rows; then dec 1 st each side every other row 3 times.

Work even until armhole measures 7½ (8, 8½)" (19, 20.5, 21.5 cm) and total measurement is 20 (21, 22)" (51, 53.5, 56 cm).

BO 8 (10, 12) sts at beg of next 2 rows and continue to work in St st on center 36 sts for 1½ inches (4 cm); Garter st for another ½ inch (1.5 cm); BO all sts loosely.

FRONT

Work same as back.

FINISHING

Sew seams.

Work slip stitch loosely around armholes with crochet hook F.

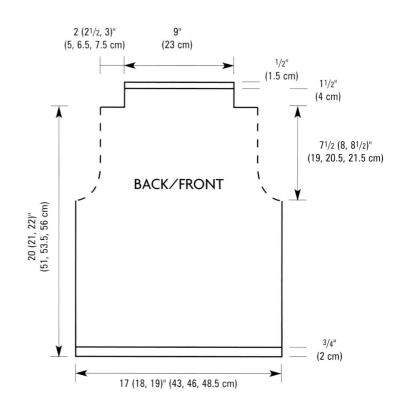

2 (2½, 3)" (5, 6.5, 7.5 cm)

9" (23 cm)

½" (1.5 cm)

1½" (4 cm)

7½ (8, 8½)" (19, 20.5, 21.5 cm)

20 (21, 22)" (51, 53.5, 56 cm)

BACK/FRONT

3/4" (2 cm)

17 (18, 19)" (43, 46, 48.5 cm)

Boatneck Tunic

SIZES

Small (medium, large)

FINISHED MEASUREMENTS

41 (43, 45)" (104, 109, 114.5 cm)

MATERIALS

Bulky weight yarn, 50% cotton/50% acrylic yarn: Approx. 1188 (1254, 1320) yds (1086.5, 1146.5, 1207 m)

14" knitting needles, size 10½ (6.5 mm), or size needed to obtain gauge.

Tapestry needle for sewing seams

GAUGE

12 sts x 18 rows = 4 inches (10 cm) square

PATTERN STITCHES

Stockinette stitch (St st): Row 1: Knit (RS), Row 2: Purl (WS)

BACK

CO 62 (64, 68) sts, work in St st to 22 (23, 24)" (56, 58.5, 61 cm). BO all sts.

FRONT

Work same as back.

SLEEVES

CO 24 (26, 28) sts, work in St st, inc 1 st each side every 6th row, to 19 (19½, 20)" (48.5, 49.5, 51 cm). BO all sts.

FINISHING

Sew shoulder seams, leaving a 10-inch (25.5 cm) neck opening.

Sew sleeve, underarm, and side seams, leaving a slit of 1½ inches (4 cm) at bottom, each side.

Raw edges will roll forward. Block sleeves and bottom edge, or work a row of single crochet to help them lie flat.

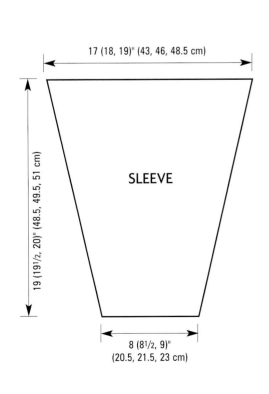

17 (18, 19)" (43, 46, 48.5 cm)

SLEEVE

19 (19½, 20)" (48.5, 49.5, 51 cm)

8 (8½, 9)" (20.5, 21.5, 23 cm)

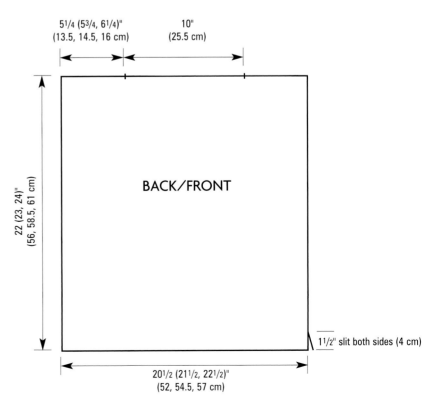

5¼ (5¾, 6¼)" (13.5, 14.5, 16 cm)

10" (25.5 cm)

BACK/FRONT

22 (23, 24)" (56, 58.5, 61 cm)

1½" slit both sides (4 cm)

20½ (21½, 22½)" (52, 54.5, 57 cm)

Exquisite Lattice Cables

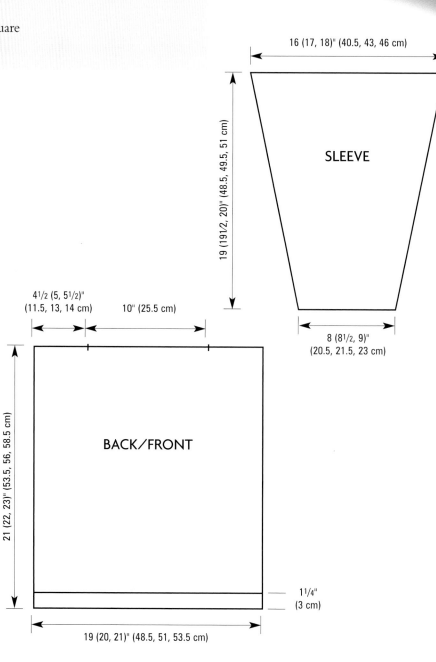

SIZES

Small (medium, large)

FINISHED MEASUREMENTS

38 (40, 42)" (96.5,101.5, 106.5 cm)

MATERIALS

Worsted weight yarn,100% merino wool: Approx. 1496 (1632, 1768) yds (1368, 1492.5, 1616.5 m)

14" knitting needles, size 7 (4.5 mm), or size needed to obtain gauge.

Cable needle

Tapestry needle for sewing seams

GAUGE

26 sts x 28 rows = 4 inches (10 cm) square

SLEEVE

16 (17, 18)" (40.5, 43, 46 cm)

19 (191/2, 20)" (48.5, 49.5, 51 cm)

8 (81/2, 9)" (20.5, 21.5, 23 cm)

BACK/FRONT

41/2 (5, 51/2)" (11.5, 13, 14 cm)

10" (25.5 cm)

21 (22, 23)" (53.5, 56, 58.5 cm)

11/4" (3 cm)

19 (20, 21)" (48.5, 51, 53.5 cm)

Eyelet Rib Sweater and Scarf

SIZES
Small (medium, large)

FINISHED MEASUREMENTS
41 (45, 49)" (104, 114, 124.5 cm)

MATERIALS
Worsted weight yarn, 50% extra-fine wool/33% angora/17% nylon:
Approx. 1392 (1479, 1566) yds (1273, 1352.5, 1432 m)
14" knitting needles, size 8 (5 mm), or size needed to obtain gauge.
Tapestry needle for sewing seams

GAUGE
In Eyelet Rib stitch using size 8 needles:
20 sts x 24 rows = 4 inches (10 cm) square

PATTERN STITCHES
Cable: Multiple of 6, plus 1 edge st each side. Row 1: Knit. Row 2: Purl.
Row 3: k3, ★ c4b, k2; rep from ★, ending row with k3. Row 4: Purl.
Row 5: k1, ★c4f, k2; rep from ★, ending row c4f, k1. Row 6: Purl.
Repeat rows 3 through 6 throughout.

Single Rib stitch: k1, p1 every row (even number of stitches)

BACK
CO 126 (132, 138) sts; Single Rib for 1¼" (3 cm).
Work in Cable to 21 (22, 23)" (53.5, 56, 58.5 cm). BO all sts in patt.

FRONT
Work same as back.

SLEEVES
CO 54 (56, 60) sts.
Work in Cable; inc 1 st each side every 5th row, to 19 (19½, 20)" (48.5, 49.5, 51 cm). BO all sts.

FINISHING
Sew shoulder seams, leaving a 10-inch (25.5 cm) neck opening.
Sew sleeve, side and underarm seams. Neck edges and cuffs will roll.

PATTERN STITCH

Eyelet Rib stitch: Multiple of 6, plus 2. Row 1: ★ p2, k2tog, yo, k2; rep from ★, end p2. Row 2: k2, ★ p2tog, yo, p2, k2; rep from ★.

BACK

CO 104 (112, 122) sts; work in Eyelet Rib until piece measures 22 (23, 24) inches (56, 58.5, 61 cm). BO all sts in patt.

FRONT

Work same as back.

SLEEVES

CO 44 (48, 50) sts; work in pattern, inc 1 st each side every 5th row, to 19 (19½, 20)" (48.5, 49.5, 51 cm)—long enough to turn back cuffs, or leave long over hands. BO all sts.

SCARF

CO 38 sts; work in pattern to 44 inches (112 cm). BO all sts.

FINISHING

Sew shoulder seams, leaving a neck opening of 9½ (10, 10½)" (24, 25.5, 27 cm). Sew in sleeves; leaving a slit opening of 1½ inches (4 cm) at bottom of each side, sew side and sleeve seams.

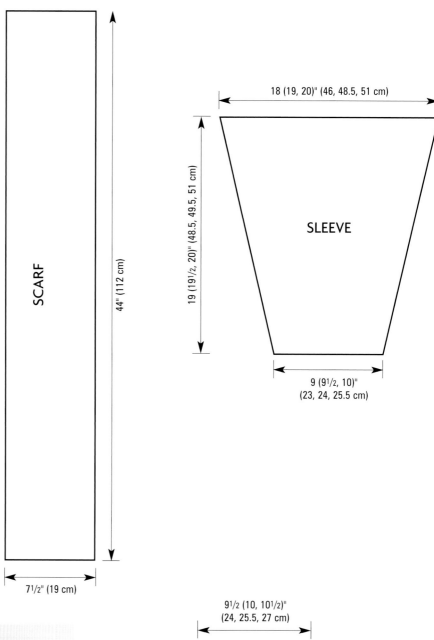

SCARF

44" (112 cm)

7½" (19 cm)

SLEEVE

18 (19, 20)" (46, 48.5, 51 cm)

19 (19½, 20)" (48.5, 49.5, 51 cm)

9 (9½, 10)" (23, 24, 25.5 cm)

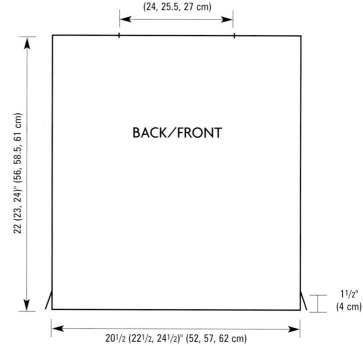

BACK/FRONT

9½ (10, 10½)" (24, 25.5, 27 cm)

22 (23, 24)" (56, 58.5, 61 cm)

1½" (4 cm)

20½ (22½, 24½)" (52, 57, 62 cm)

Cabled Boatneck

SIZES

Small (medium, large)

FINISHED MEASUREMENTS

42 (44, 46)" (106.5, 112, 117 cm)

MATERIALS

Worsted weight yarn, 50% angora/50% nylon: Approx. 1023 (1116, 1209) yds (935.5, 1020.5, 1105.5 m)

14" knitting needles, size 9 (5.5 mm), or size needed to obtain gauge.

Cable needle

Tapestry needle for sewing seams

GAUGE

Cabled pieces: 16.8 stitches x 21 rows = 4 inches (10 cm) square

Stockinette pieces: 16 stitches x 21 rows = 4 inches (10 cm) square

PATTERN STITCHES

Stockinette stitch (St st): Row 1: Knit (RS), Row 2: Purl (WS).
Single rib stitch: k1, p1 every row (even number of stitches)
Cables: See Cable pattern in Back instructions, below.

BACK

CO 88 (92, 96) sts; Single Rib for 1¼ inches (3 cm).

Begin pattern as follows:

Row 1: k8 (10, 12), ★ p1, k6, p1, k8; repeat from ★ but end k8 (10, 12).

Row 2: p8 (10, 12), ★ k1, p6, k1, p8; repeat from ★ but end p8 (10, 12).

Row 3-6: rep row 1 and 2 twice.

Row 7: As row 1, except twist the cables on each knit 6 (slip 3 sts onto cn; hold in back of work; k3 sts from left hand needle; k sts from the cn).

Row 8: Repeat row 2.

Repeat this 8-row pattern to 20¼ (21¼, 22¼)" (51.5, 54, 56.5 cm).

Single Rib for 3/4 inch (2 cm).
BO all sts in patt.

FRONT

Work same as back.

SLEEVES

CO 34 (36, 38) sts, Single rib for 1¼ inches (3 cm).

Work in St st, inc 1 st each side every 6th row, to 19 (191/2, 20)" (48.5, 49.5, 51 cm). BO all sts.

FINISHING

Sew shoulder seams, leaving a neck opening of 91/2 (10, 101/2)" (24, 25.5, 27 cm).

Sew sleeve, side, and underarm seams.

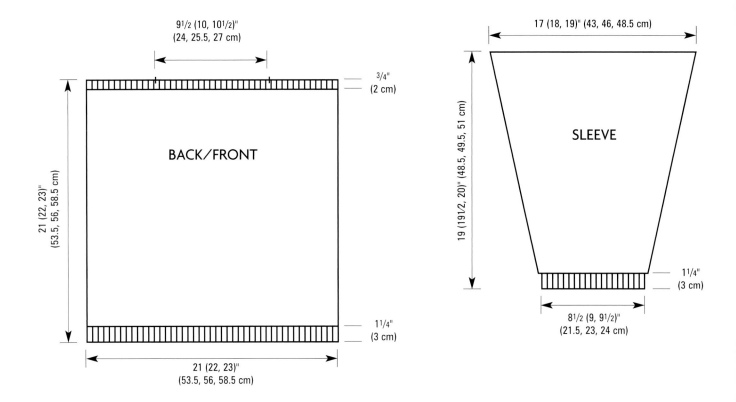

9¹/₂ (10, 10¹/₂)"
(24, 25.5, 27 cm)

3/4"
(2 cm)

BACK/FRONT

21 (22, 23)"
(53.5, 56, 58.5 cm)

1¹/₄"
(3 cm)

21 (22, 23)"
(53.5, 56, 58.5 cm)

17 (18, 19)" (43, 46, 48.5 cm)

SLEEVE

19 (19¹/₂, 20)" (48.5, 49.5, 51 cm)

1¹/₄"
(3 cm)

8¹/₂ (9, 9¹/₂)"
(21.5, 23, 24 cm)

Tweed Crew Neck

SIZES

Small (medium, large)

FINISHED MEASUREMENTS

40 (42, 44)" (101.5, 106.5, 112 cm)

MATERIALS

Worsted weight yarn, 100% silk: Approx 686 (784, 882) yds (627, 717, 806.5 m)

Sport weight yarn, (shown in 70% super kid mohair/25% polyamid/5% wool): Approx 924 (1078, 1232) yds (845, 985.5, 1126.5 m)

14" knitting needles, size 10 (6 mm), or size needed to obtain gauge.

Tapestry needle for sewing seams

GAUGE

12 sts x 18 rows = 4" (10 cm) square

PATTERN STITCHES

Stockinette stitch (St st): Row 1: Knit (RS), Row 2: Purl (WS)

Single Rib stitch: k1, p1 every row (even number of stitches)

BACK

CO 60 (64, 68) sts with 2 strands of mohair held tog; Single Rib for 1" (2.5 cm). Cont with 1 strand of mohair and 1 strand of silk held tog and work in St st to 21 (22, 23)" (53.5, 55, 58.5 cm). BO all sts.

FRONT

Work same as back to 18½ (19½, 20½)" (47, 49.5, 52 cm), ending with a p row.

Neck shaping: k22 (24, 26) sts across; with second balls of yarn (silk and mohair held tog), BO 16 sts, k22 (24, 26).

Dec 1 st each side of neck edge every other row until front measures 21 (22, 23)" (53.5, 56, 58.5 cm) at shoulder. BO all rem sts.

SLEEVES

CO 26 (28, 30) sts with 2 strands of mohair held tog; Single Rib for 2 inches (5 cm).

Cont, with 1 strand of silk and 1 strand of mohair held tog, in St st, inc 1 st each side every 6th row to 19 (19½, 20)" (48.5, 49.5, 51 cm). BO all sts.

FINISHING

Sew one shoulder seam. With 2 strands of mohair, pu 68 (72, 76) sts around neck and Single Rib for ¾" (2 cm). BO all sts in patt loosely.

Sew remaining shoulder seam, armhole, side, and sleeve seams.

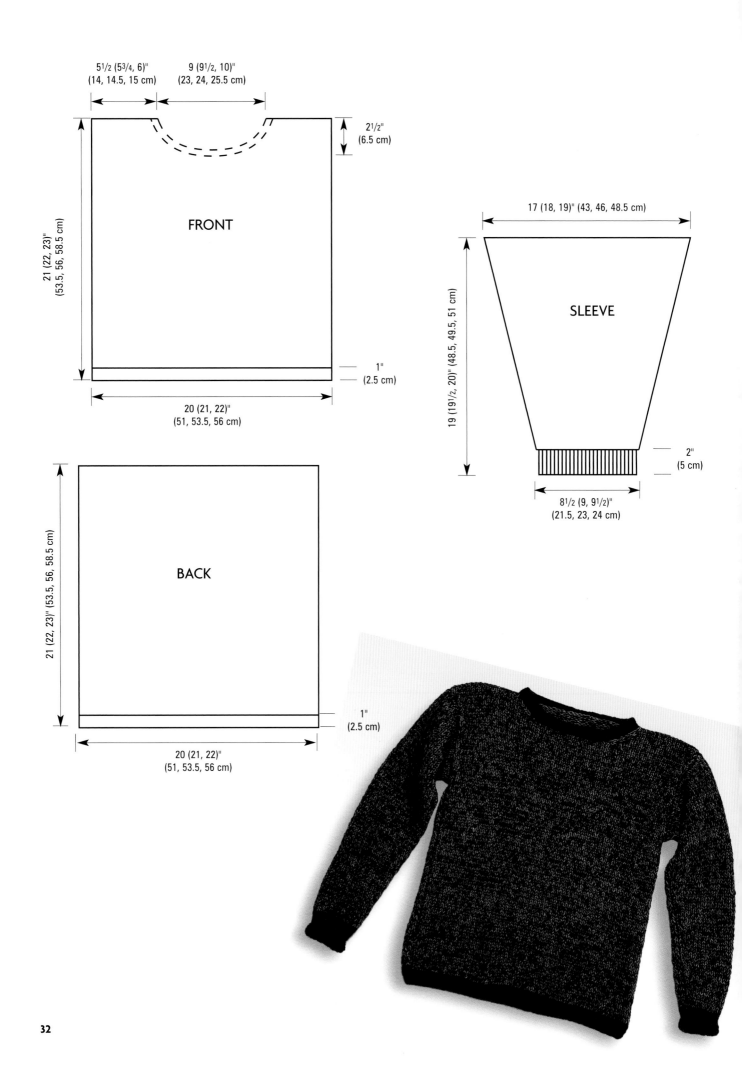

5¹/₂ (5³/₄, 6)"
(14, 14.5, 15 cm)

9 (9¹/₂, 10)"
(23, 24, 25.5 cm)

2¹/₂"
(6.5 cm)

FRONT

21 (22, 23)"
(53.5, 56, 58.5 cm)

1"
(2.5 cm)

20 (21, 22)"
(51, 53.5, 56 cm)

17 (18, 19)" (43, 46, 48.5 cm)

SLEEVE

19 (19¹/₂, 20)" (48.5, 49.5, 51 cm)

2"
(5 cm)

8¹/₂ (9, 9¹/₂)"
(21.5, 23, 24 cm)

BACK

21 (22, 23)" (53.5, 56, 58.5 cm)

1"
(2.5 cm)

20 (21, 22)"
(51, 53.5, 56 cm)

Comfy Winter Turtleneck

SIZES
Small (medium, large)

FINISHED MEASUREMENTS
41 (44, 46)" (104, 112, 117 cm)

MATERIALS
Bulky weight yarn,(shown in 100% merino wool): Approx 1056 (1188, 1320) yds (965.5, 1086.5, 1207 m)

14" knitting needles, size 11 (8 mm), or size needed to obtain gauge.

Stitch holder

Tapestry needle for sewing seams

GAUGE
12 sts x 16 rows = 4" (10 cm) square

PATTERN STITCHES
Stockinette stitch (St st): Row 1: Knit (RS), Row 2: Purl (WS)

Twisted Rib stitch: Row 1: k2 tbl (into the back of the knit sts), p2. Row 2: p2, k2 tbl (into the back of the knit sts)., Repeat these 2 rows for pattern.

BACK
CO 62 (66, 70) sts; Twisted Rib for 2½" (6.5 cm).

Work even in St st to 22 (23, 24)" (56, 58.5, 61 cm). BO all sts.

FRONT
CO 62 (66, 70) sts; Twisted Rib for 2½" (6.5 cm).

Work even in St st to 19½ (20½, 21½)" (49.5, 52, 54.5 cm).

Neck shaping: k24 (26, 28) sts, sl 14 sts onto holder. With second ball of yarn, k24 (26, 28) sts; dec 1 st each side of neck edge every other row until front is 22 (23, 24)" (56, 58.5, 61 cm). BO rem sts.

SLEEVES
CO 28 sts; Twisted Rib for 2½" (6.5 cm).

Work in St st, inc 1 st each side every 5th row, to 19 (19½, 20)" (48.5, 49.5, 51 cm). BO all sts.

FINISHING
Sew seams. Pu 68 (72, 76) sts around neck with same size needle and work Twisted Rib for

7½ inches (19 cm). BO loosely so turtleneck will go over the head easily and have a relaxed look.

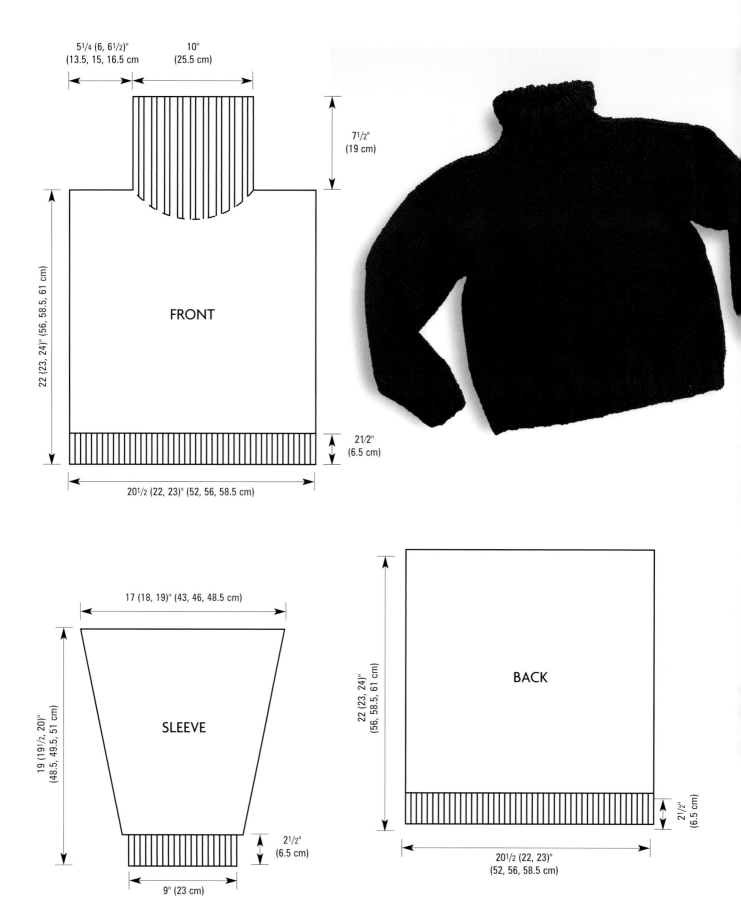

5¼ (6, 6½)"
(13.5, 15, 16.5 cm)

10"
(25.5 cm)

7½"
(19 cm)

FRONT

22 (23, 24)" (56, 58.5, 61 cm)

2½"
(6.5 cm)

20½ (22, 23)" (52, 56, 58.5 cm)

17 (18, 19)" (43, 46, 48.5 cm)

SLEEVE

19 (19½, 20)"
(48.5, 49.5, 51 cm)

2½"
(6.5 cm)

9" (23 cm)

BACK

22 (23, 24)"
(56, 58.5, 61 cm)

2½"
(6.5 cm)

20½ (22, 23)"
(52, 56, 58.5 cm)

Hooded Sweater

SIZES
Small (medium, large)

FINISHED MEASUREMENTS
38 (40, 42)" (96.5, 101.5, 106.5 cm)

MATERIALS
Sport weight yarn, (shown in 100% cashmere): Approx. 2040 (2210, 2380) yards (1865.5, 2021, 2176.5 m)

14" knitting needles, size 8 (5 mm.), or size needed to obtain gauge.

Crochet hook size D

Tapestry needle for sewing seams

GAUGE
20 sts x 34 rows = 4" (10 cm)

PATTERN STITCH
Garter stitch: knit every row.

BACK
CO 96 (100, 104) sts; sl first st at beg of each row (for an even edge) and work Garter st to 21 (22, 23)" (53.5, 56, 58.5 cm). BO all sts.

FRONT
Work same as back to 18½ (19½, 20½)" (47, 49.5, 52 cm).

Shape neck: on next row, work 39 (41, 43) sts across, join second ball of yarn and BO 18 sts, work to end of row. Working both sides at once, dec 1 st at each neck edge every other row to 21 (22, 23)" (53.5, 56, 58.5 cm). BO all rem sts.

SLEEVES
CO 44 (46, 48) sts; sl first st at the beg of each row (for an even edge) and work in Garter st, inc 1 st each side every 8th row, to 19 (19½, 20)" (48.5, 49.5, 51 cm). BO all sts.

HOOD
CO 110 sts; work in Garter st (sl first stitch at beg of each row, as above) and dec 1 st each side every 11th row. At row 85, or 10" (25.5 cm), k55 sts, attach second ball of yarn and work to end of row. Working both sides at once, work 2 rows even, then dec 1 st at each side of split (see diagram) every 3rd row (also continuing decreases at outer sides) to 110 rows, or 13" (33 cm). BO rem sts.

FINISHING
Sew center hood seam at narrow edge (folding hood in half at central split).

Sew shoulder, armhole, sleeve and side seams.

Sew long edge of hood to neckline, overlapping front edges approximately ½" (1.5 cm).

With crochet hook D, work slip stitch around edges of hood for even finish.

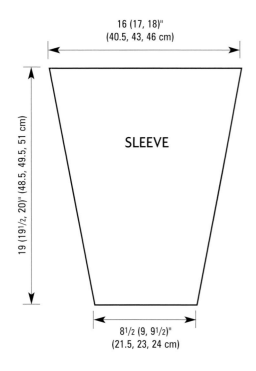

16 (17, 18)"
(40.5, 43, 46 cm)

SLEEVE

19 (19½, 20)" (48.5, 49.5, 51 cm)

8½ (9, 9½)"
(21.5, 23, 24 cm)

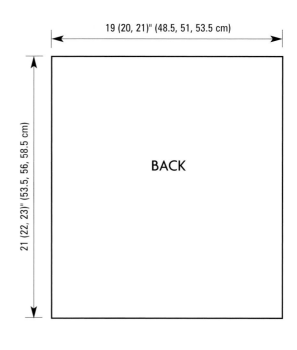

19 (20, 21)" (48.5, 51, 53.5 cm)

BACK

21 (22, 23)" (53.5, 56, 58.5 cm)

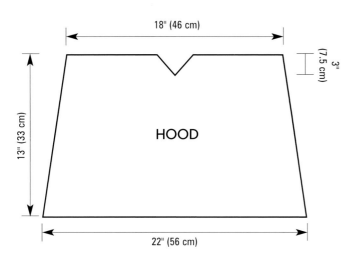

18" (46 cm)

3"
(7.5 cm)

HOOD

13" (33 cm)

22" (56 cm)

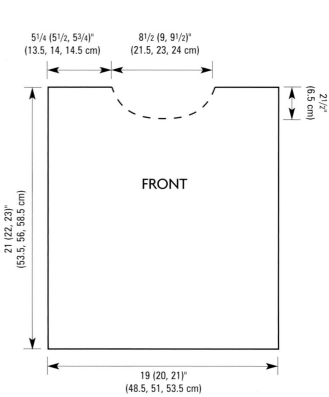

5¼ (5½, 5¾)"
(13.5, 14, 14.5 cm)

8½ (9, 9½)"
(21.5, 23, 24 cm)

2½"
(6.5 cm)

FRONT

21 (22, 23)"
(53.5, 56, 58.5 cm)

19 (20, 21)"
(48.5, 51, 53.5 cm)

Bamboo Stitch V-Neck

SIZES
Small (medium, large)

FINISHED MEASUREMENTS
36 (38, 40)" (91.5, 96.5, 101.5 cm)

MATERIALS
Sport weight yarn, (shown in 75% extra-fine merino wool/25% silk):
Approx. 1800 (1980, 2160) yards (1646, 1810.5, 1975 m)
14" knitting needles, size 6 (4 mm), or size needed to obtain gauge.
Crochet hook size E
Tapestry needle for sewing seams

GAUGE
26 sts x 32 rows = 4" (10 cm) square

PATTERN STITCH
Bamboo stitch: Multiple of 2, plus 2 edge sts. Row 1 (RS): k1 , ★ yo, k2, pass the yo over the 2 knit sts; rep from ★ ending with k1. Row 2: Purl. Repeat rows 1 and 2.

BACK
CO 118 (126, 132) sts; work in Bamboo st until piece measures 20 (21, 22)" (51, 53.5, 56 cm). BO all sts.

FRONT
Work same as back to 13 (14, 15)" (33, 35.5, 38 cm).

Neck shaping: Work 59 (63, 66) sts; join second ball of yarn and work to end to split for V. Working both sides at once, dec 1 st at neck edges every other row to same length as back 20 (21, 22)" (51, 53.5, 56 cm). BO rem sts.

SLEEVES
CO 52 (56, 60) sts; work in Bamboo st, inc 1 st each side every 6th row, until piece measures 19 (19½, 20)" (48.5, 49.5, 51 cm). BO all sts.

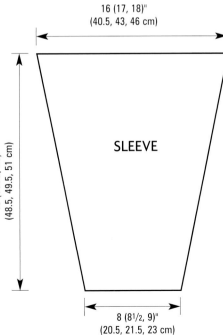

16 (17, 18)"
(40.5, 43, 46 cm)

19 (19½, 20)"
(48.5, 49.5, 51 cm)

SLEEVE

8 (8½, 9)"
(20.5, 21.5, 23 cm)

SCARF

CO 46 stitches; work in Bamboo st to 50" (127 cm). BO all sts.

FINISHING

Sew shoulder, armhole, side, and sleeve seams.

With crochet hook E and RS of neckline facing, work slip stitch evenly into every other st.

7" (18 cm)

50" (127 cm)

SCARF

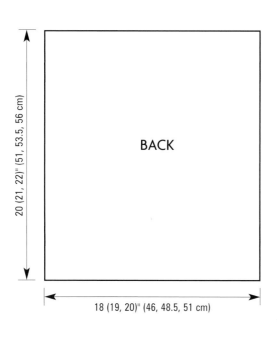

20 (21, 22)" (51, 53.5, 56 cm)

BACK

18 (19, 20)" (46, 48.5, 51 cm)

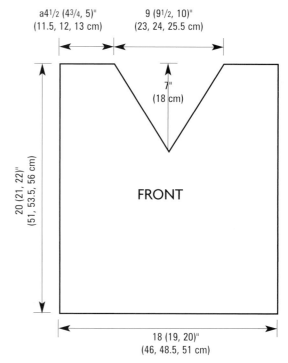

a4½ (4¾, 5)" (11.5, 12, 13 cm)

9 (9½, 10)" (23, 24, 25.5 cm)

7" (18 cm)

20 (21, 22)" (51, 53.5, 56 cm)

FRONT

18 (19, 20)" (46, 48.5, 51 cm)

Cozy Funnel Neck

SIZES

Small (medium, large)

FINISHED MEASUREMENTS

40 (42, 44)" (101.5, 106.5, 112 cm)

MATERIALS

Bulky weight yarn, (shown in 100% pure new wool): Approx. 880 (990, 1100) yards (804.5, 905.5, 1006 m)

14" knitting needles, size 15 (10 mm), or size needed to obtain gauge.

Tapestry needle for sewing seams

GAUGE

11 sts x 16 rows = 4" (10 cm) square

PATTERN STITCH

Slip Stitch Rib: (multiple of 2) Row 1: k1, sl 1 (purlwise). Row 2: Purl. Repeat these 2 rows for pattern.

BACK

CO 58 (60, 62) sts; work in Slip Stitch Rib to 22 (23, 24)" (56, 58.5, 61 cm).

Make funnel neck: BO 16 sts at the beg of next 2 rows. Cont pattern on central 26 (28, 30) sts for 1½" (4 cm). BO all sts loosely.

FRONT

Work same as back.

SLEEVES

CO 22 (24, 26) sts; work in Slip Stitch Rib, inc 1 st each side every 5th row, to 19 (20, 21)" (48.5, 51, 53.5 cm). BO all sts.

FINISHING

Sew shoulder, neck, armhole, sleeve, and side seams.

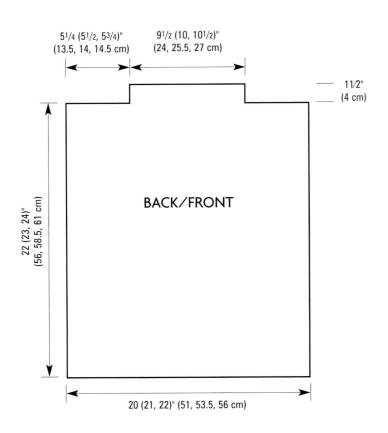

5¼ (5½, 5¾)" (13.5, 14, 14.5 cm)

9½ (10, 10½)" (24, 25.5, 27 cm)

1½" (4 cm)

22 (23, 24)" (56, 58.5, 61 cm)

BACK/FRONT

20 (21, 22)" (51, 53.5, 56 cm)

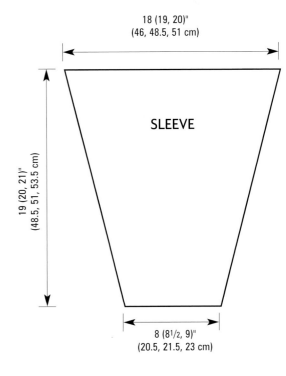

18 (19, 20)" (46, 48.5, 51 cm)

SLEEVE

19 (20, 21)" (48.5, 51, 53.5 cm)

8 (8½, 9)" (20.5, 21.5, 23 cm)

Textured Vest

SIZES AND FINISHED MEASUREMENTS

There is no set pattern for this vest. The size and finished measurements of your vest will be determined by taking a few simple measurements from a favorite, well-fitting sweater.

MATERIALS

MC: Worsted-weight mohair/wool blend yarn: Approximately 1 pound total

CC: Novelty metallic, glitter, and eyelash yarns: Remnants or small quantities

Needle size suited to your test gauge

GAUGE

With MC, knit a 6" (15 cm) square swatch.

Measure swatch carefully; the number of stitches per inch (cm) is your gauge.

PATTERN STITCH

A number of rows of Stockinette stitch in MC yarn are broken up with Garter stitch rows of novelty yarns

Note: It is especially important in this project to CO and BO loosely as the vest is knitted starting at one side and ending at opposite side edge, working rows back and forth between bottom and shoulder edges.

BACK

Measure the back of a favorite sweater across the bustline, then for length. Multiply your length measurement by your gauge and you have the number of sts to cast on.

CO with MC. For this vest, several rows of St st in the MC are broken up by rows of Garter stitch in novelty yarns. Cont until piece meas desired back width (allowing for dropped shoulders as shown), without stretching. BO loosely.

Decide back neck width by measuring your favorite sweater. It will probably be somewhere around 7" (18 cm). Subtract this meas from the

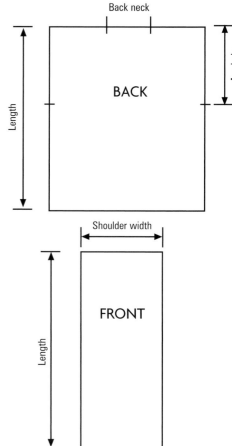

total back width, divide the result by two, and you have the width of each shoulder. (This measurement will also be the width for each front piece.)

FRONT

Note: For a spontaneous look, front pieces need not have identical stripe patterns.

CO same number of sts as for back. Knit 2 front pieces to the required width, working again from side to side. Shoulder piece measurement from back is also the width for each front piece, since shoulder seams need to match. BO loosely.

FINISHING

Join shoulder seams. Now plan arm bands.

Place markers on the front and back pieces at the point where you want the underarm seam to begin. Since this is a drop-shoulder style, armhole openings should be at least 8 inches (20 cm).

Decide on the yarn and needle size to use, then pick up an even number of sts on front and back for the arm bands. Work about 1 inch (2.5 cm) in Single rib (k1 p1). BO. Sew the underarm seam.

Tip: Sew from the underarm to bottom of garment. This prevents the seam from being pulled up.

Try vest on and consider the rest of the finishing. If you want a bottom band, place safety pins as markers at side seams and center back, and space others evenly in between. Using circular needle, pu sts around hem, using pins as guides to obtain equal number of sts between markers. Work band in same rib as armholes. Or try: Knit 1 row after pu row, then BO.

Front bands: RS facing, with circular needle, pu sts along right front, across back neck, and down the left front; proceed as for other bands. If you prefer to knit band separately, CO a few sts for a band about 1½" (4 cm) wide and knit until it is long enough to go all the way around the front edges. Sew neatly into place.

Pointed Hem Top

SIZES
Small (medium, large)

FINISHED MEASUREMENTS
Bust: 36 (40, 44)" (91.5, 101.5, 112 cm)

MATERIALS
Heavy weight yarn (shown in 35% cotton, 35% rayon, 30% nylon) (1 skein = 50 g, 98 yds[90 m]): 5 (6, 7) skeins

14" knitting needles, size 7 (4.5 mm), or in size to obtain gauge

Embellishments of choice

GAUGE
In Garter stitch:

20 sts = 5" (13 cm)

4 sts = 1" (2.5 cm)

PATTERN STITCH

Garter st: knit every row

Note: Top is begun by knitting individual triangles in Garter stitch, then joining them together. Once all the triangles have been joined, the bottom edge is asymmetrical. Either side can be worn to the front. Size and number of triangles may be adjusted as desired, as long as you have the correct number of total stitches per side.

TO MAKE A TRIANGLE

CO 2 sts; knit one row.

In Garter st, inc 1 st at the beg of the next and every row to the required number of stitches.

Leave sts on a holder.

SIDE ONE

Make a total of three triangles for each, using number of sts indicated in your size category for each triangle—Size (1st, 2nd, 3rd triangle):

Small (20, 24, 28) sts = total 72 sts

Medium (23, 27, 30) sts = total 80 sts

Large (26, 30, 32) sts = total 88 sts

When you have all the triangles, arrange them on the needle in the order most pleasing to you and knit across all the stitches.

Continue in Garter st until the piece meas about 16" (40.5 cm) at the side seam.

K22 (24, 26) sts; place rem sts on a holder. Work these sts for 2 inches (5 cm). BO these sts.

Rejoin yarn to the sts on the holder; BO 28 (32, 36) sts and work on rem 22 (24, 26) sts to match first shoulder. BO rem sts.

SIDE TWO

Make a total of four triangles for each size, using the number of sts indicated in your size category for each triangle—Size (1st, 2nd, 3rd, 4th triangle):

Small (15, 18, 18, 21) sts = total of 72 sts.

Medium (17, 20, 20, 23) sts = total of 80 sts.

Large (18, 21, 23, 26) sts = total of 88 sts.

When all the triangles are completed, continue as for the Side One.

FINISHING

Place markers 8 (8½, 9)" (20.5, 21.5, 23 cm) from top of shoulder. Join shoulder seams and side seams below markers.

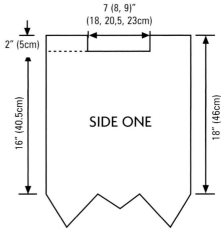

7 (8, 9)"
(18, 20,5, 23cm)

2" (5cm)

16" (40.5cm)

SIDE ONE

18" (46cm)

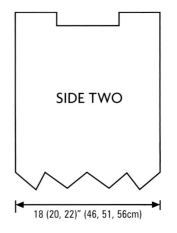

SIDE TWO

18 (20, 22)" (46, 51, 56cm)

Perfect Turtleneck

SIZES

Small (medium, large)

FINISHED MEASUREMENTS

41(44, 46)" (104, 112, 117 cm)

MATERIALS

Sport weight yarn, 75% extra-fine merino wool/25% silk: Approx. 1810 (1991, 2172) yards (1655, 1820.5, 1986 m)

14" knitting needles, size 6 (4 mm), or size needed to obtain gauge.

Tapestry needle for sewing seams

GAUGE

29 sts x 28 rows = 4" (10 cm) square

PATTERN STITCH

Single Rib: k1, p1 every row (even number of sts)

BACK

CO 148 (158, 166) sts; work in Single Rib until piece measures 22 (23, 24)" (56, 58.5, 61 cm). BO 38 (43, 47) sts at beg of next 2 rows. Cont in pattern on central 72 sts for 7½" (19 cm). BO all sts in patt.

FRONT

Work same as back.

SLEEVES

CO 62 (64, 68) sts; work in Single Rib, inc 1 st each side every 5th row, to 20 (20½, 21)" (51, 52, 53.5 cm). BO all sts.

FINISHING

Sew shoulder and turtleneck seams. Sew sleeve, side, and underarm seams.

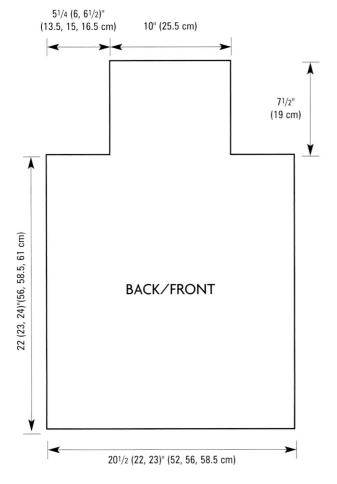

5¼ (6, 6½)" (13.5, 15, 16.5 cm)

10" (25.5 cm)

7½" (19 cm)

22 (23, 24)" (56, 58.5, 61 cm)

BACK/FRONT

20½ (22, 23)" (52, 56, 58.5 cm)

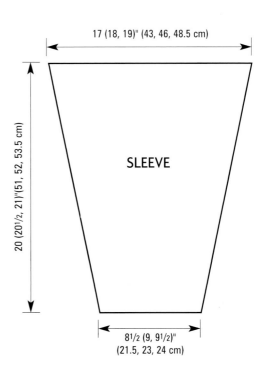

17 (18, 19)" (43, 46, 48.5 cm)

20 (20½, 21)" (51, 52, 53.5 cm)

SLEEVE

8½ (9, 9½)" (21.5, 23, 24 cm)

Easy Flap-Front Top

SIZES
Small (medium, large, extra large)

FINISHED MEASUREMENTS
Bust: 35 (38, 42, 44) inches (89, 96.5, 107, 112 cm)

Length: 16 (16½, 17, 17½)" (40.5, 42, 43, 44.5 cm)

MATERIALS
Sport weight yarn (1 skein = 50 g [154 yds/141 m]): 6 (7, 7, 8) skeins

Note: Yarn is doubled.

Knitting needles in size 9 (5.5 mm) or size needed to obtain gauge

Buttons as desired

GAUGE
In Garter stitch, using 2 strands of yarn held together:

15 sts = 4" (10 cm)

Note: Cast on pieces loosely, using a larger needle for the cast-on row if necessary.

BACK
Holding two strands of yarn together, CO 66 (72, 78, 82) sts and work in Garter st (knit every row) until the piece meas 15 (15½, 16, 16½)" (38, 39.5, 40.5, 42 cm).

Next row: k20 (22, 24, 26) sts and place on a holder, BO the center 26 (28, 30, 30) sts; k across the rem 20 (22, 24, 26) sts.

Knit 8 more rows (four Garter st ridges).

BO the shoulder sts.

Return to sts on the holder and complete other shoulder to match.

FRONT
Holding two strands of yarn together, CO 66 (72, 78, 82) sts and work in Garter st until piece meas 10 (10½, 11, 11½)" (25.5, 27, 28, 29 cm).

Next row (RS): k20 (22, 24, 26) sts and work on these sts only; place the rem sts on a holder. Knit until the piece meas the same as the back to shoulder. BO shoulder sts.

Return to sts on holder. Knit until piece meas 15 (15-½, 16, 16-½)" (38, 39.5, 40.5, 42 cm).

BO 26 (28, 30, 30) sts; work on rem 20 (22, 24, 26) sts. Knit 8 more rows. BO all rem sts.

FINISHING
Place markers on front and back 8 (8, 8½, 9)" (20.5, 21.5, 23 cm) from start of shoulder shaping.

Join shoulder seams and side seams below the markers.

You can leave top unadorned, or choose one of the options presented here. A stunning button may be secured with strong matching or contrasting thread, ribbon, or thin leather cord. A feature in itself—it also means the look can quickly be changed by untying the cord. A button can be stitched to one side of the opening and secured by a loop on the other side. The top may also be worn back-to-front.

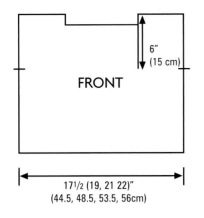

FRONT

6"
(15 cm)

17½ (19, 21 22)"
(44.5, 48.5, 53.5, 56cm)

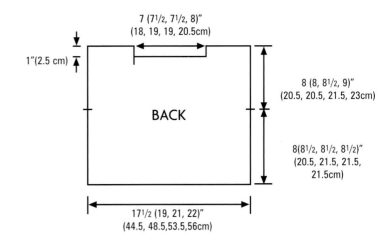

7 (7½, 7½, 8)"
(18, 19, 19, 20.5cm)

1"(2.5 cm)

BACK

8 (8, 8½, 9)"
(20.5, 20.5, 21.5, 23cm)

8(8½, 8½, 8½)"
(20.5, 21.5, 21.5, 21.5cm)

17½ (19, 21, 22)"
(44.5, 48.5,53.5,56cm)

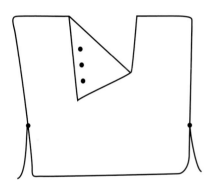

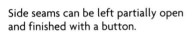

Side seams can be left partially open
and finished with a button.

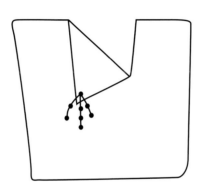

Flap can be embellished with buttons or
beads.

Flap can be worn closed withor without side
vents.

Basic Vest

SIZES
To fit bust 32 (34, 36, 38, 40, 42, 44)" (81, 86.5, 91.5, 96.5, 101.5, 107, 112 cm)

FINISHED MEASUREMENTS
Bust: 37 (39, 41, 43, 45, 47, 49)" (94, 99, 104, 109, 114.5, 119.5, 124.5 cm)

Length: 21 (21, 21, 22½, 22½, 24, 24)" (53.5, 53.5, 53.5, 57, 57, 61, 61 cm)

MATERIALS
Medium weight bouclé yarn (50 g = 1.75 oz; approximately 96 yds = 86.5 m): 6 (6, 7, 7, 8, 8, 8) skeins

14" knitting needles, sizes 6 and 8 (4 mm and 5 mm), or size to obtain gauge

Circular needle in size 6 (4 mm)

Buttons

GAUGE
In Stockinette st using larger needles: 14 sts = 4" (10 cm)

BACK
Using smaller needles, CO 60 (62, 66, 68, 72, 74, 78) sts and work in Single rib (k1, p1) for 2" (5 cm). On last rib row, inc 6 (6, 6, 8, 8, 8, 8) sts, evenly spaced, across the row for a total of 66 (68, 72, 76, 80, 82, 86) sts.

Change to larger needles; work in St st until piece measures 12 (12, 12, 13, 13, 14, 14)" (30.5, 30.5, 30.5, 33, 33, 35.5, 35.5 cm).

Armhole shaping: BO 5 (5, 6, 6, 7, 7, 8) sts at beg of next 2 rows. Dec 1 st at each side every other row 4 (5, 5, 6, 7, 7, 7) times until 48 (48, 50, 52, 52, 54, 56) sts remain. Continue knitting until back meas 21 (21, 21, 22½, 22½, 24, 24)" (53.5, 53.5, 53.5, 57, 57, 61, 61 cm).

Shoulder shaping: BO 6 (6, 6, 7, 7, 7, 7) sts at the beg of the next 2 rows, then BO 6 (6, 7, 7, 7, 7, 8) sts at beg of following 2 rows. Place rem 24 (24, 24, 24, 24, 26, 26) back neck sts on a holder.

LEFT FRONT
With smaller needles, CO 30 (31, 33, 34, 36, 37, 39) sts and work in rib as for back, inc 3 (3, 3, 4, 4, 4, 4) sts evenly across last rib row for a total 33 (34, 36, 38, 40, 41, 43) sts.

Change to larger needles and work as for back to start of armhole shaping, ending with RS facing.

Neck and shoulder shaping: Shape armhole to correspond to back armhole, and at the same time dec 1 st at neck edge on the next row and every following 4th row until 12 (12, 13, 14, 14, 14, 15) sts remain.

Continue knitting until piece meas the same as the back to start of shoulder shaping, ending with RS facing. BO 6, (6, 7, 7, 7, 7, 8) sts at beg of next row. Purl 1 row. BO 6 (6, 7, 7, 7, 7, 8) sts.

RIGHT FRONT
Work to match left front, reversing all shapings.

FINISHING

Block pieces carefully, according to yarn manufacturer's recommendations.

Join shoulder seams.

Arm bands: Using smaller needles, pu and knit approx 84 (84, 84, 88, 88, 94, 94) sts evenly around armhole edge. Work in Single rib (k1, p1) for 1" (2.5 cm). BO loosely in Single rib.

Mark position for buttons on the left front, placing the top marker ½ inch (1.5 cm) below the start of the front neck shaping and bottom marker ½ inch (1.5 cm) above the CO edge.

Space the other buttons evenly in between.

Front bands: Using circular needle, with RS facing, start at lower right front edge, pick up and knit approximately 200 (200, 200, 212, 212, 226, 226) sts all around the edges and down to the lower left front edge. Work 3 rows in Single rib (k1, p1).

Next row: work buttonholes to correspond with the marked positions of the buttons, working (k2tog, yo) as needed to maintain rib patt.

Work 3 more rows. BO in rib.

Sew the side seams.

Sew on buttons.

VARIATION SUGGESTIONS

★ Change the basic Single rib. For example, try Moss (Seed) stitch for the bands.

★ For a rolled edge, CO with smaller needles, work a few rows in St st, change to larger needles, and continue.

★ Knit sections in different colors or textures.

★ Knit the body, or part of the body, in stripes; knit the band in stripes.

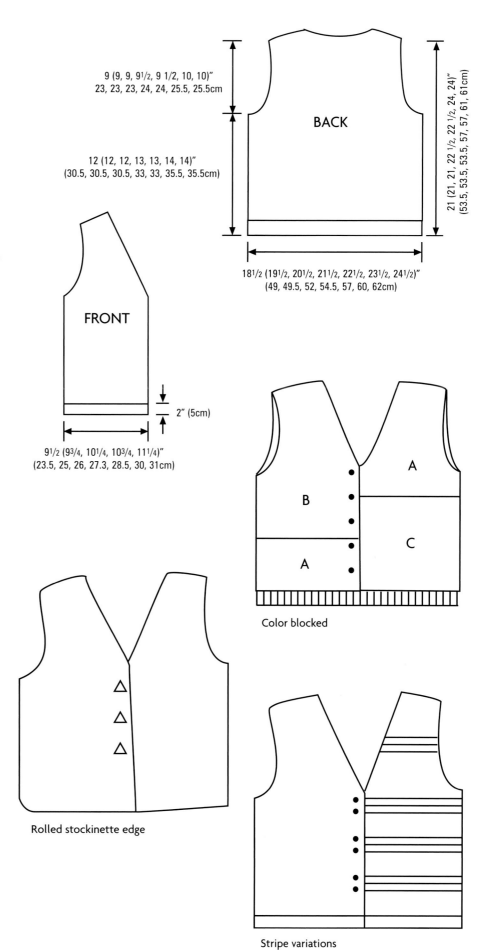

9 (9, 9, 9½, 9 1/2, 10, 10)"
23, 23, 23, 24, 24, 25.5, 25.5cm

12 (12, 12, 13, 13, 14, 14)"
(30.5, 30.5, 30.5, 33, 33, 35.5, 35.5cm)

BACK

21 (21, 21, 22 ½, 22 ½, 24, 24)"
(53.5, 53.5, 53.5, 57, 57, 61, 61cm)

18½ (19½, 20½, 21½, 22½, 23½, 24½)"
(49, 49.5, 52, 54.5, 57, 60, 62cm)

FRONT

2" (5cm)

9½ (9¾, 10¼, 10¾, 11¼)"
(23.5, 25, 26, 27.3, 28.5, 30, 31cm)

B

A

A

C

Color blocked

Rolled stockinette edge

Stripe variations

Indian Vest

SIZES

Small (medium, large)

FINISHED MEASUREMENTS

Bust: 36 (40, 44)

MATERIALS

Medium weight mohair type yarn (1 skein = 50 g [1.75 oz], approximately 95 yds [85.5 m]): 6 (7, 7) skeins

14" knitting needles, sizes 6 and 8 (4 and 5 mm), or size to obtain gauge

Embellishments of choice

GAUGE

In Stockinette st using larger needles: 18 sts = 4" (10 cm)

BACK

Using smaller needles, CO 80 (88, 98) sts and knit 12 rows (6 Garter st ridges).

Change to larger needles; work in St st for 10 (10½, 11)" (25.5, 27, 28 cm) ending with a k row.

Next row: ★ k8 (9, 11) sts, purl to last 8 (9, 11) sts, knit to end. ★

Next row: Knit.

Repeat from ★ to ★.

Armhole shaping (RS facing): BO 5 (6, 8) sts, knit to the end of the row.

Next row: BO 5 (6, 8) sts, k3, purl to last 3 sts, k3.

Next row: k3, ssk, knit to last 5 sts, k2tog, k3.

Next row: k3, purl to last 3 sts, k3. Cont dec at armhole every other row for a total of 5 (6, 7) dec, maintaining 3 sts in Garter st, until 60 (64, 68) sts remain. Cont knitting, keeping 3 sts in Garter st on each armhole edge until back measures 18½ (19½, 20½)" (47, 49.5, 52 cm).

Shape shoulders: BO 5 (5, 6) sts at beg of next 2 rows. BO 5 (6, 6) sts at beg of following 2 rows. BO 6 (6, 6) sts at beg of last 2 rows. Place rem 28 (30, 32) sts on a holder.

LEFT FRONT

Using smaller needles, CO 40 (44, 49) sts.

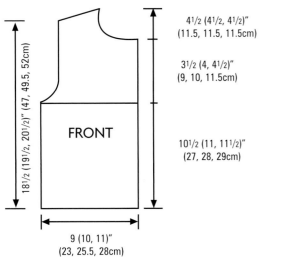

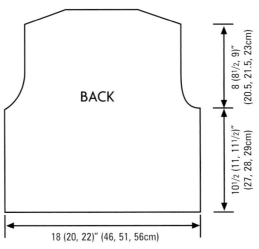

FRONT

18½ (19½, 20½)" (47, 49.5, 52cm)

9 (10, 11)" (23, 25.5, 28cm)

4½ (4½, 4½)" (11.5, 11.5, 11.5cm)

3½ (4, 4½)" (9, 10, 11.5cm)

10½ (11, 11½)" (27, 28, 29cm)

BACK

18 (20, 22)" (46, 51, 56cm)

10½ (11, 11½)" (27, 28, 29cm)

8 (8½, 9)" (20.5, 21.5, 23cm)

18½ (19½, 20½)" (47, 49.5, 52cm)

Work as given for back, incl arm-hole shaping at beg of RS rows (when armhole shaping is complete you will have 30 [32, 34] sts). Work till piece meas 14 (15, 16)" (35.5, 38, 40.5 cm) from beg.

Neck shaping: With WS facing, p12 (13, 14) sts and place these sts on a holder. Purl to last 3 sts, k3. Maintaining Garter st border at armhole edge, dec 1 st at neck edge every other row twice. Cont working on rem 16 (17, 18) sts until front meas same as the back to the start of shoulder shaping. Work shoulder shaping as for back at beg of RS rows.

RIGHT FRONT

Work as for Left Front, reversing all shapings.

FINISHING

Block pieces carefully. Join shoulder seams.

With RS facing and smaller needles, pu and knit approx 74 (78, 82) sts around neck, incl sts left on holders. Work in Garter st for ½" (1.5 cm). BO all sts.

BUTTON BAND

With smaller needles and RS facing, beg at top of neckband and pu 2 sts for every 3 rows along left front edge, ending immediately above the garter st bottom band.

Working in Garter st knit 10 more rows. BO.

Mark the position of the buttons as desired.

BUTTONHOLE BAND

With RS facing and smaller needles, pu sts to correspond to button band.

On 5th Garter st row, work buttonholes to correspond with markers: knit to position of buttonhole, yo, k2tog. Knit 5 more rows. BO.

Join side seams.

Sew on buttons.

Embellish as desired.

VARIATION:

Materials:

Felt scraps

Embroidery floss and needle

Buttons

Cut ten 1½" (4 cm) squares from red felt and pin them around bottom edge of the vest. Secure in place with blanket st, then sew a button in center of each square.

Cut 2 elephants from felt using pattern provided. Pin in position and secure with blanket st.

Appliqué pattern

Shawl Collar Vest

SIZES
Small (medium, large)

FINISHED MEASUREMENTS
Bust: 38 (42, 46)" (96.5, 107, 117 cm)

Length: 19 (19½, 20)" (48.5, 50, 51 cm)

MATERIALS
Heavy worsted weight 80% super fine merino wool, 20% nylon (1 skein = 4 oz, 112 g): 3 (3, 4) skeins

14" knitting needles, size 9 (5.5 mm), or size needed to obtain gauge

GAUGE
16 sts = 4" (10 cm) over pattern stitch

PATTERN STITCH
Box stitch:

Row 1: k2 *p2 k2; rep from * to end of row. Row 2: p2 *k2 p2; rep from * to end of row. Row 3: p2 *k2 p2; rep from * to end of row. Row 4: k2 *p2 k2; rep from * to end of row.

Repeat these four rows.

BACK
CO 78 (86, 94) sts and work in Box st until piece meas 18 (18½, 19)" (46, 47, 48.5 cm).

Shoulder shaping: BO 6 (7, 8) sts at beg of next 8 rows. BO rem 30 sts.

FRONTS
Note: You can reverse shapings, or simply work both pieces alike since the fabric is reversible.

CO 38 (42, 46) sts; work in Box st until pieces meas the same as the back to start of shoulder shaping.

With RS facing, shape shoulder at one edge as for back; 14 (14, 14) sts rem.

Collar extension: Cont working on these 14 sts (all sizes) in Box st for 4½ (4½, 4½)" (11.5, 11.5, 11.5 cm). BO loosely.

FINISHING
Place markers on fronts and back 8 (8½, 9)" (20.5, 21.5, 23 cm) from start of shoulder shaping.

Join shoulder seams.

Join ends of collar, remembering that WS of collar will be on RS of garment.

Stitch collar to the back neck edge.

Join side seams below markers.

Apply closure or buttons if desired.

4¹/₂" (11.5cm)

4¹/₂" (11.5cm)

FRONT

10¹/₂ (11¹/₂, 12¹/₂)"
(27, 29, 32cm)

7¹/₂" (19cm)

BACK

18 (18¹/₂, 19¹/₂)" (46, 47, 48.5cm)

19¹/₂ (21¹/₂, 23¹/₂)"
(49.5, 54.5, 60cm)

Cardigan with Knit-In Front Bands

SIZES

Small (medium, large, extra large)

FINISHED MEASUREMENTS

Chest: 39 (43, 47, 49)" (99, 109, 119.5, 124.5 cm)

MATERIALS

Bulky weight (50 g = approximately 48 m): 16 (16, 17, 17) balls

14" knitting needles, sizes 7 and 9 (4.5 and 5.5 mm) or size needed to obtain correct gauge

5 buttons

GAUGE

In reverse Stockinette stitch (rev St st):

12 sts x 18 rows = 4" (10 cm) square

STITCH PATTERNS

Garter stitch: knit every row.
Reverse Stockinette stitch: Row 1: Purl (RS), Row 2: Knit (WS).

BACK

Using smaller needles, CO 58 (64, 70, 74) sts.

Work 8 rows in Garter st (4 ridges).

Change to larger needles and work in rev St st until back meas 22 (23, 24, 25)" (56, 58.5, 61, 63.5 cm).

Shoulder shaping: BO 6 (7, 8, 8) at beg of next 2 rows, then 6 (7, 8, 9) at beg of following 2 rows and 7 (8, 8, 9) at beg of last 2 rows. BO remaining 20 (20, 22, 22) back neck sts.

Place markers 9 (9½, 10½, 11)" (23, 24, 27, 28 cm) down from beg of shoulder shaping to indicate armhole.

LEFT FRONT

Using smaller needles, CO 35 (38, 41, 43) sts, noting that 6 sts will form the front border.

Work 8 rows garter st.

Change to larger needles.

Next row: RS facing, purl to last 6 sts, k6.

Next row: Knit.

Cont working in rev St st, working 6 sts in Garter st at front edge on every row (place marker to remind you if necessary) until work meas same as back to armhole.

Neck shaping: RS facing, ★ work to last 8 sts; k2tog, k6. Rep from ★ every 4 rows until 25 (28, 30, 32) sts remain. When piece meas same as back to start of shoulder shaping, work shoulder at arm edge to correspond to back. Cont knitting on 6 rem front band sts for about 3½" (9 cm). Place sts on safety pin. With safety pins, mark position of buttons on left front band, placing the first ½" (12 mm) from bottom, and last just below start of neck shaping. Space rest of markers evenly in between—this is easy to

do, just count the number of Garter st ridges.

RIGHT FRONT

Knit as for the left front, reversing all shaping, working buttonholes (k2 tog, yo) in band to correspond with button markers.

SLEEVES

Using smaller needles, CO 26 (28, 28, 30) sts and work 8 rows Garter st.

Change to larger needles and rev St st.

Work increases as follows: Inc 1 st on each side of piece every 4 rows until there are 54 (58, 64, 66) sts on the needle.

Work straight until sleeve meas 17 (17½, 18, 18½)" (43, 44.5, 46, 47 cm). Adjust sleeve length here, if necessary.

BO sts loosely.

FINISHING

Join shoulder seams together. Adjust length of Garter st borders to meet in center back neck; BO and join together neatly. Sew border to back neck.

Pin sleeve in position between the markers and stitch to armhole.

Complete side and sleeve seams.

Sew on the buttons to correspond with the buttonholes.

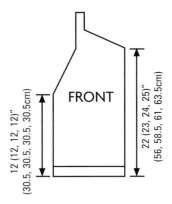

FRONT

12 (12, 12, 12)" (30.5, 30.5, 30.5, 30.5cm)

22 (23, 24, 25)" (56, 58.5, 61, 63.5cm)

6½ (6½, 6½, 7, 7)" (16.5, 16.5, 16.5, 18, 18cm)

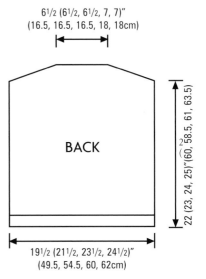

BACK

22 (23, 24, 25)" (60, 58.5, 61, 63.5)

19½ (21½, 23½, 24½)" (49.5, 54.5, 60, 62cm)

18 (19, 21, 22)" (46, 48.5, 53.5, 56cm)

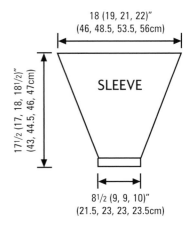

SLEEVE

17½ (17, 18, 18½)" (43, 44.5, 46, 47cm)

8½ (9, 9, 10)" (21.5, 23, 23, 23.5cm)

Shawl Collar Jacket

SIZES
Small (medium, large, extra large)

FINISHED MEASUREMENTS
Chest: 39 (43, 45, 49)" (99, 109, 114.5, 124.5 cm)

MATERIALS
Bulky weight boucle yarn (50 g = approximately 58 m):
13 (14, 15, 16) balls
14" knitting needles, size 10½ (size 6.5 mm) or size needed to obtain correct gauge.
Small amount of a smooth yarn in a matching color for seams

GAUGE
In Garter Stitch:
11 sts = 4" (10 cm)
2.75 sts = 1" (2.5 cm)

BACK
CO 54 (60, 66, 70) sts.
Work in Garter st until the back meas 25 (26, 27, 28)" (63.5, 66, 68.5, 71 cm) in length.

Shape shoulders: BO 6 (7, 7, 8) sts at beg of next 2 rows. BO 6 (7, 8, 8) sts at beg of following 4 rows. BO rem 18 (18, 20, 22) back neck sts. Meas 9 (9½, 10, 10½)" (23, 24, 25.5, 27 cm) down from the beg of shoulder shaping and place markers for underarm.

LEFT FRONT
CO 33 (36, 39, 42) sts and work until piece meas same as back to start of shoulder shaping.

Work left shoulder shaping on RS rows as for back.

Collar: Cont on rem 15 (15, 16, 18) sts for 3 (3½, 3½, 4)" inches (7.5, 9, 9, 10 cm). BO.

RIGHT FRONT
Work same as left front, reversing all shaping.

Place markers for underarm as on back.

SLEEVES
CO 26 (28, 28, 30) sts. Inc 1 st at each side of piece every 4 rows until there are 50 (52, 56, 60) sts.

Work straight until sleeve meas 17 (17½, 18, 18½)" (43, 44.5, 46, 47 cm).

Place all stitches of each sleeve on a separate circular needle or flexible cord holder until seaming jacket together to allow for ease in sleeve length adjustment.

FINISHING
Use a smooth yarn in a matching color for seams.

Join shoulder seams firmly together.

Join ends of shawl collar; remember that WS becomes RS when collar is attached to jacket.

Stitch collar to back neck edge.

Mark midpoint of sleeve and place at shoulder seam.

Pin sleeve into place between

Back vent, decorated with button, as described in coat variation.

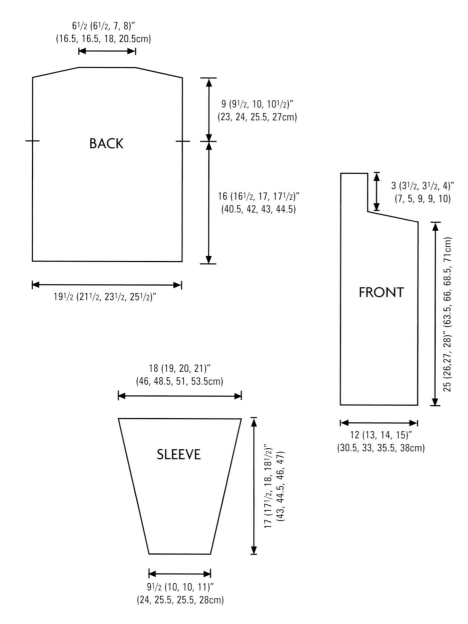

6½ (6½, 7, 8)"
(16.5, 16.5, 18, 20.5cm)

BACK

9 (9½, 10, 10½)"
(23, 24, 25.5, 27cm)

16 (16½, 17, 17½)"
(40.5, 42, 43, 44.5)

19½ (21½, 23½, 25½)"

18 (19, 20, 21)"
(46, 48.5, 51, 53.5cm)

SLEEVE

17 (17½, 18, 18½)"
(43, 44.5, 46, 47)

9½ (10, 10, 11)"
(24, 25.5, 25.5, 28cm)

3 (3½, 3½, 4)"
(7, 5, 9, 9, 10)

FRONT

25 (26,27, 28)" (63.5, 66, 68.5, 71cm)

12 (13, 14, 15)"
(30.5, 33, 35.5, 38cm)

markers; try on jacket and make any adjustment to sleeve length; then BO all sts loosely. Seam sleeve into armhole.

Join underarm and side seams.

CUFFED-SLEEVE VARIATION

CO 30 (32, 32, 34) sts and work 1"(2.5 cm) in Garter st.

Dec 1 st each end of next row.

Cont working until sleeve meas 2-½" (6.5 cm); dec 1 st at each end of next row. You will now have 26 (28, 28, 30) sts.

When sleeve meas 3" (7.5 cm), mark last row for turning row.

Inc 1 st at each end of next row and cont working sleeves as given.

To finish, seam first 3" (7.5 cm) of sleeve; remember that WS will show as RS when cuff is turned back. Complete rest of sleeve seam.

COAT VARIATION

Jacket length can easily be extended to make a coat. To lengthen jacket by 15" (38 cm) you will need an extra 5 (5, 6, 6) balls of yarn.

You can fasten the coat with a pin, add bands and buttons, or wear it edge-to-edge.

You have the option of making side vents by simply leaving the side edges unseamed for the bottom 8 to 10" (20.5 to 25.5 cm). Add a decorative button to make a feature of these vents and to secure the seam (see photograph above).

Yet another option is to add a central back vent for a more tailored look. To add the back vent you will need to work the back of the coat in two sections for the depth of the vent. See following instructions.

BACK WITH CENTER VENT

First part: CO 33 (36, 39, 41) sts and work in Garter st until the piece is 8" (20.5 cm) long.
Next row: BO 6 sts. Put this piece aside.

Second part: CO 27 (30, 33, 35) sts and work in Garter st until this piece matches the first in length (count Garter st ridges to be sure).

Joining row: Knit to end of row; using same working strand of yarn and placing the 6 BO sts behind the work at vent, knit across 27 (30, 33, 35) sts of First part. Continue knitting on these 54 (60, 66, 70) sts as for jacket back, beginning the shoulder shaping when piece is 40 (41, 42, 43)" (101.5, 104, 107, 109 cm) in length.

FRONTS

Work as for jacket but knit pieces to match length of the coat back.

SLEEVES

Work as for jacket.

FINISHING

To finish the center back vent, slipstitch the bound-off sts of the underlay to the wrong side of the back.

Sew a flat button through both thicknesses to secure the vent.

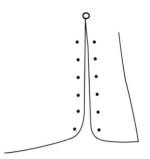

Side seam vent embellished with small buttons

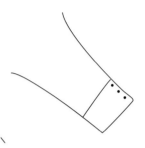

Sleeve cuffs trimmed with vertical or horizontal buttons

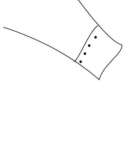

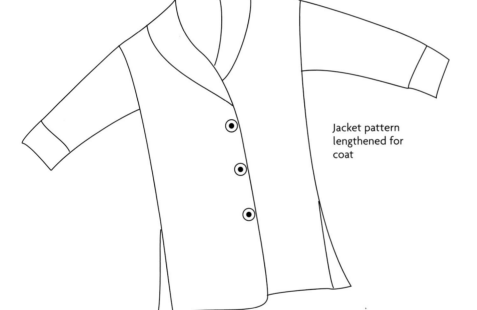

Jacket pattern lengthened for coat

Button collar trim

Fringe collar trim

Patchwork Jacket

MATERIALS

Assorted yarns: Approx 4 (4 oz =112 g) skeins

Needles in your choice of size

Gridded dressmaker's pattern paper (available at fabric and quilting stores)

Safety pins

Tapestry needle

GAUGE

Only your gauge matters here, and it can vary considerably if you are using a variety of weights and textures. Even if you make all patchwork pieces 20 stitches, the variety of sizes will be that much more interesting.

MAKING THE RECTANGLES

CO 20 stitches and work in box stitch.

Rows 1 and 2: (k2, p2) to end.

Rows 3 and 4: (p2, k2) to end.

Don't add seam stitches, as these will be pieced together both vertically and horizontally, but be sure to leave yourself yarn ends at beg and end of work to use for sewing.

ASSEMBLING THE GARMENT

You will need a pattern piece to put your modules on. Cut a template from freezer paper, craft paper or from gridded dressmaker's pattern paper (available at fabric stores and quilting stores) onto which you can easily pin the pieces and then drape the work-in-progress on yourself.

Refer to schematic on page 57, and cut pieces for the back, fronts, and sleeves; take an existing sweater that fits well, and draw the shape of its pieces; or choose a schematic from another knitting pattern you like.

Safety-pin rectangles onto the pattern pieces, arranging them like a jigsaw puzzle. Fill in gaps by knitting the missing piece, or pick up stitches and knit onto an existing rectangle. You may need to shape an area by increasing or decreasing.

When each pattern piece is filled, safety-pin the pieces together taking care not to stretch rectangles. Sew/weave them together, RS facing to avoid bulky seams. Nothing can go wrong. At the worst, you'll have to unpick a rectangle or two.

Garment edges can be left as they are because the modules lie flat and the edges are neat, or you can pick up stitches to knit on ribbing for cuffs and welts, or to add other areas of knitting. If the piece you added on doesn't look right, pull the knitting out gently and try again.

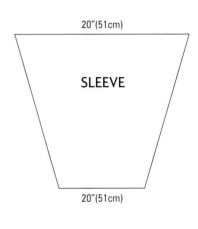

20"(51cm)

SLEEVE

20"(51cm)

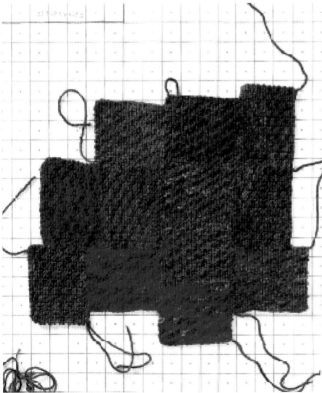

Laying rectangles on grid.

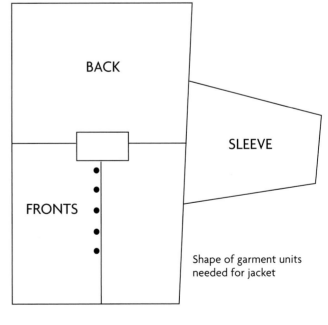

BACK

SLEEVE

FRONTS

Shape of garment units
needed for jacket

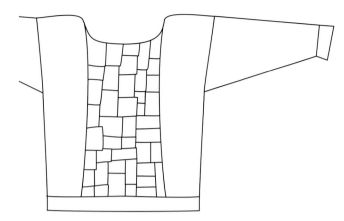

Front/back panels in patchwork

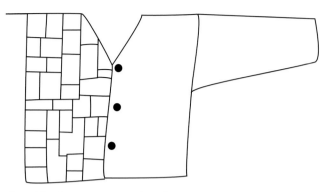

One side of garment in patchwork

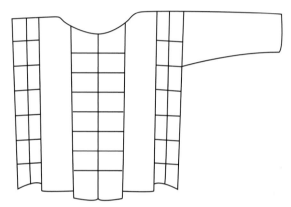

Alternating strips of patchwork and plain knitting

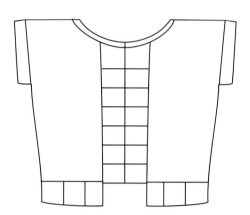

Vest with hem and front bands in patchwork

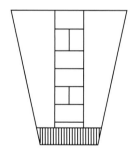

Patchwork in center panel of sleeve

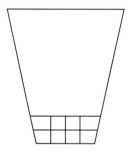

Patchwork on a turned-back cuff

Maggie Rennard Jacket

RATING

Intermediate

SIZES

Small (Medium, Large, Extra Large)

Finished measurements: 38 (40, 44, 48)" (96.5, 101.5, 112, 122 cm)

MATERIALS

Heavy weight mohair type yarn: 1080 (1120, 1170, 1260) yds (988, 1024, 1070, 1152 m)

14" knitting needles, sizes 5 and 7 (3.75 and 4.5 mm)

Cable needle (cn)

Four ¾" (2 cm) buttons

GAUGE

St st on larger needles: 17 sts and 23 rows = 4" (10 cm)

Double cable = 2½" (6.5 cm)

PATTERN STITCHES

Single rib: All rows: k1, p1.

Stockinette stitch: Row 1: Knit (RS), Row 2: Purl (WS).

Double Cable: multiple of 16 sts.

Row 1 (RS): p2, k12, p2.

Row 2 and all other WS rows: k2, p12, k2.

Row 3: p2, sl next 3 sts to cn and hold in back, k3, k3 from cn, sl next 3 sts to cn and hold in front, k3, k3 from cn, end p2.

Rows 5 and 7: p2, k12, p2.

Rep rows 1 through 8.

BACK

With smaller needles, CO 83 (87, 95, 103) sts.

Work in Single rib for 3" (7.5 cm), end with a RS row.

Purl across next row, inc 9 sts evenly spaced to give 92 (96, 104, 112) sts.

Change to larger needles.

Next row (RS): k12 (13, 17, 20), work row 1 of cable over next 16 sts, k36 (38, 38, 40) sts, work row 1 of cable over next 16 sts, end k12 (13, 17, 20).

Next row: p12 (13, 17, 20), work row 2 of cable over next 16 sts, p36 (38, 38, 40) sts, work row 2 of cable over next 16 sts, end p12 (13, 17, 20).

Work even until piece meas 1" (2.5 cm) above rib, end with a WS row.

Form pocket extensions:

On next row (RS), CO 15 sts and k them, place marker, slip 1 p-wise, work as est to end.

Next row (WS): CO 15 sts and p them, place marker, work as est to next marker, end p15.

Next row (RS): k15, sl marker, sl 1, work as est to 1 st before next marker, sl 1, sl marker, end k15.

Work even as est until pocket extensions measure 6" (15 cm), end with a WS row.

BO 15 sts at beg of next 2 rows.

Work even until piece meas 10" (25.5 cm) above rib (13"/33 cm total).

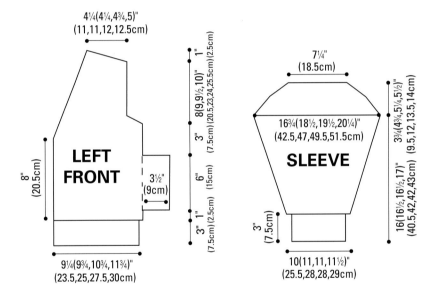

4¼(4¼,4¾,5)"
(11,11,12,12.5cm)

1"
(2.5cm)

8(9,9½,10)"
(20.5,23,24,25.5cm)

3"
(7.5cm)

6"
(15cm)

3"
(7.5cm)

1"
(2.5cm)

8"
(20.5cm)

LEFT FRONT

3½"
(9cm)

9¼(9¾,10¾,11¾)"
(23.5,25,27.5,30cm)

7¼"
(18.5cm)

16¾(18½,19½,20¼)"
(42.5,47,49.5,51.5cm)

SLEEVE

3¾(4¾,5,5½)"
(9.5,12,13.5,14cm)

16(16½,16½,17)"
(40.5,42,42,43cm)

3"
(7.5cm)

10(11,11,11½)"
(25.5,28,28,29cm)

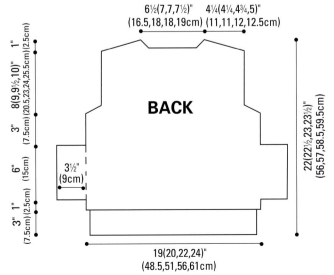

6½(7,7,7½)"
(16.5,18,18,19cm)

4¼(4¼,4¾,5)"
(11,11,12,12.5cm)

1"
(2.5cm)

8(9,9½,10)"
(20.5,23,24,25.5cm)

3"
(7.5cm)

6"
(15cm)

3"
(7.5cm)

1"
(2.5cm)

BACK

3½"
(9cm)

22(22½,23,23½)"
(56,57,58.5,59.5cm)

19(20,22,24)"
(48.5,51,56,61cm)

Armhole shaping:

BO 2 sts at beg of next 6 (6, 8, 8) rows; then dec 1 st at each edge 3 (3, 3, 5) times to give 74 (78, 82, 86) sts.

Work even as est until armhole depth measures 8 (9, 9½,10)" (20.5, 23, 24, 25.5 cm), end with a WS row.

Shoulder and back neck shaping:
Mark center 12 (14, 14, 16) sts.

Work to center sts, join a 2nd ball of yarn, BO center 12 (14, 14, 16) sts, and work to end.

Working both sides at the same time with separate balls of yarn, BO 4 sts from each neck edge twice, and at the same time, BO 8 (8, 9, 9) sts from each shoulder edge twice, then 7 (8, 8, 9) sts once.

LEFT FRONT

With smaller needles, CO 41 (43, 47, 51) sts.

Work in Single rib for 3" (7.5 cm), end with a WS row.

Purl across next row, inc 4 sts evenly spaced to give 45 (47, 51, 55) sts.

Change to larger needles.

Next row (RS): k12 (13, 17, 20), work row 1 of cable over 16 sts, k17 (18, 18, 19).

Next row: p17 (18, 18, 19) sts, work row 2 of cable over 16 sts, p12 (13, 17, 20).

Work even as est until piece meas 1" (2.5 cm) above rib, end with a WS row.

To form a pocket extension as for back, CO 15 sts at beg of next row.

Work as est until pocket extension meas same as for back, end with a WS row.

BO 15 sts at beg of next row.

Work even until piece meas 8" (20.5 cm) above rib (11"/28 cm total), end with a WS row.

Neckline shaping: Next row, dec row (RS): work to last 3 sts, k2tog, end k1.

Rep dec row after 3 more rows, then alternately every 6th and 4th row thereafter for a total of 13 (14, 14, 15) decs at this edge; at the same time, work even until front meas same as back to armhole, end with a WS row.

Armhole shaping: BO 2 sts at beg of next 3 (3, 4, 4) RS row; then dec 1 st at armhole edge 3 (3, 3, 5) times.

Work even until front meas same as back to shoulder, end with a WS row to give 23 (24, 26, 27) sts.

Shoulder shaping: BO 8 (8, 9, 9) sts at beg of next 2 RS row, then 7 (8, 8, 9) sts at beg of last RS row.

RIGHT FRONT

Work same as for left front, reversing all pattern placement and shaping.

SLEEVES

With smaller needles, CO 39 (41, 41, 43) sts.

Work in Single rib for 3" (7.5 cm), end with a RS row.

Purl across next row, inc 9 (11, 11, 11) sts evenly spaced to give 48 (52, 52, 54) sts.

Change to larger needles.

Next row (RS): k16 (18, 18, 19), work row 1 of cable, k16 (18, 18, 19).

Next row: p16 (18, 18, 19), work row 2 of cable, p16 (18, 18, 19).

Work even as est for 3 (7, 1, 3) more rows to end with a WS row.

Keeping in patt as est, inc 1 st each end of next row; then for size small, inc 1 st each end alternately every 4th and 6th row thereafter; for all other sizes, inc 1 st each end every 4th row thereafter, making a total of 14 (16, 18, 19) inc sts each end to give 76 (84, 88, 92) total sts.

Note: Work incs as follows: k2, inc 1, work to last 2 sts, inc 1, end k2. Cont until sleeve meas 16 (16½, 16½, 17)" (40.5, 42, 42, 43 cm) or to desired length, end with WS row.

Cap shaping: BO 2 sts at the beg of next 8 (12, 14, 16) rows, 3 sts at beg of next 8 rows, then rem 36 sts on the next row.

FINISHING

Sew front to back at shoulders.

Note: Left front button band, collar, and buttonhole band are worked in one continuous piece, then sewn onto sweater. Begin with left front button band.

Front band: With smaller needles, CO 7 sts.

Work in Single rib until piece, when slightly stretched, meas 11" (28 cm), end with a WS row.

Tie first scrap yarn marker at end of this row.

Shawl collar: Change to larger needles.

Work 2 rows in rib.

Inc 1 st at beg of next row, then every other row 30 more times to give 38 sts.

Tie end-of-increases scrap yarn marker on shaped edge.

Work even until shaped edge meas 12½" (31.5 cm) above first marker.

Tie shoulder marker #1 on shaped edge.

Work even for 8½ (9, 9, 9½)" (21.5, 23, 23, 24 cm) more; then tie shoulder marker #2 along shaped edge.

At this point, check the fit by aligning shaped edge of collar with garment and matching markers to shoulder seams.

Work even until shaped edge meas 12½" (31.5 cm) beyond marker #2; then tie beg-of-decreases marker on shaped edge.

Dec 1 st at neck edge every other row until 7 sts rem; then work 2 rows even.

Sl these sts onto holder.

Tie last marker.

Pin collar around jacket, aligning first marker with beg of neck shaping on left front and matching shoulder markers #1 and #2 to shoulder seams.

Match last marker to beg of neck shaping on right front.

Sew collar in place.

Sew 4 buttons evenly spaced on button band at left front.

Buttonhole band: Change to smaller needles.

Sl 7 sts from holder and work in rib until piece meas same as for left button band, working a buttonhole (yo and k2tog or p2tog as needed for rib pattern) opposite each button on left front.

Sew remaining band to right front.

Sew sleeve seams.

Sew sleeve cap in armhole, centering at shoulder seam.

Sew side seams and around pocket extensions, leaving pocket opening at side seam.

Woven-Look Cardigan

RATING

Intermediate

SIZES

Small (Medium, Large)

Finished measurements: 38½ (42, 46)" (98, 106.5, 117 cm)

MATERIALS

Worsted-weight yarn, preferably wool: 1520 (1520, 1615) yds (1390, 1390, 1477 m)

14" knitting needles, sizes 5 and 8 (3.75 and 5 mm)

Five 1" (2.5 cm) buttons

GAUGE

Pattern stitch with larger needles:

22 sts and 26 rows = 4" (10 cm)

PATTERN STITCHES

RT (right twist): k2tog, leaving sts on left-hand needle, insert right-hand needle from the front bet the ktog sts and k first st again; then slip both sts from the needle tog.

LT (left twist): With right-hand needle behind left-hand needle, skip the first st and k the 2nd st in the back loop; then insert the right-hand needle into the backs of both sts and k2tog.

Single Rib: k1, p1 every row (even number of stitches).

Pattern Stitch: Multiple of 10 sts plus 6.

Row 1 (WS): k1, ★ p4, k1; rep from ★.

Row 2: ★ p1, k4, p1, LT, RT; rep from ★ and end p1, k4, p1.

Rows 3 and 5: ★ k6, p4; rep from ★ and end k6.

Row 4: ★ p6, k1, RT, k1; rep from ★ and end p6.

Row 6: ★ p1, k4, p1, RT, LT; rep from ★ and end p1, k4, p1.

Row 7: Rep row 1.

Rows 8 and 10: p1, ★ k4, p6; rep from ★ and end k4, p1.

Row 9: K1, ★ p4, k6; rep from ★ and end p4, k1.

Repeat rows 1 through 10.

BACK

With smaller needles, CO 132 (146, 158) sts.

Work in Single rib for 1½" (4 cm), ending with a WS row.

Knit across next row and dec 26 (30, 32) sts evenly across to give 106 (116, 126) sts.

Change to larger needles and work even in pattern stitch until piece meas 9½ (10, 10½)" (24, 25.5, 26.5 cm).

Armhole shaping: Keeping in est patt, BO at the beg of row 3 sts twice, then 2 sts 6 times.

Then dec 1 each end every other row 3 times, then each end every

4th row 3 times, to leave 76 (86, 96) sts. rem.

Work even until armhole meas 7 (7½, 8)" (18, 19, 20.5 cm), ending with a WS row.

Shoulder and neck shaping: Work 31 (35, 39) sts, join another ball of yarn, BO center 14 (16, 18) sts, and work to end of row.

Working each side sep, BO at each neck edge 4 sts twice, 3 sts once and 2 sts once.

At the same time, when armhole meas 7½ (8, 81/2)" (19, 20.5, 21.5 cm), BO at each shoulder edge 6 (7, 9) sts twice, then 6 (8, 8) sts once.

LEFT FRONT

With smaller needles, CO 64 (70, 76) sts.

Work in Single rib as for back for 1½" (4 cm), ending with a WSR.

Knit across next row and dec 13 (14, 15) sts evenly across to give 51 (56, 61) sts.

Change to larger needles and beg working in pattern stitch with row 1.

On row 2 of patt, for small and large sizes, end row with LT, RT, p1.

Cont to work even in patt as est, shaping armhole at beg of RS rows only as for back, until armhole meas 5 (5½, 6)" (12.5, 14, 15 cm), ending with a RS row to give 36 (41, 46) sts.

Neck shaping: At neck edge, BO 4 sts once, 3 sts twice, 2 sts 3 times and dec 1 st 2 (3, 4) times. Work even on 18 (22, 26) sts until piece meas the same length as back, shaping shoulder as for back.

RIGHT FRONT

Work to correspond to left front, reversing all shaping.

Note: Since pattern will have alternating squares because of row beginning, it is not necessary to place pattern differently.

SLEEVES

With smaller needles, CO 52 (56, 62) sts.

Work in Single rib for 2" (5 cm), ending with a RS row.

Knit across next row and dec 1 (0, 1) sts evenly across to give 51 (56, 61) sts.

Beg pattern stitch as for left front.

Keeping in est pattern, inc 1 st each edge every 8th row 3 (2, 0) times, then every 10th row 7 (8, 10) times.

Work even on 71 (76, 81) sts until piece meas 17 (17½, 18)" (43, 44.5, 45.5 cm).

Cap shaping: BO 4 sts at the beg of the next 2 rows, 2 (3, 3) sts at beg of next 2 rows, then dec 1 st each edge every other row 9 (10, 11) times.

BO 2 sts at beg of next 6 rows, 3 sts at beg of next 2 rows.

BO rem 23 (24, 27) sts.

FINISHING

Sew shoulder and side seams.

Neck band: With RS facing and smaller needles, pu 95 (101, 107) sts evenly around neck.

Work in Single rib for 1½" (4 cm).

BO in ribbing.

Left front button band: With smaller needles and RS facing, pu 89 (95, 101) sts along left front edge, incl edge of neck band.

Row 1: k1, ★ p1, k1; rep from ★.

Row 2: k2, p1, ★ k1, p1; rep from ★ to last 2 sts and k2.

Rep these 2 rows until band meas 1½" (4 cm).

BO in ribbing.

Mark positions for 5 buttonholes evenly spaced in p sts of left front band.

Right front band: Work as for left front band for ¾" (2 cm). Work buttonholes opposite markers on left front band by working to marked p st and working yo, k2tog.

Finish to correspond to left front band.

Set in sleeves.

Sew underarm and sleeve seams.

Sew on buttons.

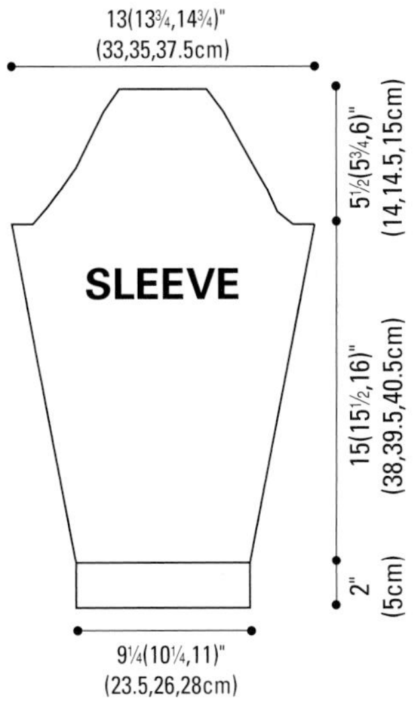

13(13¾,14¾)"
(33,35,37.5cm)
SLEEVE
5½(5¾,6)"
(14,14.5,15cm)
15(15½,16)"
(38,39.5,40.5cm)
2"
(5cm)
9¼(10¼,11)"
(23.5,26,28cm)

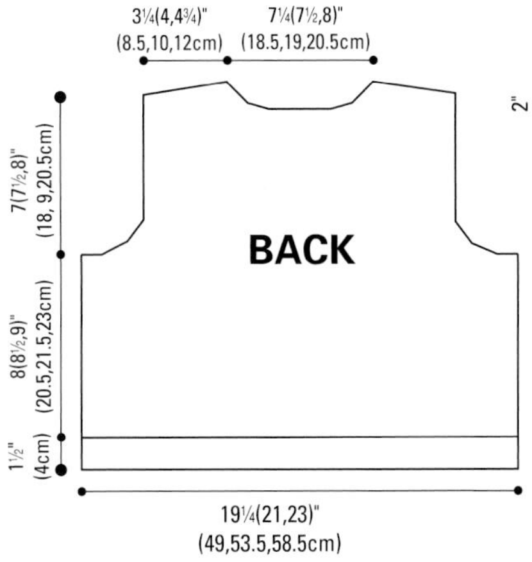

3¼(4,4¾)"
(8.5,10,12cm)
7¼(7½,8)"
(18.5,19,20.5cm)
7(7½,8)"
(18, 9,20.5cm)
BACK
8(8½,9)"
(20.5,21.5,23cm)
1½"
(4cm)
19¼(21,23)"
(49,53.5,58.5cm)

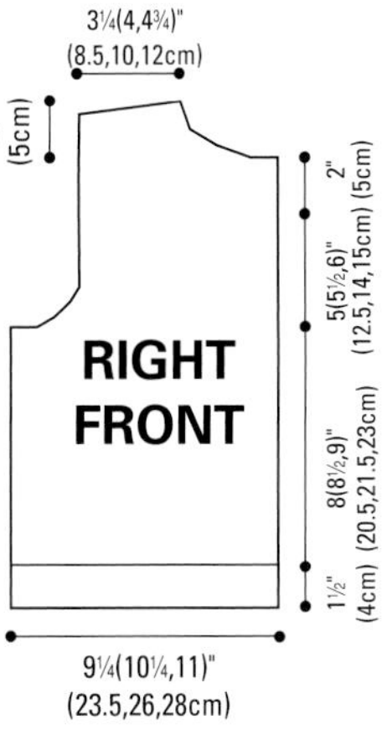

3¼(4,4¾)"
(8.5,10,12cm)
2"
(5cm)
RIGHT FRONT
2"
(5cm)
5(5½,6)"
(12.5,14,15cm)
8(8½,9)"
(20.5,21.5,23cm)
1½"
(4cm)
9¼(10¼,11)"
(23.5,26,28cm)

Deborah's Biking Cardigan

RATING

Intermediate

SIZES

Petite (Small, Medium, Large).

Finished measurements: 38¾ (40, 41½, 43½)" (98.5, 101.5, 105.5, 110.5 cm)

MATERIALS

Worsted-weight yarn for cropped version shown: 1275 (1360, 1445, 1530) yds (1166, 1244, 1321, 1399 m); 1615 (1700, 1785, 1870) yds (1477, 1554, 1632, 1710 m) for longer version

14" knitting needles, sizes 6 and 7 (4 and 4.5 mm)

Five 1" (2.5 cm) buttons

GAUGE

Charted pattern: 20 sts and 32 rows = 4" (10 cm)

PATTERN STITCHES

3 x 3 Rib: Multiple of 6 sts, plus 3.
Row 1 (WS): p3, ★ k3, p3; rep from ★.
Row 2: k3, ★ p3, k3; rep from ★.
Seed Band: Odd number of sts.
Rows 1, 2, and 3: K all sts., Row 4: P all sts.
Rows 5, 6, 7, 8, and 9: k1, ★ p1, k1; rep from ★.
Row 10: p all sts, Rows 11 and 12: k all sts.
Diamond/Zigzag Pattern:
See chart on page 66.
Moss stitch: Even number of sts.
Row 1 (WS): ★ k1, p1; rep from ★.
Row 2: k2, ★ p1, k1; rep from ★.

BACK

With larger needles, CO 105 (105, 111, 117) sts.

Work in 3 x 3 rib for 1½" (4 cm), ending with a RS row.

Purl across next row and dec 4 (2, 4, 4) sts evenly across to give 101 (103, 107, 113) sts.

Work 1 rep of Seed band.

On RS row, beg Diamond/Zigzag patt with row 1 of chart, beg where indicated for size (see chart and key).

Work even until row 24 of chart is complete, then rows 17 through 24 once more, ending with a WS row.

Work 1 rep of Seed band.

Cont as est, alternating Diamond/Zigzag patt and Seed band.

Work even until piece meas 9½" (24 cm) for cropped version or 15" (38 cm) for longer version (adding 44 more rows).

End with WS row 8 of Diamond/Zigzag patt.

Armhole shaping: BO 2 sts at the beg of the next 8 (8, 8, 6) rows, then 3 sts at the beg of the next 0 (0, 0, 2) rows to give 85 (87, 91, 95) sts.

Work even until armhole meas 7½ (8, 8½, 9)" (19, 20.5, 21.5, 23 cm), ending with a WS row.

Shoulder and neck shaping: Work across 35 (35, 37, 38) sts, join another ball of yarn, BO center 15 (17, 17, 19) sts, and work to end. Working each side sep, BO at each shoulder edge 8 (8, 9, 9) sts twice, then 9 (9, 9, 10) sts once, and at the same time, BO 5 sts at each neck edge twice.

LEFT FRONT

With larger needles, CO 51 (51, 57, 57) sts.

Work in 3 x 3 rib as for back, ending with a RS row.

P across next row and dec 4 (2, 6, 4) sts evenly across to give 47 (49, 51, 53) sts.

Work Seed band as for back.

Work Diamond/Zigzag pattern where indicated on chart.

Work same as back to armhole, ending with a WS row.

Armhole shaping: BO 2 sts at the beg of the next 4 (4, 4, 3) RS rows, then 3 sts at the beg of the next 0 (0, 0, 1) RS rows to give 39 (41, 43, 44) sts.

Work even as est until armhole meas 5½ (6, 6½, 7)" (14, 15, 16.5, 18 cm), ending with a RS row.

Neck shaping: BO at neck edge 2 (4, 4, 4) sts once, 3 sts once, 2 sts three times; then dec 1 st each RS row 3 times to give 25 (25, 27, 28) sts.

Work even until armhole meas the same as back, ending with a WS row.

Shoulder shaping: BO 8 (8, 9, 9) sts at the beg of the next 2 (2, 3, 2) RS row, then 9 (9, 0, 10) sts at the beg of next RS row.

RIGHT FRONT

Work as for left front, beg where indicated on Diamond/Zigzag chart and reversing all shaping.

SLEEVES

With larger needles, CO 51 (51, 57, 57) sts.

Work in 3 x 3 rib for 1½" (4 cm), ending with a RS row.

Purl across next row and inc 12 (12, 8, 10) sts evenly across to give 63 (63, 65, 67) sts.

Beg Diamond/Zigzag pattern where indicated on chart.

Cont as est until 8 rows are complete, ending with a WS row.

Inc 1 st each end of the next row and every following 10th (8th, 8th, 6th) row 11 (14, 15, 17) times to give 85 (91, 95, 101) sts.

At the same time, cont until row 16 of chart is complete above the rib, ending with a WS row; then work Seed band.

Working inc sts into est patts, cont to alternate 32 rows of chart and Seed band.

Work even until piece meas 15½" (39.5 cm) above rib (17"/43 cm total), ending with WS row 8 of chart.

Cap shaping: BO 2 sts at the beg of the next 24 (26, 28, 30) rows; then BO 3 sts at the beg of the next 4 rows.

BO rem 25 (27, 27, 29) sts on the next row.

FINISHING

Sew shoulder and side seams.

With RS facing and starting at right front, use smaller needles to pu 75 (81, 81, 87) sts evenly around entire neckline edge to left front.

Work in 3 x 3 rib for ¾" (2 cm).

Left front button band: With smaller needles, CO 8 sts.

Work in moss st until band, when slightly stretched, meas the same as front edge incl neckline rib; then BO all sts.

Sew to left front, stretching slightly to fit.

Sew 5 buttons evenly spaced along band.

Right front buttonhole band:

With RS facing and smaller needles, pu 105 (108, 111, 114) sts for cropped version or 135 (138, 141, 144) sts for longer version.

Next row (WS): p3 (0, 3, 0) sts, ★ k3, p3; rep from ★.

Work 3 x 3 rib as est for 2 more rows.

On next row, work a 4-st buttonhole opposite each button: (BO 4 sts on this row and CO 4 sts on the next row above the BO sts.)

Cont rib until band meas 1" (2.5 cm); then BO all sts.

Sew sleeve seams.

Sew sleeve cap in armhole, centering it at shoulder seam.

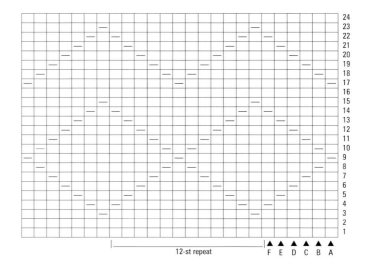

12-st repeat   F E D C B A

KEY

▢ = Knit on RS, purl on WS

— = Purl on RS, knit on WS

Odd number rows are RS rows; read right to left

Even number rows are WS rows; read left to right

A: Beg back large, left front small
B: Beg back medium
C: Beg back small
D: Beg back petite, sleeve large
E: Beg sleeve medium, left front large
F: Beg all right fronts, left front medium, sleeve petite and small

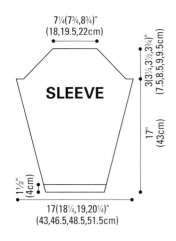

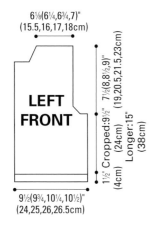

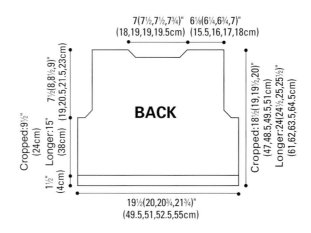

Zigzag Eyelet Cardigan

RATING
Experienced

SIZES
Small (Medium, Large)
Finished measurements: 34 (37, 39½)" (86.5, 94, 100.5 cm)

MATERIALS
Worsted-weight cotton yarn:
Color A: 500 (525, 560) yds (457, 480, 512 m)
Color B: 165 (175, 185) yds (151, 160, 169 m)
Color C and F, each: 240 (260, 280) yds (219, 238, 256 m)
Color D and E, each: 80 (85, 93) yds (73, 78, 85 m)
29" circular knitting needles: sizes 3 and 6 (3 and 4 mm)
Two small stitch holders
Five ⅞" (2.2 cm) buttons

GAUGE
St st on larger needles:
6 sts and 7 rows = 1" (2.5 cm)

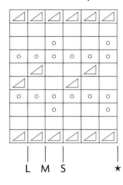

CHART A: 3-st rep

L M S ★

COLOR KEY
⊠ = Color E
☐ = Color C
○ = Color D
◿ = Color B

CHART B: 3-st rep

L M S ★

PATTERN STITCHES

P2tog-b:
p1, sl the st back on left needle, with right needle sl next st over the purled st and off the left needle, and slip the st back to right needle.

Ssk:
Slip the first and second sts knitwise, one at a time, then insert the tip of the left-hand needle into the fronts of these 2 sts from the left, and knit them together.

2 x 2 Rib: Multiple of 4 sts, p2
Row 1: ★ k2, p2; rep from ★, end k2. Row 2: ★ p2, k2; rep from ★, end p2.

Zigzag Eyelet Pattern:
Multiple of 8 sts, plus 6.
Row 1 (RS): k3, ★ k6, k2tog, yo; rep from ★, end k3.
Row 2: p3, ★ p1, yo, p2tog, p5; rep from ★, end p3.
Row 3: k3, ★ k4, k2tog, yo, k2; rep from ★, end k3.
Row 4: p3, ★ p3, yo, p2tog, p3; rep from ★, end p3.
Row 5: k3, ★ k2, k2tog, yo, k4; rep from ★, end k3.

Row 6: p3, ★ p5, yo, p2tog, p1; rep from ★, end p3.
Row 7: k3, ★ k2tog, yo, k6; rep from ★, end k3.
Row 8: p3, ★ p6, p2tog-b, yo; rep from ★, end p3.
Row 9: k3, ★ k1, yo, ssk, k5; rep from ★, end k3.
Row 10: p3, ★ p4, p2tog-b, yo, p2; rep from ★, end p3.
Row 11: k3, ★ k3, yo, ssk, k3; rep from ★, end k3.
Row 12: p3, ★ p2, p2tog-b, yo, p4; rep from ★, end p3.
Row 13: k3, ★ k5, yo, ssk, k1; rep from ★, end k3.
Row 14: p3, ★ p2tog-b, yo, p6; rep from ★, end p3.
Row 15: Knit all sts.
Row 16: Purl all sts.
Repeat rows 1 through 16.

BODY
(Make in one piece, knitting back and forth on circular needle.)
With color A and smaller needles, CO 214 (230, 246) sts and work back and forth in 2 x 2 rib for ¾" (2 cm).
Buttonhole row (RS only): Work 3 sts, BO the next 2 sts, work to end.
Next row: Inc 2 sts to replace the 2 BO on previous row.
Work until rib measures 2½" (6.5 cm).
Next row (RS): Work 8 sts and place them on a st holder.
Note: (Applies to body only). To read charts on RS rows, repeat from ★ to S, end at S (M, L). On WS rows, start at S (M, L) and work to ★, then repeat from S to ★.
Change to larger needles and work in St st according to chart A until there are 8 sts left on needle; transfer these 8 stitches to a st holder. There should be 198 (214, 230) sts on needle.

Work 48 (52, 56) sts, place marker for side seams, work next 102 (110, 118) sts, place marker, work across last 48 (52, 56) sts to end, still working from chart A.

When 10 rows have been completed, work 16 rows Zigzag pattern in color F.

Work 10 rows according to chart B, then 16 rows in Zigzag pattern in color A.

Cont working in this sequence until 63 (66, 69) rows (within third zigzag stripe) after rib have been completed.

Armhole split: Cont patt as est, work across until 2 sts before marker, join 2nd ball of yarn, BO next 4 sts, work across to 2 sts before next marker, join a 3rd ball of yarn, BO the next 4 sts, work to end.

Work 1 more row across 3 separate pieces.

Next row: dec 1 st each side of each armhole.

Cont working for 43 (46, 49) more rows and beg shaping neck on front edges only: BO 4 sts at each neck edge, 3 sts at each neck edge every other row twice, then 1 st every row 4 times.

When decreases have been completed, work 6 more rows and BO rem 31 (35, 39) sts.

At the same time, when you begin to shape front neck, work 11 rows on the back following the pattern.

Next row: BO center 18 sts for back of neck, then 4 sts from each neck edge every other row twice to give 31 (35, 39) sts.

BO all sts.

SLEEVES

With color A and smaller needles, CO 38 (40, 42) sts.

Work in 2 x 2 rib for 2¼" (5.5 cm).

In last row of rib, inc 16 (20, 24) sts to give 54 (60, 66) sts.

Change to larger needles and work in St st, starting with 10 rows of

chart B; then cont working in sequence as for body.

Work 3 (6, 9) rows; then inc 1 st each edge and cont to do this every 5th row until there are 92 (98, 104) sts on needle.

Work even until 17 (17½, 18)" (43, 44.5, 45.5 cm) above rib.

Cap shaping: BO 3 sts at beg of next 2 rows.

Work 1 more row and dec 1 st each edge on next 7 rows.

BO all sts.

FINISHING

Left side: With smaller needles, pu the 8 sts from holder and work in 2 x 2 rib until band measures 1" (2.5 cm) shorter than entire front.

Put sts back on st holder.

Right side: With smaller needles, pu 8 sts from holder and work 2 x 2 rib until right band measures same as left band, making 3 more buttonholes as for first buttonhole on body ribbing, evenly spaced and allowing for 5th buttonhole on neck band.

Put 8 sts back on st holder.

Sew shoulder seams and set in sleeves.

Sew underarm seams.

With smaller needles and color A, pu 8 sts from first st holder, 15 sts from front neck, 30 sts from back neck, 15 sts from other front neck, and 8 sts from the 2nd st holder (76 sts in all).

Work in 2 x 2 rib for ½" (1.5 cm) and make 5th buttonhole.

Cont in rib until neck band measures 1" (2.5 cm).

BO all sts.

Stitch down front bands.

Sew on 5 buttons.

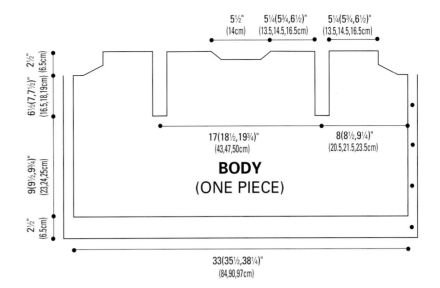

5½" (14cm)   5¼(5¾,6½)" (13.5,14.5,16.5cm)   5¼(5¾,6½)" (13.5,14.5,16.5cm)

2½" (6.5cm)   6½(7,7½)" (16.5,18,19cm)

17(18½,19¾)" (43,47,50cm)   8(8½,9¼)" (20.5,21.5,23.5cm)

BODY
(ONE PIECE)

9(9½,9¾)" (23,24,25cm)

2½" (6.5cm)

33(35½,38¼)" (84,90,97cm)

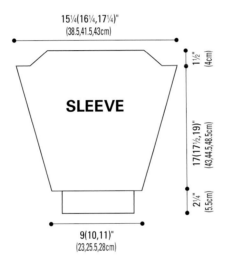

15¼(16¼,17¼)" (38.5,41.5,43cm)

1½" (4cm)

SLEEVE

17(17½,19)" (43,44.5,48.5cm)

2¼" (5.5cm)

9(10,11)" (23,25.5,28cm)

Geometric Swing Jacket

RATING

Experienced

SIZES

Small (Medium, Large)

Finished measurements: 46 (48, 50)" (117, 122, 127 cm)

MATERIALS

Heavy worsted-weight wool:

Color A (MC): 1200 (1220, 1235) yds (1097, 1115, 1129 m)

Color B: 320 (360, 380) yds (293, 329, 347 m)

Color C: 95 yds (87 m)

Color D: 620 (645, 665) yds (567, 590, 608 m)

14" knitting needles, sizes 5, 8, and 9 (3.75, 5, and 5.5 mm) or use circular needles in proper sizes to work body.

Stitch holders

Five 1¼" (3 cm) buttons

GAUGE

St st on larger needles:

18 sts and 22 rows = 4" (10 cm)

PATTERN STITCHES

Stockinette stitch:
Row 1: Knit (RS), Row 2: Purl (WS).

2 x 2 Ribbing:
Row 1 (RS): k2, p2.
Row 2: p2, k2.

Pocket Backs: (Make 2.)
With color A and largest needles, CO 22 sts.

Work in St st for 6" (15 cm).,
Place on holder.

BODY

(Make in one piece, knitting back and forth if using circular needle.)

Hem: With medium-sized needles and color A, CO 216 (232, 248) sts. Work in St st until piece meas 1½" (4 cm).

Front facings: Next row: CO 10 sts at the beg and end of the row to give 236 (252, 268) sts. Change to largest needles; then follow graph for color changes and buttonhole placement.

Note: For body chart, work rows 1 to 53 as follows: work to center; then cont working 16 st rep to end of row, ending with same st as you began and omitting buttonholes. Work rows 54 to 180 as follows: work to center; then work chart in reverse, beg at center, from left to right, omitting buttonholes. Work buttonholes as follows (WS): Work to last 18 sts.

BO next 4 sts, work next 8 sts, BO next 4 sts, work 2 sts.

Next row: CO 4 sts over each BO st on previous row.

Complete chart for lower body.

Pocket row: See chart on page 73. Work 31 (35, 39) sts, place the next 22 sts on holder, work 22 sts

8(9,10)"
(20.5,23,25.5cm)

10(10¼,10½)"
(25.5,26,26.5cm)

BODY
(ONE PIECE)

46(48,50)"
(117,122,127cm)

of pocket back, work to last 53
(57, 61) sts, place next 22 sts on
holder, work 22 sts of pocket back,
work to end.

Follow graph for color changes,
neck, and armhole shaping.

SLEEVES

With smallest needles and color A,
CO 44 (46, 48) sts.

Work 2 x 2 rib for 5" (12.5 cm).

In last row, inc 6 (6, 8) sts evenly
across.

Change to largest needles and
work in St st, following graph for
color changes and shaping.

POCKET TOPS (make 2)

With smallest needles and color A,
pu 22 sts from holder and work in
2 x 2 rib for 1" (2.5 cm). BO all sts.

Sew pocket backs and tops carefully
in place.

FINISHING

Sew shoulder seams.

Turn under hem and stitch in place.

Sew collar tog at center back.

Set collar in neckline, sleeves in
armholes, and sew underarm seams.

Fold under front facings and sew in
place.

Sew on buttons.

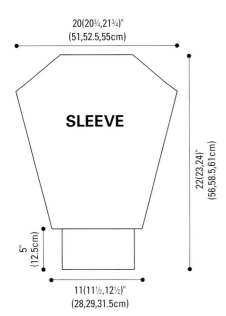

20(20¾,21¾)"
(51,52.5,55cm)

SLEEVE

22(23,24)"
(56,58.5,61cm)

5"
(12.5cm)

11(11½,12½)"
(28,29,31.5cm)

BODY
(Rows 1 to 53)

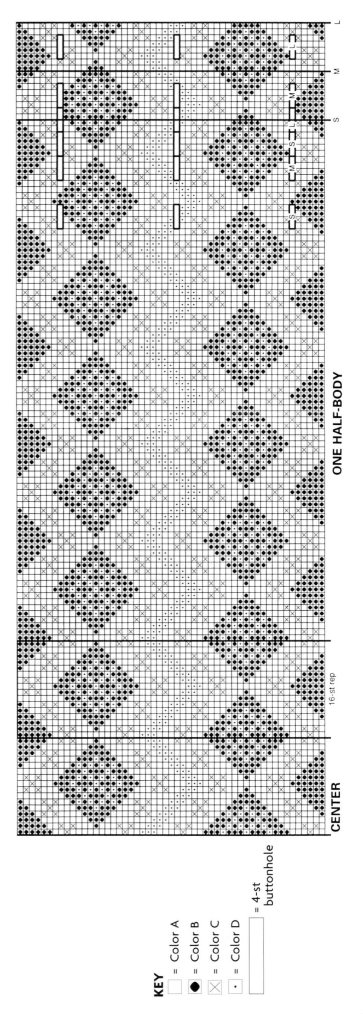

ONE HALF-BODY

16-st rep

CENTER

= 4-st
buttonhole

KEY

□ = Color A
● = Color B
☒ = Color C
· = Color D

71

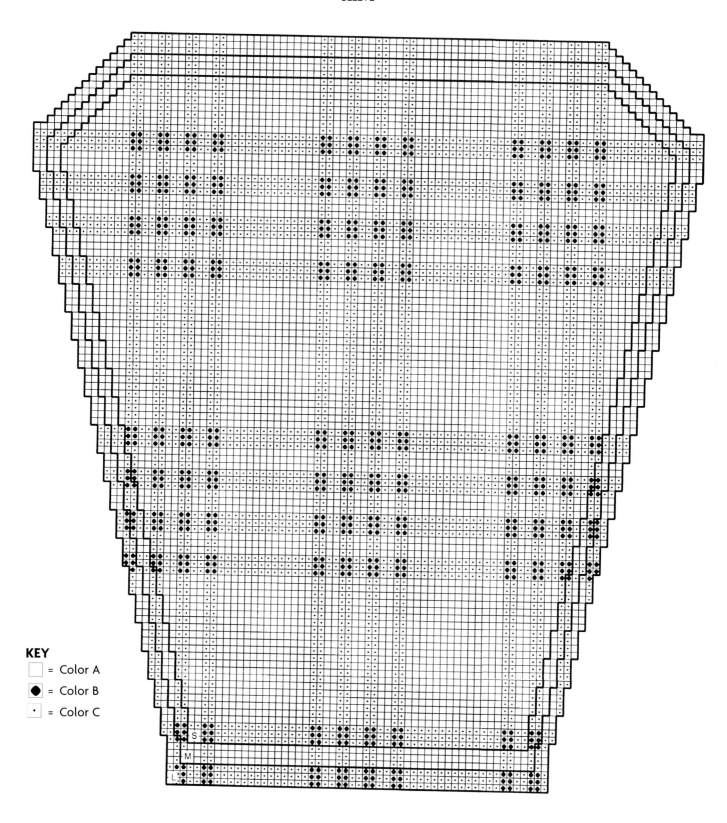

KEY

☐ = Color A

◆ = Color B

· = Color C

BODY
(Rows 54 to 180)

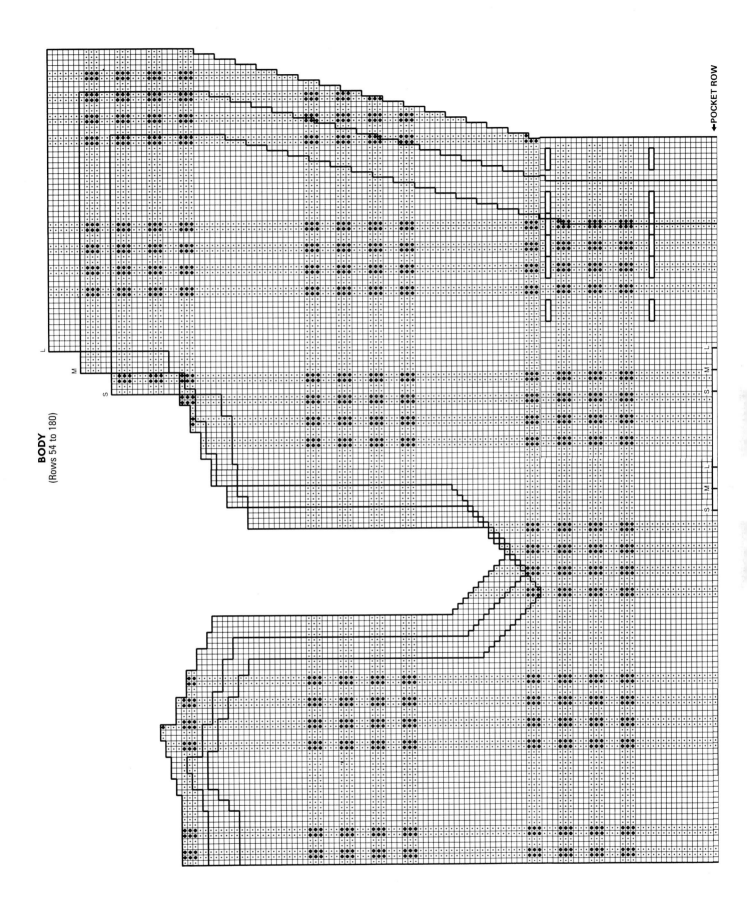

Sunflower Splendor

RATING
Experienced

SIZES
Small (Medium, Large)
Finished measurements: 46 (48, 50)" (117, 122, 127 cm)

MATERIALS
Worsted-weight wool yarn:
Main Color (MC): 1045 (1080, 1140) yds (956, 988, 1042 m)
Color A: 190 yds (174 m)
Colors B, C, and D, each: 95 yds (87 m) each of
14" knitting needles, sizes 7 and 8 (4.5 and 5 mm)
Two stitch markers
Five ¾" (2 cm) drapery rings
Crochet hook in size F
Tapestry needle

GAUGE
St st with larger needles:
20 sts and 26 rows = 4" (10 cm)

PATTERN STITCHES
Seed stitch:
Row 1 (RS): ★ k1, p1; rep from ★.
All other rows: p the k sts, k the p sts.

Seed stitch Points:
CO 2 sts. Row 1: k1, p1.
Row 2: inc 1 (k in front and in back loop of st) in first st, k1.
Rows 3 and 4: inc in first st, (p1, k1) across row.
Rows 5 and 6: inc in first st, (k1, p1) across row.
Rep rows 3 to 6 until you have 12 sts. Cut yarn and push these 12 sts to end of needle.
With other needle, CO 2 sts, and rep sequence until desired number of points have been worked.

BACK
With smaller needles and MC, CO 114 (120, 126) sts and work 8 rows in Seed st.
Change to larger needles and work 0 (3, 6) rows St st.
Work chart for back.
After completing chart, work a further 0 (3, 6) rows in St st.
Shoulder shaping: BO 12 (12, 14) sts at beg next two rows, 13 (14, 15) sts at beg next two rows, and 13 (15, 15) sts at beg next two rows.
BO rem 38 sts.

RIGHT FRONT
With smaller needles and MC, CO 57 (60, 63) sts and work 8 rows Seed st.
Change to larger needles and work St st for 0 (3, 6) rows.
Work chart for right front until piece meas 11½ (12½, 13½)" (29, 31.5, 34 cm).

Shape neck: Cont on chart as est, at neck edge, dec 1 st every other row 19 times to give 38 (41, 44) sts rem for shoulder.
At the same time, after completing chart, work 0 (3, 6) rows St st; then shape shoulder to correspond to back.

LEFT FRONT
Work as for right front, using chart for left front and reversing all shaping.

RIGHT SLEEVE
With smaller needles and MC, work 4 Seed st points.
Keeping in patt, work Seed st across all 4 points, joining them to give 48 sts for cuff.
Cont in Seed st, and at the same time, dec 1 st each edge every 4th row 3 times.
Cont in Seed st until cuff measures 3 (3, 3½)" (7.5, 7.5, 9 cm) from base of points (the first joining row).
Change to larger needles and beg working in St st.
Inc 1 st each edge every other row 6 times, every 4th row 14 times, and every 6th row 3 times to give 88 sts.
At the same time, when you have 58 sts, work chart for sleeve with Color A for sunflower and Color D for leaf.
Position chart as follows: On RS row, k6, pm, work chart (51 sts), pm, k1.
After completing chart, cont in St st until piece meas 14½ (15, 15½)" (37, 38, 39.5 cm) from top of cuff.
BO all sts.

LEFT SLEEVE
Work as for right sleeve, but work chart with Color B for sunflower and Color D for leaf.

FINISHING
Block all pieces according to yarn directions.
Sew shoulder seams.

Cont in Seed st for a total of 8 rows.

BO 59 (63, 67) sts at beg next row, work 118 sts Seed st, and BO rem 59 (63, 67) sts.

Rejoin yarn and cont in Seed st on the rem 118 sts.

BO 1 st at beg of next 2 rows, 2 sts at beg next 10 rows, 9 sts at beg next 4 rows, 10 sts beg next 2 rows; then BO rem 40 sts.

Sew collar to jacket, placing buttonholes along right front and attaching center 40 sts on collar to back neckline.

Pointed border: With smaller needles, work 12 Seed st points. Work across all 12 points and cont in Seed st.

Work two more rows and BO all sts.

Sew border to collar from start of shawl collar shaping around the edge to the corresponding point on second side.

Gently block pointed border and shawl collar.

Mark 9¼" (23.5 cm) from shoulder seam on fronts and back.

Sew sleeves bet markers, matching center of sleeve to shoulder seam.

Sew side and sleeve seams.

Gently block seams.

Sew on buttons.

Crochet buttons: With desired color, work in single crochet around drapery ring to fill ring completely. Pull yarn through the last loop, leaving a 12" (30.5 cm) tail.

Thread yarn tail through tapestry needle.

Take needle through back of every other stitch and pull yarn tightly to fill in center of ring; use MC to pull sts tog in center of ring, if desired.

COLLAR

With smaller needles and MC, CO 236 (244, 252) sts and work 3 rows Seed st.

Row 4: Work 5 buttonholes as follows: Seed 2 sts, BO 2 sts, ★ Seed 12 (13, 14) sts, BO 2 sts; rep from ★ twice more, Seed 11 (12, 13) sts, BO 2 sts, work in Seed st to end of row.

Row 5: Work in Seed st to first BO sts.

CO 2 sts over each pair of BO sts in row 4.

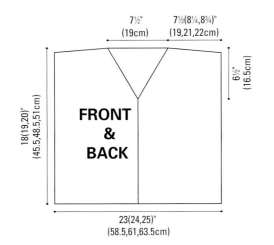

FRONT & BACK

7½" (19cm)

7½(8¼,8¾)" (19,21,22cm)

6½" (16.5cm)

18(19,20)" (45.5,48.5,51cm)

23(24,25)" (58.5,61,63.5cm)

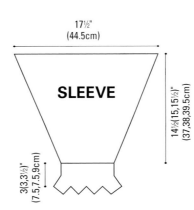

SLEEVE

17½" (44.5cm)

14½(15,15½)" (37,38,39.5cm)

3(3,3½)" (7.5,7.5,9cm)

KEY

☐ = MC, k on RS, p on WS

⊟ = MC, p on RS, k on WS

◎ = St st, color D

● = St st, color A

☒ = St st, color C

⬡ = St st, color B

75

SLEEVE

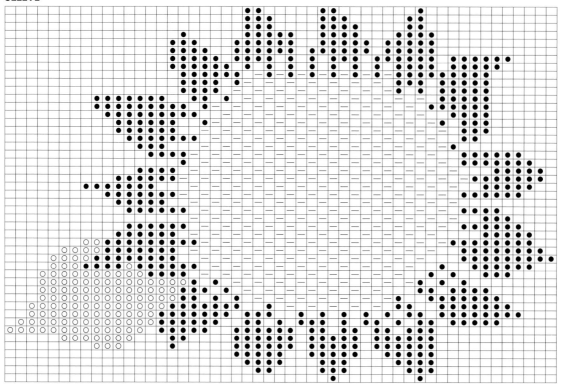

	LEFT FRONT		RIGHT FRONT	

L M S   BACK   S M L

Sweaters
for Men
and
Women

Roomy Cabled Aran Cardigan

KNITTING RATING

Experienced

SIZES

Small (Medium, Large)

Finished measurements: 46 (48, 52)" (117, 122, 132 cm)

MATERIALS

Aran-weight yarn: 1550 (1580, 1760) yds (1417, 1445, 1609 m)

14" knitting needles, sizes 5 and 7 US (3.75 and 4.5 mm)

Cable needle (cn)

Nine ¾" (2 cm) buttons

GAUGE

Rev St st: 16 sts x 25 rows = 4" (10 cm) square

Diamond cable = 4½" (11.5 cm)

Ribbed cable = 2½" (6.5 cm)

Square cable = 1¾" (4.5 cm)

PATTERN STITCHES

T4L: sl next 3 sts to cn and hold in front of work, p1, k3 from cn

T4R: sl next st to cn and hold in back of work, k 3 sts from left-hand needle, p1 from cn

T7F: sl next 4 sts to cn and hold in front, k3, sl last st from cn to left needle and p it, k3 from cn

Reverse Stockinette stitch: (RSS)

Row 1 (WS): Knit all sts.

Row 2: Purl all sts.

Diamond Cable: Multiple of 27 sts.

Row 1 (WS): k10, p3, k1, p3, k10.

Row 2: p10, T7F, p10.

Row 3 and all WSR: Work all sts as they appear, unless otherwise stated.

Rows 4 and 6: p10, k3, p1, k3, p10.

Rows 7 through 18: Rep rows 1 through 6 twice.

Rows 19 and 20: Rep rows 1 and 2.

Row 21: k10, p3, k1, p3, k10.

Row 22: p9, T4R, p1, T4L, p9.

Row 23: k9, p3, k3, p3, k9.

Row 24: p8, T4R, p3, T4L, p8.

Row 25: k8, p3, k2, p1, k2, p3, k8.

Row 26: p7, T4R, p2, k1, p2, T4L, p7.

Row 27: k7, p3, k2, p3, k2, p3, k7.

Row 28: p6, T4R, p2, k3, p2, T4L, p6.

Row 29: k6, p3, k2, p5, k2, p3, k6.

Row 30: p5, T4R, p2, k5, p2, T4L, p5.

Row 31: k5, p3, k2, p7, k2, p3, k5.

Row 32: p4, T4R, p2, T7F, p2, T4L, p4.

Row 33 and all rem WSR: Work all sts as they appear, unless otherwise stated.

Row 34: p3, T4R, p2, T4R, p1, T4L, p2, T4L, p3.

Row 36: p2, T4R, p2, T4R, p3, T4L, p2, T4L, p2.

Row 38: p1, T4R, p2, T4R, p5, T4L, p2, T4L, p1.

Row 40: T4R, p2, T4R, p7, T4L, p2, T4L.

Row 42: T4L, p2, T4L, p7, T4R, p2, T4R.

Row 44: p1, T4L, p2, T4L, p5, T4R, p2, T4R, p1.

Row 46: p2, T4L, p2, T4L, p3, T4R, p2, T4R, p2.

Row 48: p3, T4L, p2, T4L, p1, T4R, p2, T4R, p3.

Row 50: p4, T4L, p2, T7F, p2, T4R, p4.

Row 51: k5, p3, k2, p7, k2, p3, k5.

Row 52: p5, T4L, p2, k5, p2, T4R, p5.

Row 54: p6, T4L, p2, k3, p2, T4R, p6.

Row 56: p7, T4L, p2, k1, p2, T4R, p7.

Row 58: p8, T4L, p3, T4R, p8.

Row 60: p9, T4L, p1, T4R, p9.

Rep rows 1 through 6, then 1 and 2, then 21 through 60 for pattern (total of 48 rows for rep).

Rep these 48 rows for remainder of design.

Square Cable: Multiple of 8 sts.

Row 1 and all WS rows: p2, k4, p2.

Rows 2, 6, 8: k2, p4, k2.

Row 4: sl 2 sts to cn and hold in front, k2, p2 from cn, sl 2 to cn and hold in back, p2, k2 from cn.

Rep rows 1 through 8.

Ribbed Cable: Multiple of 13 sts.

Row 1 (WS): p2, k2, p2, k1, p2, k2, p2.

Rows 2, 6, 8, 10, 12, 14: k2, p2, k2, p1, k2, p2, k2.

Row 4: sl 4 sts to cn and hold in back, k2, sl last 2 sts from cn to left needle and p2, k2 from cn, p1, sl 4 sts to cn and hold in front, k2, sl last 2 sts from cn to left needle and p2, k2 from cn.

Rep rows 1 through 14.

BACK

With smaller needles, CO 115 (119, 127) sts.

Est cable sequence as follows: Work 4 (5, 7) in RSS, work Ribbed cable over 13 sts, work 2 (2, 3) in RSS, work Ribbed Cable over 13 sts, work 2 (2, 3) in RSS, work Square Cable over 8 sts, work 2 (3, 3) in RSS, work Diamond Cable over 27 sts, work 2 (3, 3) in RSS, work Square Cable over 8 sts, work 2 (2, 3) in RSS, work Ribbed Cable over 13 sts, work 2 (2, 3) in RSS, work ribbed cable over 13 sts, work 4 (5,7) in RSS.

Work 12 rows of Diamond, Square, and Ribbed Cables as given in pattern instructions.

left: Unisex Loose-Fitting Vest with Pockets; right: Roomy Cabled Aran Cardigan.

Change to larger needles and work in est patt until piece meas 25½ (26½, 27½)" (64.5, 67.5, 70 cm).

Shape neck: Work 44 (46, 50) sts, BO center 27 sts, work to end.

BO 2 (2, 3) sts at neck edge every other row twice to give 40 (42, 44) sts at shoulder.

When piece meas 27 (28, 29)" (68.5, 71, 73.5 cm), BO all sts.

LEFT FRONT

With smaller needles, CO 54 (56, 60) sts.

Est cable sequence as follows: Work 2 (2, 4) sts in RSS, work Ribbed Cable over 13 sts, work 1 (2, 3) sts in RSS, work Square Cable over 8 sts, work 1 (2, 3) sts in RSS, work Diamond Cable over 27 sts, work 2 sts in RSS.

Work 12 rows of Diamond, Square, and Ribbed Cables as given in pattern instructions.

Change to larger needles and work in est patt until piece meas 20 (20½, 21)" (51, 52, 53.5 cm).

V-neck Shaping: Dec 1 st at neck edge alternately every other row 4 (2, 4) times, then every 4 rows 10 (12, 12) times to give 40 (42, 44) sts at shoulder.

When piece meas same as back, BO all shoulder sts.

RIGHT FRONT

Work same as for left front, reversing cable placement and V-neck shaping.

To place cables: Work 2 sts in RSS, work Diamond Cable over 27 sts, work 1 (2, 3) sts in RSS, work Square Cable over 8 sts, work 1 (2, 3) in RSS, work 13 sts in Ribbed Cable, work 2 (2, 4) in RSS.

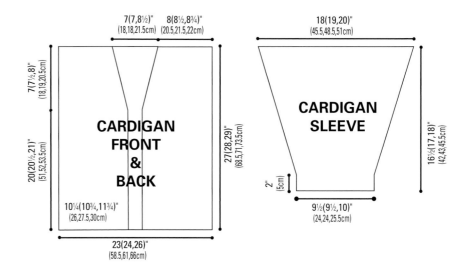

CARDIGAN FRONT & BACK

7(7,8½)" (18,18,21.5cm) 8(8½,8¾)" (20.5,21.5,22cm)

7(7½,8)" (18,19,20.5cm)

20(20½,21)" (51,52,53.5cm)

27(28,29)" (68.5,71,73.5cm)

10¼(10¾,11¾)" (26,27.5,30cm)

23(24,26)" (58.5,61,66cm)

CARDIGAN SLEEVE

18(19,20)" (45.5,48.5,51cm)

16½(17,18)" (42,43,45.5cm)

2" (5cm)

9½(9½,10)" (24,24,25.5cm)

SLEEVES

With smaller needles, CO 49 (49, 51) sts.

Est cables as follows: Work 2 sts in RSS, work square cable over 8 sts, work 1 (1, 2) in RSS, work Diamond Cable over 27 sts, work 1 (1, 2) sts in RSS, work square cable over 8 sts, work 2 sts in RSS.

Work 12 rows of Diamond and Square Cables as given in pattern instructions.

Change to larger needles and beg inc in RSS as follows: Inc 1 st each end every 4 rows 10 (12, 11) times, then every 5 rows 9 (9, 11) times to give 87 (91, 95) sts.

When piece meas 16½ (17, 18)" (42, 43, 45.5 cm), BO all sts.

FINISHING

Sew shoulder seams.

Meas down 9 (9½, 10)" (23, 24, 25.5 cm) in front and back and mark.

Sew sleeves bet markers.

Sew side and sleeve seams.

Cable band: Using smaller needles, CO 14 sts.

Work in cabled button band patt as follows:

All WS rows: k2, p3, k4, p3, k2.

Rows 2, 6, 8, 10: p2, k3, p4, k3, p2.

Row 4: p2, slip 3 sts to cn and hold in front, k2, sl last st on cn to left needle and k it, p2 from cn; sl 2 sts to cn and hold in back, p2, k1, k2 from cn, p2.

Work two pieces, each equal in length to meas from bottom of sweater to center back of neck when slightly stretched.

Work 9 evenly-spaced buttonholes on one piece, beg 1" (2.5 cm) up from bottom of sweater (on the 8th row) to V-neck shaping and placing buttonhole every 16th row.

Buttonholes: On row 8 (RS), p2, k3, p1, BO 2 sts, p1, k3, p2.

Row 9: CO 2 sts where BO was done to complete buttonhole.

Attach front bands to sweater, joining them at center back of neck.

Sew on 9 buttons.

Unisex Loose-Fitting Vest with Pockets

KNITTING RATING
Experienced

SIZES
Small (Medium, Large, Extra Large)

Finished measurements: 40 (44, 48, 52)" (101.5, 112, 122, 132 cm)

MATERIALS
Aran-weight yarn: 704 (880, 880, 1056) yds (644, 805, 805, 966 m)

14" knitting needles, size 8 US (5 mm)

Five 1" (2.5 cm) buttons

GAUGE
Rib st: 15 sts and 27 rows = 4" (10 cm)

PATTERN STITCHES

Garter rib stitch:

Row 1 (RS): k2, p4, ★ k2, p3; rep from ★, end k2, p4, k2.

Row 2: sl first st as if to p with yarn in front, p across row, sl last st as if to p, end with yarn in front.

Full-Fashioned Decreases:

In order to make a decorative shaping detail at neckline and armhole shaping, follow the instructions below. Always work dec on RSR.

Right-leaning decreases:

On RS, work to specified number of sts, k2tog, work to end of row or until next dec should be worked.

Left-leaning decreases:

On RS, k specified number of sts, ssk, k to end of row or until next dec should be worked.

BACK
CO 74 (84, 89, 94) sts.

Work in Garter Rib until piece meas 14½ (15, 15, 15½)" (37, 38, 38, 39.5 cm) and you have completed a WSR.

BO 6 sts at beg of next 2 rows, ending with a WSR.

Full-fashioning: On every RSR, work 6 sts as est in patt, work left-leaning dec, work across in patt until 8 sts rem, work right-leaning dec, and work to end.

Cont to work dec every RSR until 6 sts total have been dec in full-fashioned method until 50 (60, 65, 75) sts rem.

When piece meas 24 (24½, 25, 25½)" (61, 62, 63.5, 64.5 cm), beg working in garter st (knit all rows).

Work until piece meas 25 (25½, 26, 26½)" (63.5, 64.5, 66, 67.5 cm). BO all sts.

RIGHT FRONT
CO 39 (44, 49, 54) sts.

Work in Garter rib until piece meas 7" (18 cm).

Insert pocket: On RS, work across 12 sts, PM: work next 20 sts, sl 20 sts just worked back onto left needle and work them in scrap yarn, cont working in MC to end of row.

Work in Garter rib until piece

meas 14½ (15, 15, 15½)" (37, 38, 38, 39.5 cm).

Underarm and neck shaping:

On WS, BO first 6 sts and work to end.

Next row: At neckline edge, work 6 sts as est in patt, work left-leaning dec, work across until 8 sts rem, work right-leaning dec.

Cont working dec every RSR, making a total of 6 full-fashioned dec at armhole.

At neckline dec every other row 1 (2, 3, 0) times, then every 8 rows 8 (8, 8, 0) times, then every 6 rows 0 (0, 0, 12) times to leave 18 (22, 26, 30) sts at shoulder.

When piece meas same as back, BO all sts.

LEFT FRONT
Work same as right front, but reverse shaping and work buttonholes into front band.

Work first buttonhole when piece meas 1" (2.5 cm), then every 3⅜ (3½, 3½, 3⅝)" (8.6, 9, 9, 9.2 cm).

Buttonholes: Work until 5 sts rem, BO next 2 sts, complete row.

Next row: CO 2 sts over BO sts.

Work total of 5 buttonholes evenly between bottom and beg of neck shaping.

Pocket opening: When piece meas 7" (18 cm), work pocket row.

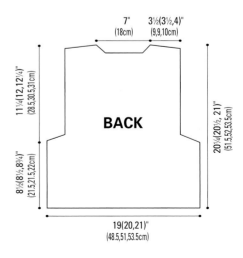

On RS, work across 8 (13, 18, 24) sts, PM: work 20 sts, sl these 20 sts back to left-hand needle and work sts with contrast color scrap yarn, work in MC to end.

Cont as est until piece meas 14½ (15, 15, 15½)" (37, 38, 38, 39.5 cm) and you have completed a WS row.

Armhole and neckline shaping: BO 6 sts and work to end.

Work 1 WSR.

Next row: At armhole edge, work 6 sts as est in Garter rib, work left-leaning dec at armhole, work across until 8 sts rem, work right-leaning dec.

Cont dec at armhole every RS row for 6 times total.

At neckline dec every other row 1 (2, 3, 0) times, then every 8 rows 8 (8, 8, 0) times, then every 6 rows 0 (0, 0, 12) times to leave 18 (22, 26, 30) sts at shoulder.

When piece meas same as back, BO all sts.

FINISHING

Sew shoulder and side seams.

To finish pocket: unravel scrap yarn; pu bottom sts and BO neatly in patt; pu top sts and work into patt or St st as desired.

Work until piece meas 5" (12.5 cm); then BO.

Sew to underside of garment to complete pocket.

Sew on buttons.

Left: Autumn Leaves Cardigan; right: Cabled Raglan Pullover

Autumn Leaves Cardigan

KNITTING RATING

Experienced

SIZES

Small (Medium, Large)

Finished measurements: 42 (46, 50)" (106.5, 117, 127 cm)

MATERIALS

Sportweight yarn in five leaf colors, each: 115 yds (105 m)

Main color (MC): 1725 (1725, 1840) yds (1577, 1577, 1682 m)

14" knitting needles: size 5 US (3.75 mm)

36" (91.5 cm) circular needle in size 2 US (2.75 mm)

Cable needle (cn)

Seven ⅜" (1 cm) buttons.

GAUGE

St st with larger needles: 23 sts = 4" (10 cm)

PATTERN STITCHES

(See charts p. 84–85 for feature stitches.)

Reverse Stockinette stitch (RSS):

Row 1 (RS): Purl all sts.

Row 2 (WS): Knit all sts.

Moss stitch: Odd number of sts.

Row 1: ★ k1, p1; rep from ★, end k1.

Rows 2 and 3: ★ p1, k1; rep from ★, end p1.

Row 4: ★ k1, p1; rep from ★, end k1.

Twisted rib:

Row 1: ★ k1, p1, all sts tbl; rep from ★.

Row 2: ★ p1, k1, all sts tbl; rep from ★.

BACK

CO 118 (130, 142) sts.

Work Twisted rib for 1" (2.5 cm), ending with a WSR.

Using the intarsia method (see p. 9), work Leaves chart through row 50 as follows: k3 (4, 5) sts, Leaf 1 (17 sts), k3 (5, 7) sts, Leaf 2 (12 sts), k3 (5, 7) sts, Leaf 3 (19 sts), k2 (5, 6) sts, Leaf 4 (20 sts), k2 (4, 6) sts, Leaf 5 (12 sts), k2 (4, 6) sts, Leaf 6 (19 sts), k3 (4, 5) sts.

Next row (RS): Knit across, adding 20 sts evenly spaced to give 138 (150, 162) sts.

Next row (WS): Est cable patterns as follows: Work 11 (17, 23) sts in Moss st, [★ work 4-st cable, 5 sts Acorn chart, 4-st cable ★, 19 sts Leaf chart, rep bet ★s once], work 26 sts Diamond cable, rep bet [ ]s, work 11 (7, 23) sts in Moss st.

Cont as est until piece meas 12½ (12, 11½)" (31.5, 30.5, 29 cm).

Armhole shaping: BO 6 sts at the beg of the next 2 rows.

Cont until the 8th rep of Acorn has been worked.

Shoulder and back neck shaping: On RSR, BO 13 (15, 17) sts; then work across 31 (35, 39) sts in est patt.

Working this shoulder only, BO 13 (15, 17) sts once more, 14 (16, 18) sts once, and at the same time, BO 4 sts once at neck edge.

BO center 38 sts and work the other shoulder to match.

Note: When finishing shoulders, do not beg new Acorn or Leaf patterns.

LEFT FRONT

CO 59 (65, 71) sts.

Work Twisted rib for 1" (2.5 cm), ending with a WSR.

Using the intarsia method (refer to p. 9), work Leaves chart through row 50 as follows: k3 (4, 6) sts; Leaf 1 (17 sts); k3 (5, 7) sts; Leaf 2 (12 sts); k3 (5, 7) sts; Leaf 3 (19 sts); k2 (3, 3) sts.

Next row (RS): Knit, inc 13 sts evenly spaced to give 72 (78, 84) sts.

Next row (WS): Est cable patterns as follows: Work 26 sts of front Diamond cable chart, ★ 4-st cable, 5 sts Acorn chart, 4-st cable ★, 9 sts Leaf chart; rep bet ★ once more, and work 11 (17, 23) sts in Moss st.

Armhole and Neck shaping:

When piece meas 12", (30.5 cm), Dec 1 st at neck edge every 4 rows 12 times, then every other row 14 times.

At the same time, shape armhole and shoulder as for back.

RIGHT FRONT

Work as for left front, reversing all shaping and cable charts and working Leaves chart as follows: k2 (2, 3), Leaf 4 (20 sts), k2 (4, 6) sts, Leaf 5 (12 sts), k2 (4, 6) sts, Leaf 6 (19 sts), k2 (4, 5) sts.

SLEEVES

CO 52 (52, 56) sts.

Work Twisted rib for 1" (2.5 cm), ending with a WSR.

Work rows 1 to 4 of colored Leaves chart (for the second sleeve, work rows 47 to 50).

Next row (RS): Knit, inc 12 sts evenly spaced to give 64 (64, 68) sts.

Next row (WS): Est cable patterns as follows: Work 4 (4, 6) sts in RSS, 4-st cable, 46 sts in Diamond cable, 4-st cable, and 4 (4, 6) sts in RSS.

Add 1 st each edge in the next row and every 4 rows 18 times, then every 6 rows 3 (6, 7) times.

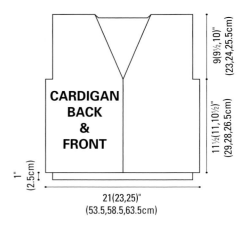

CARDIGAN BACK & FRONT

9(9½,10)" (23,24,25.5cm)

11½(11,10½)" (29,28,26.5cm)

1" (2.5cm)

21(23,25)" (53.5,58.5,63.5cm)

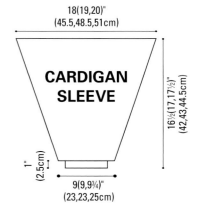

18(19,20)" (45.5,48.5,51cm)

CARDIGAN SLEEVE

16½(17,17½)" (42,43,44.5cm)

1" (2.5cm)

9(9,9¾)" (23,23,25cm)

LEAVES CHART

KEY

☐ = MC

◆ = COLOR A

☐ = COLOR B

◇ = COLOR C

● = COLOR D

— = COLOR E

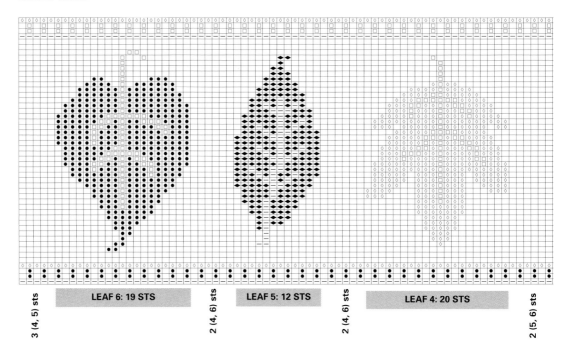

3 (4, 5) sts | LEAF 6: 19 STS | 2 (4, 6) sts | LEAF 5: 12 STS | 2 (4, 6) sts | LEAF 4: 20 STS | 2 (5, 6) sts

FRONT DIAMOND CABLE CHART

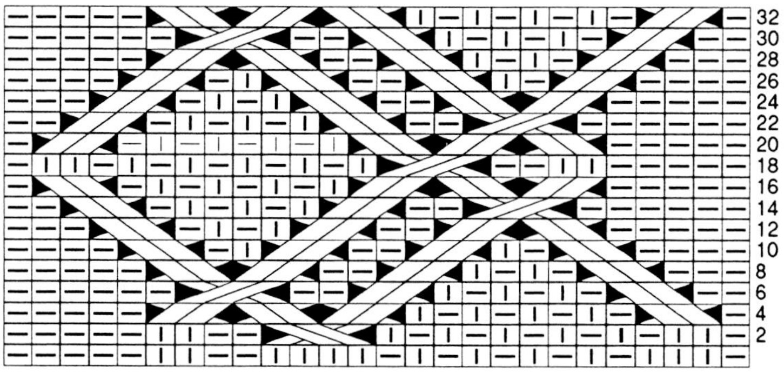
32
30
28
26
24
22
20
18
16
14
12
10
8
6
4
2

LEAF CHART

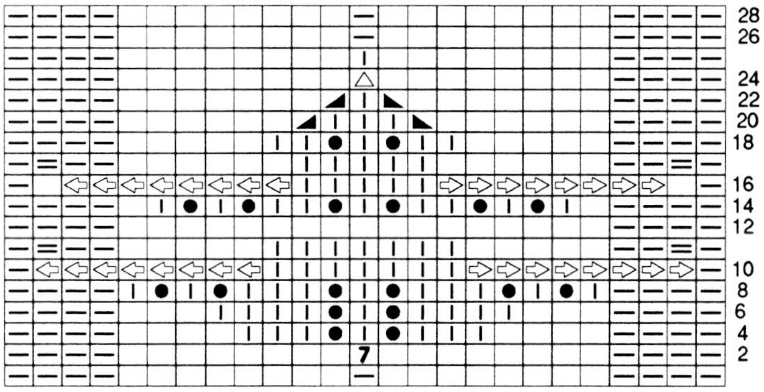
28
26
24
22
20
18
16
14
12
10
8
6
4
2
7

ACORN CHART

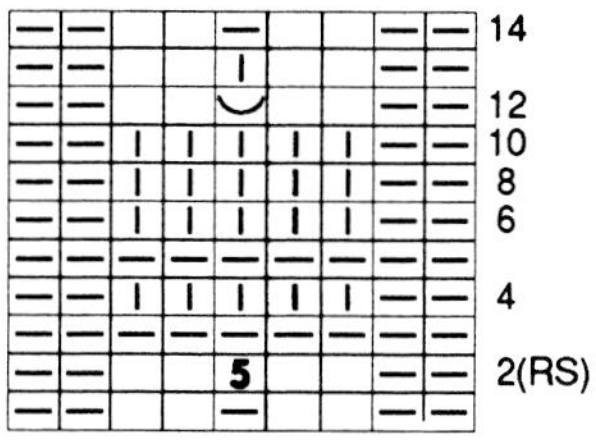
14
12
10
8
6
4
2(RS)
5

4-ST CABLE

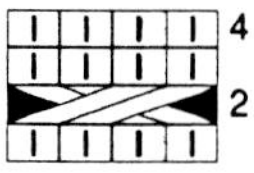
4
2

KEY

I = Knit on RS, p on WS

— = Purl on RS, k on WS

5 = (K1, p1, k1, p1, k1) into 1 st

7 = (K1, p1, k1, p1, k1, p1, k1) into 1 st

= Knit 5 sts tog

● = M1(p.u. horizontal strand & k into the back of it)

= Place 3 sts on cn and hold in back, ssk, k1, k2tog, turn, p3, turn, sl 1 knitwise, k2tog, psso, p3, from cn

= Place 5 sts on cn and hold in front, p3 from cn, ssk, k1, k2tog, turn, p3, turn, k3tog

≡ = p2tog

= Ssk-slip the first and 2nd sts one at a time knitwise; then insert the tip of the left hand needle into the fronts of these 2 sts and knit them tog from this position

= K2tog

△ = Sl 2 sts tog (as if to knit them tog), k1, psso

= Sl 2 sts to cn and hold in back, k2, k2 from cn

=Sl 2 sts to cn and hold in front, k2, k2 from cn

= Sl 1 st on cn and hold in back, k2, p1 from cn

= Sl 2 sts to cn and hold in front, p1, k2 from cn

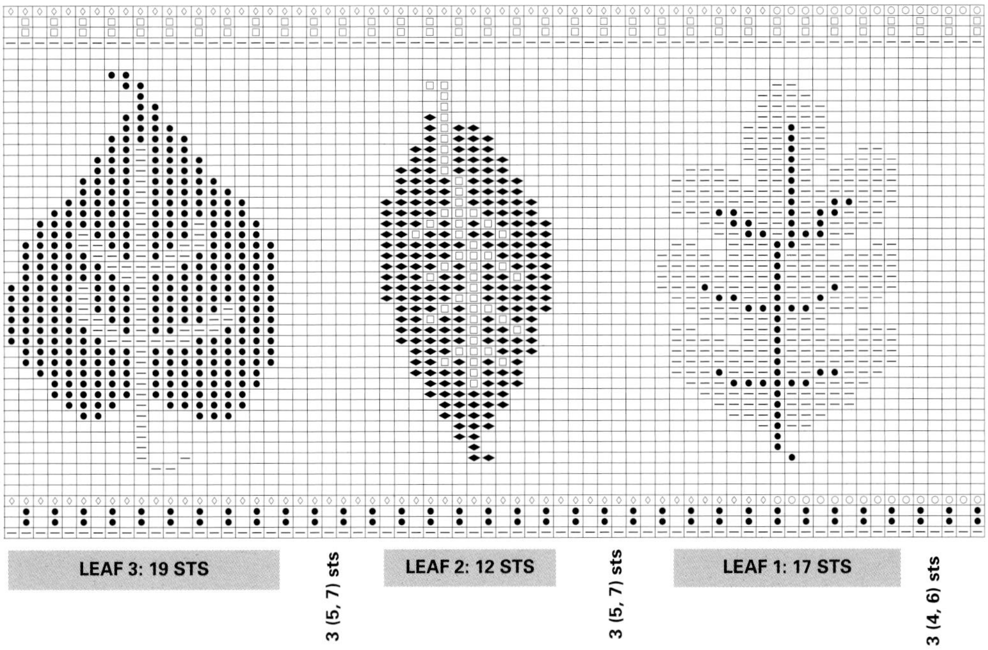
LEAF 3: 19 STS
3 (5, 7) sts
LEAF 2: 12 STS
3 (5, 7) sts
LEAF 1: 17 STS
3 (4, 6) sts

DIAMOND CABLE CHART: (for back and sleeves)

At the same time, when sleeve meas 3½ (3½, 4)" (9, 9, 10 cm), beg Leaf chart over RSSs.

As more sts are added, work another 4-st cable, 5 sts Acorn chart, 4-st cable, 4 (7, 10) sts in Moss st.

When sleeve meas 17½ (18, 18½)" (44.5, 45.5, 47 cm), BO all sts.

Note: Beg Acorn chart only in row 1 or 15 of Leaf chart so that the 2 charts will end together at the top of the sleeve. When 4 Leaf charts have been worked, do not start another Leaf or Acorn chart.

FINISHING

Block all pieces.

Sew shoulder seams.

Neck band and buttonholes:
With circular needle, pu 71 sts from left front to beg of neck shaping, 58 sts up left front to shoulder, 46 sts across back neck, 58 sts down right front neck to beg of neck shaping, pm, and 71 sts down right front to CO edge to give 304 sts.

With RS facing, k 1 row.

Row 2: Purl to marker; then place buttonholes as follows: ★ BO 2 sts, p9; rep from ★ until 7 buttonholes

have been worked.

Row 3 (RS): Knit, CO 2 sts over BO sts on previous row.

Row 4 (WS): Knit to form fold line.

Work 4 more rows in St st, beg with a k row and working buttonholes on 3rd and 4th rows to correspond to those previously worked.

Fold front band on fold line and slip-stitch into place on WS.

Set in sleeves.

Sew side and sleeve seams.

Sew on buttons.

Cabled Raglan Pullover

KNITTING RATING
Experienced

SIZES
Small (Medium, Large)

Finished measurements: 46½ (50, 54)" (118, 127, 137 cm)

MATERIALS
Worsted-weight wool yarn: 2280 (2375, 2470) yds (2085, 2172, 2259 m)

14" knitting needles, sizes 4 and 7 US (3.25 and 4.5 mm)

16" (40.5 cm) circular needle in size 4 US (3.25 mm)

Cable needle (cn)

Stitch holders

GAUGE
RSS with larger needles: 20 sts and 26 rows = 4" (10 cm)

PATTERN STITCHES
See chart below for cable patterns.

Garter stitch:

All rows: Knit all sts.

Reverse Stockinette stitch (RSS):

Row 1 (RS): Purl all sts.

Row 2: Knit all sts.

2 x 2 Rib: Multiple of 4 sts plus 2. Row 1 (WS): k2, ★ p2, k2; rep from ★.

Row 2: p2, ★ k2, p2; rep from ★.

Decrease Methods:

Double decrease (RS row): p3, sl 1, k2tog, psso, work to last 6 sts, k3tog, p3.

Single decrease (RS row): p3, sl 1, k1, psso, work to last 5 sts, k2tog, p3.

BACK
With smaller needles, CO 142 (142, 174) sts.

Work 4 rows in Garter st, ending with WS facing.

Work 2 x 2 rib for 13 rows.

Work 4 more rows in garter st (ending with RS facing).

Change to larger needles and work set-up row:

Small: ★ p1, inc1, p1, k2, p6, (k1, inc1) twice, p6, k2; rep from ★ to last 2 sts, end p1, inc1, p1 to give 164 sts.

Medium: ★ (p1, inc1) twice, k2, p6, (k1, inc1) twice, p6, k2; rep from ★ to last 2 sts, end (inc, p1) twice to give 172 sts.

Large: ★ p1, inc1, p2, p2tog, k2, p6, (k1, inc1) twice, p6, k2; rep from ★ to last 6 sts, end p2tog, p2, inc1, p1 to give 180 sts.

Note: The cable panel vertical knit sts should line up over the knit sts of the 2 x 2 rib.

Foundation row (WS): ★ Work 3 (4, 5) sts in RSS, beg row 1 of chart, work next 20 sts in cable patt; rep from ★ 6 times, end 3 (4, 5) sts in RSS.

Cont to follow chart as est until piece meas 14½ (15, 15½)" (37, 38, 39.5 cm).

Raglan shaping: Maintaining cable patt as est, BO 3 sts at beg of next 2 rows to give 158 (166, 174) sts.

Alternate single and double decs at either end of all RS rows until 73 (77, 77) rows have been worked, then all double decs until 85 (89, 91) rows have been completed.

At the same time, maintain 3 sts at each side in RSS.

On all WS rows: K3, work in est patt until 3 sts rem, k3.

BO rem 26 (28, 32) sts for back neck.

FRONT
Work as for back until 72 (76, 76) rows have been completed to give 50 (52, 60) sts.

Neckline shaping:

BO center 14 (16, 20) sts, and work rem sts in est patt.

BO 3 sts at each neck edge 3 times to give 3 sts rem on each side.

Place these sts on holders for neck finishing.

RIGHT SLEEVE
With smaller needles, CO 62 (62, 78) sts and work as for back, ending with RS facing.

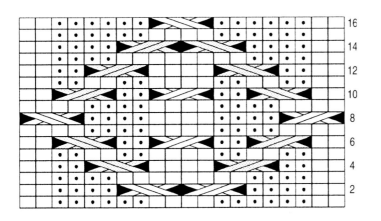

KEY
☐ = K2tog

⊡ = Sl 2 sts tog (as if to knit them tog), k1, psso

= Sl 2 sts to cn and hold in back, k2, k2 from cn

= Sl 2 sts to cn and hold in front, k2, k2 from cn

= Sl 1 st on cn and hold in back, k2, p1 from cn

= Sl 2 sts to cn and hold in front, p1, k2 from cn

Change to larger needles and work set-up row as for back to give 72 (76, 80) sts.

Foundation row (WS): ★ Work 3 (4, 5) sts in RSS, beg row 1 of chart, work next 20 sts in cable patt; rep from ★ twice, end 3 (4, 5) sts in RSS.

At the same time, keeping in patt, inc 1 st each edge every other row 25 (25, 26) times, then every 4 rows 11 (12, 12) times to give 144 (150, 156) sts.

Cont to work even until piece meas 18 (18½, 19)" (45.5, 47, 48.5 cm), end with a WS row.

Raglan shaping: BO 3 sts at the beg of the next 2 rows to give 138 (144, 150) sts.

Alternate single and double decs with RSS border (as for back) until 79 (83, 85) rows have been completed and 18 (20, 20) sts rem.

Shape cap: BO 6 (7, 7) sts at the beg of each RS row twice, then 6 sts once.

LEFT SLEEVE

Work the same as right sleeve until 18 (20, 20) sts rem.

BO 6 (7, 7) sts at the beg of each WS row twice, then 6 sts once to reverse angle of cap shaping.

FINISHING

Block all pieces to finished measurements.

Sew raglan seams.

With smaller circular needle, pu

and k92 (96, 100) sts evenly spaced around neck; p 1 row, k 1 row, p 1 row.

Work 2 x 2 rib over an even number of sts, beg with ★, for 1½" (4 cm).

P 1 row, k 1 row.

BO loosely in p.

Raglan bands: (make 4) With smaller needles, CO 84 (88, 92) sts. Work in 2 x 2 rib over an even number of sts, beg with ★, for 5 rows.

BO all sts loosely.

Sew band neatly over top of RSS raglan border.

Sew side and sleeve seams.

Block seams lightly.

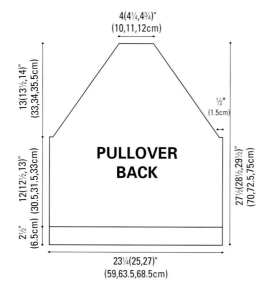

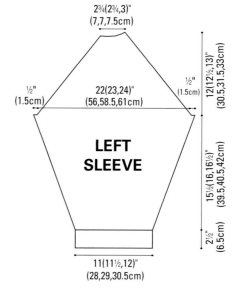

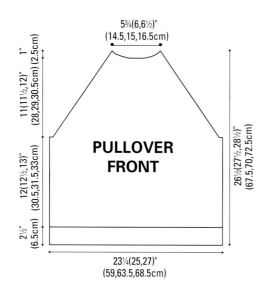

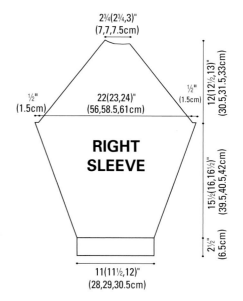

Aran Pullover with Neckline Variations

KNITTING RATING

Advanced

SIZES

Small (Medium, Large)

Finished measurements: 40 (44, 48)" (101.5, 112, 122 cm)

MATERIALS

Light worsted-weight yarn:

Man's shawl collar: Cashmere/Wool, 100 g = approx 226 yds (207 m): 7 (7, 8) hanks, or total of 1450 (1580, 1800) yds (1325, 14445, 1646 m)

Woman's crewneck: Cotton/Wool, 100 g = approx 226 yds (207 m): 7 (7, 8) hanks, or total of 1450 (1580, 1800) yds (1325, 14445, 1646 m)

14" knitting needles, sizes 5 and 7 US (3.75 and 4.5 mm)

16" (40.5 cm) circular needle in size 5 U.S. (3.75 mm)

Cable needle (cn)

GAUGE

St st and RSS: 25 sts and 25 rows = 4" (10 cm)

Boxy cable = 2¼" (5.5 cm)

Enclosed cable = 2¼" (5.5 cm)

Open braid cable = 2" (5 cm)

4-St cable = ¾" (2 cm)

Open cable = 1" (2.5 cm)

Ribbed cable = 4¼" (11 cm)

Trinity stitch: 24 sts = 4" (10 cm)

PATTERN STITCHES

T3B: sl next st to cn and hold in back, k2, p1 from cn.

T3F: sl next 2 sts to cn and hold in front, p1 from left-hand needle, k2 from cn.

T4L: sl next 3 sts to cn and hold in front, p1, k3 from cn.

T4R: sl next st to cn and hold in back, k3 sts from left-hand needle, p1 from cn.

T4B: sl next 2 sts to cn and hold in back, k2, p2 from cn.

T4F: sl next 2 sts to cn and hold in front, p2 from left-hand needle, k2 from cn.

C4B: sl next 2 sts to cn and hold in back, k2, k2 from cn.

C4F: sl next 2 sts to cn and hold in front, k2, k2 from cn.

C6B: sl next 3 sts to cn and hold in back, k3, k3 from cn.

C6F: sl next 3 sts to cn and hold in front, k3, k3 from cn.

Stockinette stitch (St st):

Row 1: Knit (RS)

Row 2: Purl (WS)

Trinity Stitch: Multiple of 4 sts.

Row 1 (WS): ★ (k1, p1, k1) into first st, p next 3 sts tog; rep from ★.

Rows 2 and 4 (RS): Purl all sts.

Row 3: ★ p3tog, (k1, p1, k1) into next st; rep from ★.

Reverse Stockinette stitch (RSS):

Row 1: Knit (WS)

Row 2: Purl (RS)

4-Stitch Cable: Multiple of 4 sts.

Rows 1 and 3 (WS): p4.

Row 2: C4F.

Row 4: k4.

Enclosed Cable: Multiple of 12 sts.

Row 1 (WS): k2, p8, k2.

Row 2: p2, C4B twice, p2.

Row 3 and all WSR: Work all sts as they appear.

Row 4: T4B, C4B, T4F.

Row 6: k2, p2, k4, p2, k2.

Row 8: k2, p2, C4B, p2, k2.

Rows 9 to 16: Rep rows 5 to 8 twice.

Row 18: k2, p2, k4, p2, k2.

Row 20: T4F, C4B, T4B.

Rep rows 1 through 20.

Boxy Cable: Multiple of 12 sts.

Row 1 (WS): p4, k4, p4.

Row 2: C4F, p4, C4B.

Row 3 and all WSR: Work all sts as they appear.

Row 4: k2, T3F, p2, T3B, k2.

Row 6: k2, p1, T3F, T3B, p1, k2.

Row 8: k2, p2, C4B, p2, k2.

Row 10: k2, p1, T3B, T3F, p1, k2.

Row 12: k2, T3B, p2, T3F, k2.

Rep rows 1 through 12.

Open Braid Cable: Multiple of 10 sts.

Row 1 (WS): p2, k6, p2.

Rows 2 and 4: k2, p6, k2.

Row 3 and all WSRs: Work all sts as they appear.

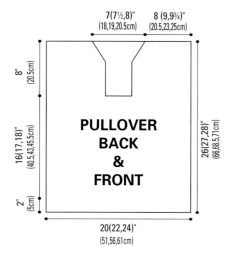

PULLOVER BACK & FRONT

7(7½,8)"
(18,19,20.5cm)

8 (9,9¾)"
(20.5,23,25cm)

8"
(20.5cm)

16(17,18)"
(40.5,43,45.5cm)

26(27,28)"
(66,68.5,71cm)

2"
(5cm)

20(22,24)"
(51,56,61cm)

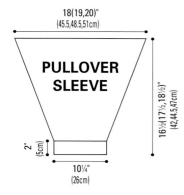

PULLOVER SLEEVE

18(19,20)"
(45.5,48.5,51cm)

16½(17½,18½)"
(42,44.5,47cm)

2"
(5cm)

10¼"
(26cm)

Row 6: sl 2 sts to cn and hold in front, p2, k2, k2 from cn, T4B.

Rows 8, 12, and 16: p2, k2, C4B, p2.

Rows 10 and 14: p2, C4F, k2, p2.

Row 18: sl 4 sts to cn and hold in back, k2, p4 from cn, T4F.

Rows 20, 22, and 24: k2, p6, k2.

Rep rows 1 through 24.

Open Cable: Multiple of 5 sts.

Row 1 (WS): p2, k1, p2.

Rows 2, 4, and 6: k2, p1, k2.

Row 3 and all WSR: Work all sts as they appear.

Row 8: sl 3 sts to cn and hold in back, k2, sl last st on cn to left-hand needle and p it, k2 from cn.

Ribbed Cable: Multiple of 22 sts.

Row 1 (WS): p2, k2, p6, k2, p6, k2, p2.

Row 2: k2, p2, k6, p2, k6, p2, k2.

Row 3 and all WSRs except row 19: Work all sts as they appear.

Row 4: k2, p2, C6F, p2, C6B, p2, k2.

Row 6: Rep row 2.

Rows 7 to 18: Rep rows 1 to 6 twice.

Row 19 (transition row): p6, k2, p2, k2, p2, k2, p6.

Rows 20 and 24: k6, p2, k2, p2, k2, p2, k6.

Row 22: C6B, p2, k2, p2, k2, p2, C6F.

Rows 25 to 36: Rep rows 19 to 24 twice.

Rep rows 1 through 36.

BACK

With smaller needles, CO 108 (118, 130) sts.

Purl 1 RSR.

Knit across next WSR, inc 14 (16, 16) sts evenly to give 122 (134, 146) sts.

Beg Trinity st, keeping first and last sts in RSS for 12 rows.

Change to larger needles and est cable sequence on WSR: Work 2 sts in RSS, work Enclosed cable over 12 sts, work 2 in RSS, work Boxy cable over 12 sts, work 2 in RSS, work Open Braid cable over 10 sts, work 2 in RSS, work Open cable over 5 sts, work 3 in RSS, work Ribbed cable over 22 sts, work 3 in RSS, work Open cable over 5 sts, work 2 in RSS, work Open Braid cable over 10 sts, work 2 in RSS, work Boxy cable over 12 sts, work 2 in RSS, work Enclosed cable over 12 sts, work 2 in RSS.

Small:

Work 122 sts as given for cable sequence above.

Medium:

Work 2 sts in RSS, work 4-St cable, work cable sequence above over 122 sts, work 4-St cable, work 2 sts in RSS to give 134 sts.

Large:

[Work 2 sts in RSS, work 4-St cable] twice, work cable sequence above over 122 sts, [work 4-St cable, work 2 sts in RSS] twice to give 146 sts.

When piece meas 26 (27, 28)" (66, 68.5, 71 cm), BO all sts.

SHAWL COLLAR FRONT

Work same as back.

When piece meas 18 (19, 20)" (45.5, 48.5, 51 cm), shape neck: Work 49 (55, 61) sts, join 2nd ball of yarn, BO center 24 sts, and work to end.

Work each side sep in est patt until piece meas 22 (23, 24)" (56, 58.5, 61 cm).

Dec for neckline: BO 1 st at neck edge every other row 3 (4, 8) times, then every 4 rows 4 (4, 2) times to give 42 (47, 51) sts at shoulder.

When piece meas same as back, BO all shoulder sts.

CREWNECK FRONT

Work same as back.

When piece meas 24 (25, 26)" (61, 63.5, 66 cm), shape neck: Work 50 (55, 59) sts, join 2nd ball of yarn, BO center 22 (24, 28) sts, and work to end.

Working each side sep as est, dec for neckline every other row 4 sts once, 2 sts once, 1 st twice to give 42 (47, 51) sts at shoulder.

When piece meas same as back, BO all sts.

SLEEVES

With smaller needles, CO 44 (44, 48) sts.

Purl 1 RSR.

Knit across next RSR, inc 10 (10, 6) sts evenly across to give 54 sts.

Beg Trinity st, keeping first and last sts in RSS for 10 rows.

Change to larger needles and est cables on WSR: Work 2 in RSS, work Boxy cable over 12 sts, work 2 in RSS, work Ribbed cable over 22 sts, work 2 in RSS, work Enclosed cable over 12 sts, work 2 in RSS.

Work in est patt, inc into Trinity st but keep first and last st in RSS to make seaming easier.

Inc 1 st each end every other row 0 (0, 2) times, then every 4 rows

21 (23, 24) times to give 96 (100, 106) sts.

Work in est patt until piece meas 16½ (17½,18½)" (42, 44.5, 47 cm) or desired length; then BO all sts.

FINISHING

Sew shoulder seams.

Meas down 9 (9½, 10)" (23, 24, 25.5 cm) in front and back and mark.

Sew sleeves bet markers.

Sew side and sleeve seams.

SHAWL COLLAR

With RS facing and circular needle, pu 154 (154, 158) sts evenly at neckline, leaving center bottom cable sts free.

Row 1 (WS): ★ p2, k2; rep from ★, end p2.

Row 2: ★ k2, p2; rep from ★, end k2.

Work in 2 x 2 rib for 4¼" (11 cm) or until piece fits across opening.

BO all sts.

Overlap and sew edges at lower center front.

CREWNECK

With RS facing and circular needle, pu 90 (94, 100) sts evenly around neck and k in trinity st for 4 rows, then in RSS for 2 rows, dec 6 (8, 10) sts on last row.

BO all sts.

Fair Isle–Fronted Vest

KNITTING RATING

Experienced

SIZES

Extra Small (Small, Medium, Large, Extra Large)

Finished measurements: 38 (40, 42, 44, 46)" (96.5, 101.5, 106.5, 112, 117 cm)

MATERIALS

Sport-weight alpaca yarn: Colors A, C, and D 115 yds (105 m) each

Color B: 500 (510, 525, 550, 575) yds (457, 466, 480, 503, 526 m)

Color E: 230 yds (210 m)

14" knitting needles, sizes 5 and 7 US (3.75 and 4.5 mm)

16" circular needle size 5 US (3.75 cm) Two stitch holders

Seven ¾" (2 cm) buttons

GAUGE

St st on larger needles: 24 sts and 24 rows = 4" (10 cm)

Textured stitch on larger needles: 20 sts and 28 rows = 4" (10 cm)

Left: Fair Isle-Fronted Vest; right: Cropped Aran.

PATTERN STITCHES

Stockinette stitch (St st)

Row 1 (RS): Knit.

Row 2 (WS): Purl.

In the rnd: k all sts.

Fair Isle stitch:

Work in St st as shown on chart, carrying non-active yarn loosely behind work (refer to page 8).

Twisted Single rib: Odd number of sts.

Row 1: ★ p1, k1 tbl (through back of loop); rep from ★, end p1.

Row 2: k1, ★ p1, k1; rep from ★.

Textured stitch: Multiple of 4 sts.

Row 1: Knit all sts.

Row 2 and all WSR: Purl all sts.

Row 3: k2, p2.

Row 5: Knit all sts.

Row 7: p2, k2.

Rep rows 1 through 8.

BACK

With smaller needles and color B, CO 77 (81, 85, 91, 95) sts.

Work in Twisted Single rib for 1½" (4 cm).

In last row of rib, inc 7 (11, 11, 9, 9) sts evenly across to give 84 (92, 96, 100, 104) sts.

Change to larger needles and work in textured st.

At the same time, inc 1 st each end every 10 rows 5 (4, 5, 5, 6) times to give 94 (100, 106, 110, 116) sts.

Armhole shaping: When piece meas 11½ (12, 12½, 13, 13½)" (29, 30.5, 31.5, 33, 34 cm), BO 5 sts at beg of next 2 rows, then dec 1 st each end every 2nd row 10 times to give 64 (70, 76, 80, 86) sts.

Shoulder shaping: When piece meas 21 (22, 22½, 23, 24)" (53.5, 56, 57, 58.5, 61 cm), BO 6 (7, 8, 8, 9) sts at beg of next 2 rows, BO 7 (7, 8, 9, 9) sts at beg of next 2 rows, and BO 7 (8, 9, 9, 10) sts at beg of next 2 rows.

BO rem back neck sts.

Pockets (make 2)

Using Color E and larger needles, CO 24 sts.

Work in St st until piece meas 4" (10 cm).

Slip sts to holder.

RIGHT FRONT

With Color B and smaller needles, CO 51 (53, 57, 59, 61) sts.

Work in Twisted Single rib for 1½" (4 cm).

In last row of rib, inc 6 (7, 6, 9, 10) sts to give 57 (60, 63, 68, 71) sts.

Change to larger needles and beg Fair Isle pattern on RS on first st.

Work charts in following sequence: A, B, C, D, E, A, B, F, G, D, E, A, B, H, G, I, E, A, B, H.

Note: Each chart is repeated across the width of the front.

Insert pocket back: When piece meas 5½" (14 cm) and you beg a WS row, work 15 sts; sl next 24 sts to holder; work in est patt across the 24 sts of a pocket back; work to end.

Cont in patt as est until piece meas 11½ (12, 12½, 13, 13½)" (29, 30.5, 31.5, 33, 34 cm).

Armhole and neck shaping: BO 6 sts at armhole edge. Then BO 1 st at armhole edge every other row 12 times to dec armhole edge by 18 sts total.

At the same time, BO 1 st at neck edge now and every 4th row 15 (16, 15, 17, 18) times total to give 24 (26, 30, 31, 33) sts rem at shoulder.

Shoulder shaping: When piece meas 21 (22, 22½, 23, 24)" (53.5, 56, 57, 58.5, 61 cm) at armhole edge, BO 8 (7, 10, 10, 11) sts twice, then 8 (8, 10, 11, 11) rem sts.

LEFT FRONT

Work same as right front, reversing shaping and pocket placement.

To beg Fair Isle patt and make

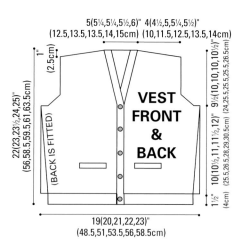

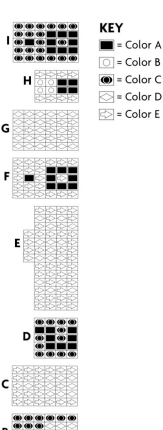

KEY

= Color A

= Color B

= Color C

= Color D

= Color E

center front match exactly, beg on first st on the WSR.

FINISHING

Button band: With Color B and smaller needles, CO 11 sts.

Row 1 (RS): k1, ⋆ k1 tbl, p1; rep from ⋆.

Row 2: ⋆ k1, p1; rep from ⋆, end k1.

Rep rows 1 and 2 until piece meas same as from bottom of vest front to center back of neck while stretching slightly.

Sew purl st edge of band to vest.

Place markers for buttons 1" (2.5 cm) from bottom of vest and at first center front neck dec. Evenly space rem 5 markers for other buttons.

Buttonhole band: Work as for button band, working buttonholes opposite markers.

Row 1 (RS): ⋆ p1, k1 tbl; rep from ⋆, end k1.

Row 2: ⋆ k1, p1; rep from ⋆, end k1.

Work buttonhole by BO center st, then CO 1 st over BO st in next row.

Sew purl st edge of band to vest.

Armhole bands: Using circular needle, pu 85 (89, 89, 89, 93) sts evenly around armhole.

Work in Twisted Single rib for 1" (2.5 cm). BO all sts.

Sew side seams.

POCKETS

Using smaller needles and color B, pu sts on holder.

Work in Twisted Single rib for 1" (2.5 cm), dec 1 st in first row to give odd number of sts. BO all sts. Tack at edges.

Sew pocket backs to inside.

Sew on buttons.

Cropped Aran

KNITTING RATING

Experienced

SIZES

Small (Medium, Large)

Finished measurements: 44 (48, 52)" (112, 122, 132 cm)

MATERIALS

Worsted-weight cotton yarn: 1150 (1300, 1350) yds (1052, 1189, 1234 m)

14" knitting needles, sizes 5 and 7 US (3.75 and 4.5 mm)

16" (40.5 cm) circular needle in size 5 U.S. (3.75 mm)

Cable needle (cn)

GAUGE

Double Moss st with larger needles: 18 sts and 23 rows = 4" (10 cm)

Cable pattern: 20 sts = 4" (10 cm)

PATTERN STITCHES

Double Moss stitch: Odd number of sts.

Row 1: ⋆ p1, k1; rep from ⋆, end p1.

Row 2: ⋆ k1, p1; rep from ⋆, end k1.

Row 3: ⋆ k1, p1; rep from ⋆, end k1.

Row 4: ⋆ p1, k1; rep from ⋆, end p1.

Center Cable Pattern:

Multiple of 70 sts.

See chart on page 94.

Cabled rib stitch:

Rnds 1 and 3: p5, k4.

Rnd 2: p5, sl 1 st to cn and hold in front, k1, k1 from cn, sl 1 st to cn and hold in back, k1, k1 from cn.

Rnd 4: p5, sl 1 st to cn and hold in back, k1, k1 from cn, sl 1 st to cn and hold in front, k1, k1 from cn.

BACK

With smaller needles, CO 108 (120, 132) sts.

Work 19 (25, 31) sts in Double Moss st, work center cable patt over 70 sts, end with 15 (25, 31) sts in Double Moss st.

When 2" (5 cm) are complete, change to larger needles, and cont as est.

When piece meas 19 (20, 21)" (48.5, 51, 53.5 cm) or desired length, BO all sts.

FRONT

Work same as back.

When piece meas 17 (18, 19)" (43, 45.5, 48.5 cm), shape neck: Work 41 (46, 50) sts, join 2nd ball of yarn, and BO center 26 (28, 30) sts. Work to end.

At neck edge, BO 1 st every other row 5 times to give 36 (41, 45) sts at shoulder.

When piece meas same as back, BO all sts.

SLEEVES

With smaller needles, CO 35 (35, 39) sts.

Work in Double Moss st for 2" (5 cm).

Change to larger needles and inc 1 st each end every 2nd row 0 (2, 0) times, then every 4th row 23 (23, 25) times to give 81 (85, 89) sts.

When piece meas 16 (17, 17½)" (40.5, 43, 44.5 cm) or desired length, BO all sts.

FINISHING

Sew shoulder seams.

With circular needle, pu 90 (90, 99) sts evenly around neckline. PM at shoulder for beg of row.

Work Cabled rib st in rnd for 3" (7.5 cm).

If neckline seems too loose, p2tog at p5 section of pattern.

When piece meas 3½" (9 cm), BO all sts.

Meas 9 (9½, 10)" (23, 24, 25.5 cm) down from shoulder in front and back.

Sew sleeve bet these points.

Sew underarm and side seams.

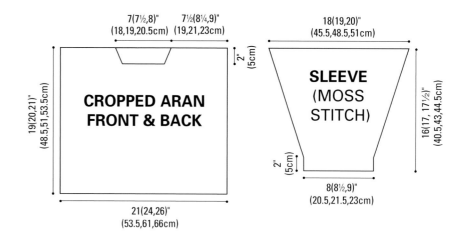

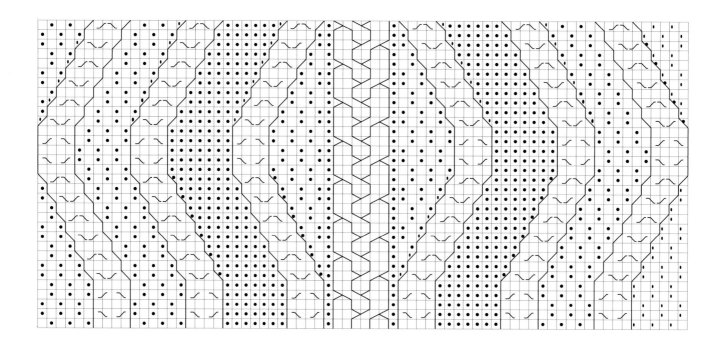

• = P on RS, k on WS

 = Sl 2 sts to cn and hold in back, k2, k2 from cn

= Sl 2 sts to cn and hold in front, k2, k2 from cn

= Sl 1 st to cn and hold in back, t2r, t2l, p1 from cn

= Sl 1 st to cn and hold in back, t2l, t2r, p1 from cn

= Sl 4 sts to cn and hold in front, p1, t2r, t2l from cn

= Sl 4 sts to cn and hold in front, p1, t2l, t2r from cn

= Sl 1 st to cn and hold in back, t2r, t2l, k1 from cn

= Sl 1 st to cn and hold in back, t2l, t2r, k1 from cn

Sweaters
for the
Family

Diamond Cable Pullover and Cardigan

KNITTING RATING

Intermediate

SIZES

Adult: Small (Medium, Large, Extra Large)

Child: <2 (4, 6, 8)>

Finished measurements: 40 (44, 48, 52)" (101.5, 112, 122, 132 cm) <27 (29, 30, 32)" (68.5, 73.5, 76, 81.5 cm)>

Note: Cardigan is sized for adults only.

MATERIALS

Bulky or Mohair type yarn:

Diamond Cable Pullover: 1143 (1143, 1270, 1397) yds (1045, 1045, 1161, 1277 m) <508 (508, 635, 750) yds (465, 465, 581, 686 m)>

Cardigan: 1260 (1350, 1350, 1440) yds (1152, 1234, 1234, 1317 m)

14" knitting needles, sizes 8 and 10 US (5 and 6 m)

16" (40.5 cm) circular needle, size 8 (5 mm)

Cable needle (cn)

GAUGE

Broken rib stitch on larger needles: 16 sts = 4" (10 cm)

Big and Little cable: 24 sts = 5" (12.5 cm) when blocked

PATTERN STITCHES

2 x 2 Ribbing: Multiple of 4 sts plus 2.

Row 1 (RS): ★ k2, p2 ★; rep bet ★s, end k2.

Row 2: ★ p2, k2 ★; rep bet ★s, end p2.

3 x 1 Broken rib: Multiple of 4 sts plus 3.

Row 1 (RS): ★ p3, k1 ★; rep bet ★s, end p3.

Row 2: Purl all sts.

Big and Little Cable: 26 sts and 40 rows.

Note: For child's version, omit rows 17 through 28.

PRC: sl next st to cn, hold in back, k3, p1 from cn

PLC: sl next 3 sts to cn, hold in front, p1, k3 sts from cn

C4B: sl next 2 sts to cn, hold in back , k2, k2 from cn

C6B: sl next 3 sts to cn, hold in back, k3, k3 from cn

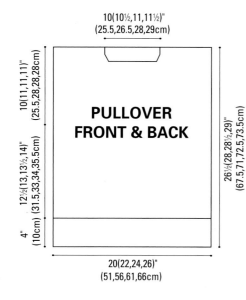

10(10½,11,11½)"
(25.5,26.5,28,29cm)

10(11,11,11)"
(25.5,28,28,28cm)

PULLOVER FRONT & BACK

26½(28,28½,29)"
(67.5,71,72.5,73.5cm)

12½(13,13½,14)"
(31.5,33,34,35.5cm)

4"
(10cm)

20(22,24,26)"
(51,56,61,66cm)

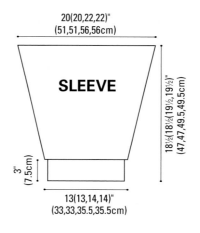

20(20,22,22)"
(51,51,56,56cm)

SLEEVE

18½(18½,19½,19½)"
(47,47,49.5,49.5cm)

3"
(7.5cm)

13(13,14,14)"
(33,33,35.5,35.5cm)

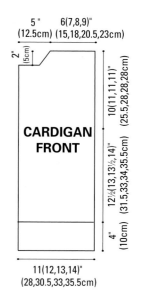

5 "
(12.5cm)

6(7,8,9)"
(15,18,20.5,23cm)

2"

(5cm)

10(11,11,11)"
(25.5,28,28,28cm)

CARDIGAN FRONT

12½(13,13½,14)"
(31.5,33,34,35.5cm)

4"
(10cm)

11(12,13,14)"
(28,30.5,33,35.5cm)

Row 1 (RS): k1, p9, k6, p9, k1.

Row 2 and all even rows: Work sts as they appear.

Row 3: k1, p9, C6B, p9, k1.

Row 5: k1, p8, PRC, PLC, p8, k1.

Row 7: k1, p7, PRC, k2, PLC, p7, k1.

Row 9: k1, p6, PRC, k4, PLC, p6, k1.

Row 11: k1, p5, PRC, p1, C4R, p1, PLC, p5, k1.

Row 13: k1, p4, PRC, p2, k4, p2, PLC, p4, k1.

Row 15: k1, p3, PRC, p3, C4R, p3, PLC, p3, k1.

Row 17: k1, p2, PRC, p4, k4, p4, PLC, p2, k1.

Row 19: k1, p1, PRC, p5, C4R, p5, PLC, p1, k1.

Row 21: k1, PRC, p6, k4, p6, PLC, k1.

Row 23: k1, PLC, p6, C4R, p6, PRC, k1.

Row 25: k1, p1, PLC, p5, k4, p5, PRC, p1, k1.

Row 27: k1, p2, PLC, p4, C4R, p4, PRC, p2, k1.

Row 29: k1, p3, PLC, p3, k4, p3, PRC, p3, k1.

Row 31: k1, p4, PLC, p2, C4R, p2, PRC, p4, k1.

Row 33: k1, p5, PLC, p1, k4, p1, PRC, p5, k1.

Row 35: k1, p6, PLC, C4R, PRC, p6, k1.

Row 37: k1, p7, PLC, k2, PRC, p7, k1.

Row 39: k1, p8, PLC, PRC, p8, k1.

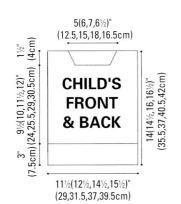

Lower Left: Diamond Cable Cardigan; right: Diamond Cable Pullover

Diamond Cable Pullover and Cardigan

CHILD'S SLEEVE

10½(11¾,13¼,13¾)" (26.5,30,33.5,35cm)

8(8½,8¾,9)" (20.5,21.5,22,23cm)

2" (5cm)

7¾(8¾,9¾,10¼)" (19.5,22,25,26cm)

BACK

With smaller needles, CO 74 (82, 86, 94) <42 (46, 50, 50)> sts.

Work 2 x 2 ribbing for 4" (10 cm) <2" (5 cm)>.

On last row of rib (WS), inc 9 <5 (5, 9, 13)> sts evenly to give 83 (91, 95, 103) <47 (51, 59, 63)> sts.

Change to larger needles and work in 3 x 1 Broken rib patt until piece meas 16½ (17, 17½, 18)" (42, 43, 44.5, 45.5 cm) <8¾ (8¾, 9¾, 9¾)" (22, 22, 25, 25 cm)> from beg.

Mark for armholes: Work until piece meas 26½ (28, 29, 29)" (67.5, 71, 73.5, 73.5 cm) <14 (14½, 16, 16½)" (35.5, 37, 40.5, 42 cm)> and BO all sts.

PULLOVER FRONT

With smaller needles, CO 78 (86, 90, 94) <46 (50, 54, 54)> sts.

Work 2 x 2 ribbing for 4" (10 cm) <2" (5 cm)>.

On last row (WS), inc 16 (16, 20, 24) <12 (10, 12, 14)> sts evenly to give 94 (102, 110, 118) <58 (60, 66, 68)> sts.

Change to larger needles and set up patt as foll: p2 <0 (1, 0, 1)>, k1 <1>, work 31 (35, 39, 43) <15 (15, 19, 19)> sts in 3 x 1 Broken rib, 26 sts in Big and Little cable, 31 (35, 39, 43) <15 (15, 19, 19)> sts in 3 x 1 Broken rib, k1 <1>, p2 <0 (1, 0, 1)>.

Work as for back until piece meas

22½ (23, 24½, 25)" (57, 59.5, 62, 63.5 cm) <9½ (10, 11½, 12)" (24, 25.5, 29, 30.5 cm)> from beg.

Neck shaping: Work 30 (33, 37, 40) <15 (15, 17, 17)> sts, sl center 34 (36, 36, 38) <28 (30, 32, 34)> sts to holder, join another ball of yarn, and work rem 30 (33, 37, 40) <15 (15, 17, 17)> sts as est. Working each side sep, BO 1 st at each neck edge every other row 5 <2> times to give 25 (28, 32, 35) <13 (13, 15, 15)> sts at each shoulder.

When piece meas same as back, BO all sts.

CARDIGAN LEFT FRONT

With smaller needles, CO 38 (42, 46, 50) sts.

Work in 2 x 2 ribbing for 4" (10 cm), ending on a RSR.

On the next row (WS), inc 7 sts evenly to give 45 (49, 53, 57) sts.

Change to larger needles.

Next row (RS): p2, k1, work 15 (19, 23, 27) sts in 3 x 1 Broken rib, 26 sts in cable pattern, ending k1.

Work as for back until piece meas 24-½ (26, 27, 27)" (62, 66, 68.5, 68.5 cm) from beg, ending on a RSR.

Neck shaping: On next row (WS), BO 14 sts at beg of row, work as est to end.

Dec 2 sts at neck edge every other row 5 times.

Work until piece meas 26½ (28, 29, 29)" (67.5, 71, 73.5, 73.5 cm) from beg and BO all sts.

CARDIGAN RIGHT FRONT

Work as for left front, reversing pattern as follows after change to large needles.

RS: k1, k26 sts in cable pattern,

work 15 (19, 23, 27) sts in 3x1 Broken rib, k1, p2.

Work in patt as est.

Reverse neck shaping.

SLEEVES

With smaller needles, CO 42 (42, 46, 46) <26 (30, 34, 38)> sts.

Work in 2 x 2 ribbing for 3" (7.5 cm) <2" (5 cm)>.

Inc 9 (9, 13, 13) <5> sts evenly in last row to give 51 (51, 59, 59) <31 (35, 39, 43)> sts.

Change to larger needles and work in 3 x 1 Broken rib, inc 1 st each end every 4th row 15 <6 (6, 7, 8)> times to give 81 (81, 89, 89) <43 (47, 53, 59)> sts.

When piece meas 18½ (18½, 19½, 19½)" (47, 47, 49.5, 49.5 cm) <8 (8½, 8¾, 9)" (20.5, 21.5, 22, 23 cm)> from beg, BO all sts.

PULLOVER FINISHING

Sew shoulder seams.

With circular needle, pu 76 (80, 80, 84) <60 (64, 72, 72)> sts evenly around neckline, including those sts on stitch holder(s). Work in 2 x 2 rib for 2½" (6.5 cm) <1½" (4 cm)>. BO loosely in ribbing.

CARDIGAN FINISHING

★ With smaller needles, pu 94 (98, 102, 102) sts evenly along right front edge.

Work in 1 x 1 rib for 5 rows ★ making 6 buttonholes in row 2 (by yo, k2tog). BO loosely in ribbing.

Rep bet ★ for left front.

Pu 92 (96, 96, 100) sts around neckline and work in 1 x 1 rib for ¾" (2 cm). BO loosely in ribbing.

Set in sleeves bet markers.

Sew underarm and side seams.

Block gently if desired.

Color Options Group

KNITTING RATING

Experienced

SIZES

1 (2, 4, 6, 8, 10)

Finished measurements: 20 (22, 24, 28, 32, 36)" (51, 56, 61, 71, 81.5, 91.5 cm)

MATERIALS

Bulky wool:

Colors A, C, and D, each: 130 (130, 130, 260, 260, 260) yds (119, 119, 119, 238, 238, 238 m)

Color B: 260 yds (238 m)

Color E: 130 yds (119 m)

14" knitting needles, sizes 7 and 9 US (4.5 and 5.5 mm)

Tapestry needle for working duplicate stitch

Markers relating to your 5 chosen colors to fill in template squares

GAUGE

St st on larger needles: 16 sts and 20 rows = 4" (10 cm)

PATTERN STITCHES

Garter ridge

Due to the different numbers of rows in Fair Isle patterns, you may end on a RSR or a WSR. Work Garter ridge as follows:

End on RSR: Beg with WS facing, p 2 rows.

End on WSR: Beg with RS facing, k 2 rows.

Garter ridges are worked over 2 rows in specified colors or color of your choice. Many of the sequences require multiple Garter ridges on top of each other.

Duplicate stitch

Where there are very small areas of a color in a patt, work this color in duplicate st (see page 9) to avoid carrying many colors behind work.

Stockinette stitch

Row 1 (RS): k all sts.

Row 2 (WS): P all sts.

Child's Color Option Pullover

Note: This pattern is designed to help you begin designing color-work patterns on your own. If you are following the pattern exactly, you will be determining your own starting points as explained in the directions that follow.

BACK

With smaller needles, CO 40 (44, 48, 56, 64, 72) sts.

Work 4 Garter ridges of: D/B/E/A, or any color sequence you desire.

Change to larger needles and beg working in Pattern A (see page 102).

To Center Pattern: (example given is for size 4 on patt A) Take total number of sts for size you are making—size 4 has a total of 48 sts in front or back—and divide this by patt rep (48 divided by 20 = 2 rep with 8 sts rem).

Divide rem sts by 2 to determine the number of sts for which you must compensate in order to center the patt (8 divided by 2 = 4).

Begin your patt 4 sts before end of patt A, work 2 complete reps of patt, and end with 4 sts of the beg of patt. Use this method to figure the centering of all patterns used.

Work patt A over 21 rows.

Work Garter ridges (2 rows) in Color E, then A.

Work patt B (see page 102) over 9 rows.

Work 1 Garter ridge in Color D.

Omit patt C for sizes 1 and 2; otherwise, work patt C (see page 103) over 12 rows.

Work Garter ridges (2 rows) in Color C, then B.

Work 13 (23, 18, 28, 18, 18) rows in patt D (see page 103).

Work 1 Garter ridge in C.

Omit patt E for sizes 1 (2, 4, 6); work patt E (see page 103) over 15 (20) rows for sizes 8 and 10.

BO all sts.

FRONT

Work as for back until piece meas 8 (10, 12, 14, 15, 16)" (20.5, 25.5, 30.5, 35.5, 38, 40.5 cm).

Work 10 (11, 13, 16, 20, 23) sts, join a 2nd ball of yarn, BO center 20 (22, 22, 24, 24, 26) sts, and work to end.

Working each side sep, BO 1 st at each neck edge every other row 4 times to give 6 (7, 9, 12, 16, 19) sts at shoulder.

When piece meas same as back at shoulders, BO all sts.

SLEEVES

With smaller needles, CO 26 (26, 28, 28, 28, 30) sts.

Left sleeve: Work Garter ridges in following sequence: A/C/B/A. Change to larger needles and beg working patt F (see page 103), centering in middle of sleeve.

At the same time, work in St st, inc 1 st each end every 4th row 2 (8, 3, 6, 10, 10) times, then every 6th row 7 (1, 7, 6, 4, 5) times to give 44 (44, 48, 52, 56, 60) sts.

When piece meas 11 (11½, 12, 13, 14, 15)" (28, 29, 30.5, 33, 35.5, 38 cm), BO all sts.

Right sleeve: Work Garter ridges as follows: D/B/A/C.

Work as for left sleeve, using patt F on page 103.

FINISHING

Sew one shoulder seam.

With smaller circular needle, pu 56 (56, 58, 62, 68, 72) sts evenly around neckline.

Work in Garter ridge as follows: B/A/C/A; then BO sts loosely.

Weave in all loose ends.

Sew other shoulder and neck seam.

Using cross-stitch embroidery techniques, decorate the different pieces with multicolored embroidery.

If you planned to work some of the colors in duplicate stitch, do this now.

Mark underarm points 5½ (5½, 6, 6½, 7, 7½)" (14, 14, 15, 16.5, 18, 19 cm) down in front and back from shoulder.

Set in sleeves bet points.

Sew underarm and side seams.

7(7½,7½,8,8,8½)"
(18,19,19,20.5,20.5,21.5cm)

2"
(5cm)

7(9,11, 13,14,15)"
(18,23,28,33,35.5,38cm)

CHILD'S PULLOVER

10(12,14,16,17,18)"
(25.5,30.5,35.5,40.5,43,45.5cm)

1"
(2.5cm)

10(11,12,14,16,18)"
(25.5,28,30.5,35.5,40.5,45.5cm)

11(11,12,13,14,15)"
(28,28,30.5,33,35.5,38cm)

CHILD'S SLEEVE

11(11½, 12,13,14,15)"
(28,29,30.5,33,35.5,38cm)

1"
(2.5cm)

6½(6½,7,7,7,7½)"
(16.5,16.5,18,18,18,19cm)

Adult Color Option Cardigan

SIZES

Small (Medium, Large)

Finished measurements: 46 (50, 54)" (117, 127, 137 cm)

MATERIALS

Bulky wool:

Colors A and D, each: 260 yds (238 m)

Colors B, C, and E, each: 520 yds (475 m)

14" knitting needles: sizes 7 and 9 US (4.5 and 5.5 mm)

36" (91.5 cm) circular needles in sizes 7 and 9 US (4.5 and 5.5 mm)

Very long stitch holders (or scraps of yarn)

Tapestry needle for duplicate stitch

Eight 1½" (4 cm) buttons

GAUGE

St st on larger needles: 16 sts and 20 rows = 4" (10 cm)

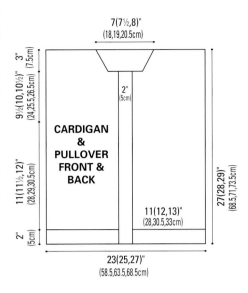

BODY

Note: Body is knit in one piece without side seams to armholes, then split into back and two fronts, which are worked separately.
With smaller circular needle, CO 180 (196, 212) sts.

Working back and forth on needle, k7 Garter ridges of: A/C/D/B/A/E/D, or in any color sequence you desire.

Change to larger circular needle and beg working in Fair Isle pattern (patts A and B page 102; C–K page 103).

To determine how to center and where to start pattern, see explanation on page 100.

Work in the following pattern sequence, or take creative license and change color sequences to suit yourself.

Work pattern H for 26 rows.

Work one Garter ridge in E.

Work one Garter ridge in C.

Work in pattern J for 6 rows.

Work one Garter ridge in C.

Work one Garter ridge in A.

Work pattern C for 12 rows.

Work one Garter ridge in A.

Work pattern I for 17 rows.

Work one Garter ridge in A.

Work one Garter ridge in C.

Work pattern J for 6 rows.

Work one Garter ridge in C.

Work one Garter ridge in B.

Work pattern K for 20 rows.

Work one Garter ridge in B.

Work pattern B for 9 rows.

Work pattern D for rem 3½ (4½, 5½)" (9, 11.5, 14 cm) of sweater.

When piece meas 17½ (18, 18½)" (44.5, 45.5, 47 cm), split work for armholes: Work 44 (48, 52) sts for one front, place sts on holder; work 92 (100, 108) sts for back, and place rem 44 (48, 52) sts on holder for other front.

BACK

Work 92 (100, 108) sts in patts until piece meas 27 (28, 29)" (68.5, 71, 73.5 cm) from bottom edge; BO all sts.

RIGHT FRONT

Work 44 (48, 52) sts at each side of opening in patts corresponding to back until piece meas 24 (25, 26)" (61, 63.5, 66 cm) from bottom edge.

Shape neck: BO 8 (9, 10) sts at neck edge. Work 1 row even.
BO 1 st at neck edge every other row 4 times to give 32 (35, 38) sts

at shoulder.

When piece meas same as back, BO all sts.

LEFT FRONT

Work to correspond with right front, reversing neck shaping.

SLEEVES

Make two different sleeves: With smaller needles, CO 34 (36, 38) sts and work in Garter ridge in colors to correspond with body of sweater.

Inc 4 sts evenly across last row to give 38 (40, 42) sts.

Change to larger needles and work in patterns given below while inc 1 st each end every 4th row 19 (20, 21) times to give 76 (80, 84) sts.

Sleeve A: Work in pattern G for 8" (20.5 cm).

Work one Garter ridge in Color A.

Work in pattern C for 12 rows.

Work one Garter ridge in E.

Work in pattern D for rem 5 (5½, 6)" (12.5, 14, 15 cm) of sleeve.

Sleeve B: Work in pattern F for 21 rows.

Work one Garter ridge in color C.

Work in pattern E for 16 rows.

Work one Garter ridge in E.

Work in pattern D for rem 8 (8½, 9)" (20.5, 21.5, 23 cm) of sleeve.

FINISHING

Sew shoulder seams.

Sew sleeve seams.

Sew sleeves into armhole openings.

Cardigan band: With RS facing, use smaller circular needle and color E to pu 110 (115, 120) sts along front edge, PM, pu corner st, PM, pu 85 (90, 95) sts around neckline, PM, pu corner st, PM, pu 110 (115, 120) sts down rem front of cardigan edge.

Knit 1 row in color E, completing first Garter ridge.

Work rem Garter ridges in the following sequence: A/B/D/C/A.

To miter corner sts: Work to marker, inc 1 by backward loop method (k1, keep st on needle, k1 into back of same st) before next marker. Work this inc every RSR at top corners of cardigan.

Buttonhole placement: Using safety pins, mark work 2" (5 cm) up from bottom of cardigan—this number seems large, but the button is 1½" (4 cm) in diameter.

Mark 2 sts down from marked st at top of cardigan. Then evenly space and mark for 6 more buttonholes.

Work to marked st on side of band that will have the buttonholes, BO next 3 sts, cont working to the next marker, and so forth.

To finish buttonhole on next row: CO 3 sts where sts were BO on previous row.

Sew on buttons.

MATERIALS

Same yarn and tools as for Adult's Cardigan. No buttons needed.

BACK

With smaller circular needle, CO 92 (100, 108) sts.

Work as for body of cardigan, following same color sequences.

When piece meas 27 (28, 29)" (68.5, 71, 73.5 cm), BO all sts.

FRONT

Work same as back.

When piece meas 24 (25, 26)" (61, 63.5, 66 cm), shape neck.

Work 36 (39, 42) sts, join a 2nd ball of yarn, BO center 20 (22, 24)

sts, and work to end.

Working each side sep, BO 1 st at neck edge every other row 4 times.

When piece meas same as back to shoulder, BO all sts.

FINISHING

Sew shoulder seams.

Sew sleeve seams.

Sew sleeves into armhole openings.

With smaller needles, pu 84 (86, 90) sts evenly around neck.

Work in Garter ridges to correspond with bottom of sweater.

BO loosely.

Note: To avoid carrying long sections of colors not being used, work extra colors in duplicate stitch when your sweater is completed.

GARTER RIDGE ROW
In any color, you will work two rows:

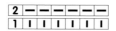

▬ = Purl on RS, knit on WS

Ι = Knit on RS, purl on WS

PATTERN A (over 20 sts and 19 rows)

PATTERN B (over 20 sts and 9 rows)

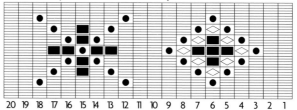

PATTERN C (over 20 sts and 12 rows)

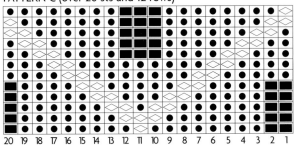

20 19 18 17 16 15 14 13 12 11 10 9 8 7 6 5 4 3 2 1

PATTERN D (over 6 sts and 6 rows)

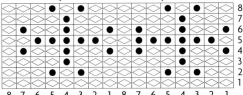

6 5 4 3 2 1 6 5 4 3 2 1

COLOR KEY

- ● = Color A (dark)
- ◇ = Color B (light)
- ☰ = Color C (medium)
- ★ = Color D (dark)
- ■ = Color E (light or medium)

PATTERN E (over 8 sts and 8 rows)

8 7 6 5 4 3 2 1

PATTERN G (over 8 sts and 8 rows)

8 7 6 5 4 3 2 1 8 7 6 5 4 3 2 1

PATTERN I (over 20 sts and 17 rows)

20 19 18 17 16 15 14 13 12 11 10 9 8 7 6 5 4 3 2 1

PATTERN J (over 7 sts and 6 rows)

7 6 5 4 3 2 1

FINISHING FOR BOTH SWEATERS

Weave in all loose ends.

Using cross-stitch embroidery techniques, decorate selected areas with multicolored embroidery.

If you planned to work some of the colors in duplicate stitch, do this now.

(Duplicate stitch can be used to outline an entire motif with a darker or lighter color to provide greater contrast between patterns.)

PATTERN F (over 10 sts and 6 rows)

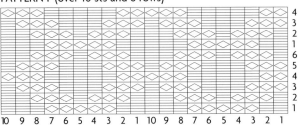

10 9 8 7 6 5 4 3 2 1 10 9 8 7 6 5 4 3 2 1

PATTERN H (over 30 sts and 26 rows)

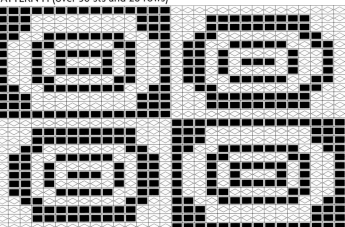

PATTERN K (over 17 sts and 20 rows)

17 16 15 14 13 12 11 10 9 8 7 6 5 4 3 2 1

American Aran Pullover

KNITTING RATING
Experienced

SIZES
Adult: Small (Medium, Large, Extra Large)

Child: <6 (8, 10, 12, 14)>

Finished measurements: 42½ (48, 53, 57½)" (108, 122, 134.5, 146 cm) <28 (34½, 38, 40, 42½)" (71, 87.5, 96.5, 101.5, 108 cm)>

MATERIALS
Worsted-weight wool or wool/mohair yarn:

Adult: 1710 (1710, 1805, 1900) yds (1564, 1564, 1650, 1737 m)

Child: <855 (950, 1045, 1140, 1235) yds (782, 869, 956, 1042, 1129 m)>

14" knitting needles, sizes 5 and 8 US (3.75 and 5 mm)

15 or 19" circular needle, size 5 US (3.75 mm)

Cable needle (cn)

GAUGE
Twist stitch cable pattern: 19 sts and 25 rows = 4" (10 cm)

Braid cable = 4½" (11.5 cm)

Open cable = 3¼" (8.5 cm)

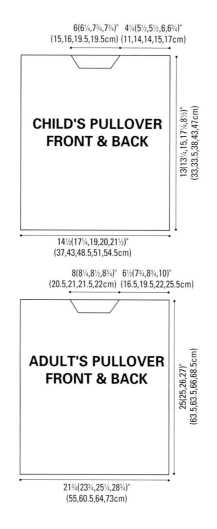

6(6¼,7¾,7¾)" 4¼(5½,5½,6,6¾)"
(15,16,19.5,19.5cm) (11,14,14,15,17cm)

CHILD'S PULLOVER FRONT & BACK

13(13¼,15,17¼,8½)"
(33,33.5,38,43,47cm)

14½(17¼,19,20,21½)"
(37,43,48.5,51,54.5cm)

8(8¼,8½,8¾)" 6½(7¾,8¾,10)"
(20.5,21,21.5,22cm) (16.5,19.5,22,25.5cm)

ADULT'S PULLOVER FRONT & BACK

25(25,26,27)"
(63.5,63.5,66,68.5cm)

21¾(23¾,25¼,28¾)"
(55,60.5,64,73cm)

PATTERN STITCHES

Reverse Stockinette stitch (RSS)

Row 1 (WS): Knit all sts.

Row 2: Purl all sts.

Twist stitch: Multiple of 2 sts.

Row 1 (WS): p2.

Row 2: TW2 (skip first st, k 2nd st without removing from needle, k first st and remove both from needle).

Twist stitch rib: Multiple of 5 sts plus 3.

Row 1 (WS): ★ k3, p2 ★; rep bet ★, end k3.

Row 2: ★ p3, TW2 ★; rep bet ★s, end p3.

Twist stitch rib: Multiple of 5 sts.

Row 1 (WS): ★ p3, k2 ★; rep bet ★.

Row 2: ★ p3, TW2 ★; rep bet ★.

Twist stitch body bib: Multiple of 6 sts plus 4.

On larger needles:

Row 1 (WS): ★ k4, p2 ★; rep bet ★, end k4.

Row 2: ★ p4, TW2 ★; rep bet ★, end p4.

Open Cable: Multiple of 21 sts.

BC3/2: sl 2 sts to cn and hold in back, k3, p2 sts from cn.

FC3/2: sl 3 sts to cn and hold in front, p2, k3 from cn.

FC3/1: sl 3 sts to cn and hold in front, p1, k3 from cn.

BC3/1: sl 1 st to cn and hold in back, k3, p1 from cn.

Row 1 (WS): k6, p6, k9.

Row 2: p9, sl 3 sts to cn and hold in back, k3, k3 from cn, p6.

Row 3 and all WS rows: Work all sts as they appear.

Row 4: p7, BC3/2, BC3/1, p5.

Row 6: p5, BC3/2, p3, FC3/1, p4.

Row 8: p3, BC3/2, p6, FC3/1, p3.

Row 10: p3, k3, p9, k3, p3.

Row 12: p3, FC3/1, p6, BC3/2, p3.

Row 14: p4, FC3/1, p3, BC3/2, p5.

Row 16: p5, FC3/1, BC3/2, p7.

Row 18: p6, sl 3 sts to cn and hold in back, k3, k3 from cn, p9.

Row 20: p5, BC3/1, FC3/2, p7.

Row 22: p4, BC3/1, p3, FC3/2, p5.

Row 24: p3, BC3/1, p6, FC3/2, p3.

Row 26: p3, k3, p9, k3, p3.

Row 28: p3, FC3/2, p6, BC3/1, p3.

Row 30: p5, FC3/2, p3, BC3/1, p4.

Row 32: p7, FC3/2, BC3/1, p5.

Braid Cable: Mulitple of 30 sts.

BC: sl 2 sts to cn and hold in back, k2, k2 from cn.

BC2/1: sl 1 st to cn and hold in back, k2, p1 from cn.

FC2/2: sl 2 sts to cn and hold in front, p2, k2 from cn.

BC2/2: sl 2 sts to cn and hold in back, k2, p2 from cn.

FC2/1: sl 2 sts to cn and hold in front, p1, k2 from cn.

FC: sl 2 sts to cn and hold in front, k2, k2 from cn.

Row 1 (WS): k1, ★ k4, p4 ★; rep bet ★ 3 times, k5.

Row 2: k1, ★ p4, BC ★; rep bet ★ 3 times, p5.

Row 3 and all WS rows: Work all sts as they appear.

Row 4: p4, BC2/1, FC2/2, BC2/2, FC2/2, BC2/2, FC2/1, p4.

Row 6: p3, BC2/1, p3, FC, p4, FC, p3, FC2/1, p3.

Row 8: p3, k2, p2, BC2/2, FC2/2, BC2/2, FC2/2, p2, k2, p3.

Row 10: p3, k2, p2, k2, p4, BC, p4, k2, p2, k2, p3.

Row 12: p3, k2, p2, FC2/2, BC2/2, FC2/2, BC2/2, p2, k2, p3.

Row 14: p3, FC2/1, p3, FC, p4, FC, p3, BC2/1, p3.

Row 16: p4, FC2/1, BC2/2, FC2/2, BC2/2, FC2/2, BC2/1, p4.

BACK

With smaller needles, CO 103 (113, 123, 133) <63 (73, 83, 83, 93)> sts.

Knit 3 rows.

Work Twist stitch rib, beg with a WSR.

When piece meas 2½" (6.5 cm) <1½" (4 cm)> incl Garter stitch, inc 31 (33, 35, 37) <27 (31, 29, 35, 31)> sts evenly across in RSR to give 134 (146, 158, 170) <90 (104, 112, 118, 124)> sts.

Change to larger needles; est cabled patt on WSR as follows:

Adult: ★ k4 in RSS, p2 for TW ★; rep bet ★ 0 (1, 2, 3) more times (over 6 (12, 18, 24) sts), work Open Cable over 21 sts, p2 for TW, work Open Cable over 21 sts, p2 for TW, work braid cable over 30 sts, p2 for TW, work Open Cable over 21 sts, p2 for TW, work Open Cable for 21 sts, ★ p2 for TW, k4 in RSS ★; rep bet ★ 0 (1, 2, 3) more times (over 6 (12, 18, 24) sts).

Child: k0 (2, 0, 3, 0) in RSS, ★ k4, p2 for TW ★; rep bet ★ 0 (1, 2, 2, 3) more times (over 6 (12, 18, 18, 24) sts), work Open Cable over 21 sts, p2 for TW, work Braid Cable over 30 sts, work p2 for TW, work Open Cable over 21 sts, ★ p2 for TW, k4 in RSS ★; rep bet ★ 0 (1, 2, 2, 3) more times (over 6 (12, 18, 18 24) sts), end with k0 (2, 0, 3, 0) sts in RSS.

Work as est in patt, twisting the 2 St sts every RSR and keeping other sts in RSS.

Work even until piece meas 25 (25, 26, 27)" (63.5, 63.5, 66, 68.5 cm) <13 (14, 16, 18, 19)" (33, 35.5, 40.5, 45.5, 48.5 cm)> BO all sts.

FRONT

Work same as back until piece meas 22 (22, 23, 24)" (56, 56, 58.5, 61 cm) <11 (12, 14, 15½, 17)" (28, 30.5, 35.5, 39.5, 43 cm)>.

Shape neck: Work 49 (54, 59, 64) <30 (37, 41, 44, 47)> sts, join 2nd ball of yarn, BO center 36 (38, 40,

19(19¾,21,22¼)"
(48.5,50,53.5,56.5cm)

ADULT'S SLEEVE

17(17,18,19,)"
(43,43,45.5,48.5cm)

2½"
(6.5cm)

9½(11¾,12¼,12¾)"
(24,30,31,32.5cm)

15¾(16½,17¾,19)"
(40,42,45,48.5cm)

CHILD'S SLEEVE

11(12,13,14)"
(28,30.5,33,35.5cm)

1½"
(4cm)

8¼(9¼,10¾,10¾)"
(21,23.5,27.5,27.5cm)

42) <30> sts, and work to end. Working each side sep, BO 1 st every other neck edge 9 <5 (5, 6, 7, 7)> times to give 40 (45, 50, 55) <25 (32, 35, 37, 40)> sts at shoulder.

When piece meas same as back, BO all sts.

SLEEVES

With smaller needles, CO 39 (43, 48, 48) <33 (38, 38, 43, 43)> sts.

Knit 3 rows, ending with a RSR.

Work in Twist stitch rib for 2" (5 cm) <1½" (4 cm)> incl Garter st rows.

When you have finished a RSR, change to larger needles and inc on WS as follows: ★ k2, inc 1, k1, p2 ★; rep bet ★, ending with k2, inc 1, k1 to give 46 (52, 58, 58) <39 (45, 45, 51, 51)> sts.

Cont to work in Twist stitch rib for sleeve as est in last row by working k4 on WSR and p4 on RSR to accomodate inc in last

row.

At the same time, inc 1 st each end every 5th row 10 (9, 13, 9) <10 (8, 7, 10, 3)> times, then every 4th row 11 (12, 8, 15) <5 (7, 10, 7, 17)> times, incorporating new sts into patt to give 90 (94, 100, 106) <69 (75, 79, 85, 91)> sts.

When piece meas 17 (17, 18, 19)" (43, 43, 45.5, 48.5 cm) <10½ (11, 12, 13, 14)" (26.5, 28, 30.5, 33, 35.5 cm)>, BO all sts.

FINISHING

Sew side and shoulder seams.

With circular needle, pu 105 (110, 115, 120) <70 (75, 80, 85, 90)> sts evenly around neck.

Work in rnd in Twist stitch ribbing for 4" (10 cm) <1½" (4 cm)>, ending with a Twist rnd.

Knit 3 rows in Garter stitch.

BO all sts in purl.

Cabled Ladder Guernseys

KNITTING RATING

Intermediate

SIZES

Adult: Extra Small (Small, Medium, Large, Extra Large)

Child: <Small (Medium, Large, Extra Large)>

Finished measurements: 38½ (42, 47, 51, 54½)" (98, 106.5, 119.5, 129.5, 138.5 cm); <20½ (26, 29, 34)" (52, 66, 73.5, 86.5 cm)>

MATERIALS

Medium weight yarn for:

Tunic (adult): 1016 (1143, 1143, 1270, 1397) yds (929, 1045, 1045, 1161, 1277 m)

Standard length (adult): 889 (1016, 1143, 1270, 1270) yds (813, 929, 1045, 1161, 1161 m)

Child's pullover: <450 (508, 635, 762) yds (411, 464, 581, 697 m)>

14" knitting needles, sizes 5 and 8 US (3.75 and 5 mm)

16" (40.5 cm) circular needle, in size 5 US (3.75 mm)

Cable needle (cn)

GAUGE

St st with larger needles: 16 sts and 24 rows = 4" (10 cm)

Cabled ladder pattern: 21 sts and 24 rows = 5" (12.5 cm)

PATTERN STITCHES

Stockinette stitch (St st)

Row 1 (RS): Knit.

Row 2 (WS): Purl.

Garter ridge and ribbing:

See charts on page 109.

Cabled Ladder pattern:

Multiple of 18 sts.

See chart on page 109.

BACK

With smaller needles, CO 72 (80, 88, 96, 100) <40 (52, 56, 68)> sts.

Work Garter st ribbing as follows:

Adult pullover or tunic–work rows 1 through 10 twice; end with rows 1 and 2 to give a total of 22 rows.

Child pullover–<work rows 1 through 10 once; end with rows 1 through 7 to give a total of 17 rows.>

Garter rib should meas approx 3" (7.5 cm) <2½" (6.5 cm)>.

In last row of rib, inc 5 (4, 6, 6, 9) <1 (0, 2, 0)> sts evenly across to give 77 (84, 94, 102, 109) <41 (52, 58, 68)> sts.

Change to larger needles and est Garter st ridge at side seams: Work 4 sts in Garter ridge, PM, work 69 (76, 86, 94, 101) <33 (44, 50, 60)> sts in St st, PM, work rem 4 sts in Garter ridge.

Work in est patt until piece meas:

Adult pullover–11 (12, 12, 12, 13)" (28, 30.5, 30.5, 30.5, 33 cm)

Tunic–8 (9, 9, 9½, 9½)" (20.5, 23, 23, 24, 24 cm)

Child–<7½ (8½, 8½, 9)" (19, 21.5, 21.5, 23 cm)>

In last WSR of St st, inc 5 (6, 6, 6, 7) <3 (2, 4, 4)> sts evenly across to give 82 (90, 100, 108, 116) <44 (54, 62, 72)> sts.

Now est Cabled Ladder patt as follows: Beg with st 9 (5, 9, 5, 1) <1 (5, 1, 5)>, work to end of graph; then work 4 (4, 5, 5, 6) <2 (2, 3, 3)> rep of patt, ending last rep with st 18 (4, 18, 4, 8) <8 (4, 8, 4)> to give 82 (90, 100, 108, 116) <44 (54, 62, 72)> sts.

Work in pattern until piece meas:

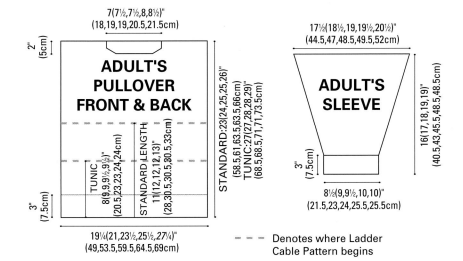

7(7½,7½,8,8½)"
(18,19,19,20.5,21.5cm)

2"
(5cm)

ADULT'S PULLOVER FRONT & BACK

17½(18½,19,19½,20½)"
(44.5,47,48.5,49.5,52cm)

ADULT'S SLEEVE

STANDARD:23(24,25,25,26)"
(58.5,61,63.5,63.5,66cm)
TUNIC:27(27,28,28,29)"
(68.5,68.5,71,71,73.5cm)

16(17,18,19,19)"
(40.5,43,45.5,48.5,48.5cm)

TUNIC
8(9,9,9½,9½)"
(20.5,23,23,24,24cm)

STANDARD LENGTH
11(12,12,12,13)"
(28,30.5,30.5,30.5,33cm)

3"
(7.5cm)

3"
(7.5cm)

8½(9,9½,10,10)"
(21.5,23,24,25.5,25.5cm)

19¼(21,23½,25½,27¼)"
(49,53.5,59.5,64.5,69cm)

– – – Denotes where Ladder Cable Pattern begins

Adult pullover–23 (24, 25, 25, 26)"
(58.5, 61, 63.5, 63.5, 66 cm)

Tunic–27 (27, 28, 28, 29)" (68.5,
68.5, 71, 71, 73.5 cm)

Child pullover–<13 (14, 15, 16)"
(33, 35.5, 38, 40.5 cm)>

BO all sts.

FRONT

Work as for back until piece meas:

Adult's standard version: 21 (22, 23,
23, 24)" (53.5, 56, 58.5, 58.5, 61 cm)

Tunic: 25 (25, 26, 26, 27)" (63.5,
63.5, 66, 66, 68.5 cm)

Child's sweater: <11 (12, 13, 14)"
(28, 30.5, 33, 35.5 cm)>

Shape neck: Work 30 (33, 38, 41,
44) <12 (17, 20, 24)> sts, join a 2nd
ball of yarn.

BO center 22 (24, 24, 26, 28) <20
(20, 22, 24)> sts, and work to end.

Working each side sep, BO 1 st at
neck edge every other row 4 <4>
times to give 26 (29, 34, 37, 40) <8
(13, 16, 20)> sts at shoulder.

When piece meas same as back at
shoulders, BO all sts.

SLEEVES

With smaller needles, CO 34 (36,
38, 40, 40) <26 (28, 30, 32)> sts.

Work in Garter ridge as done on
body for 3" (7.5 cm) <2½" (6.5
cm)>.

In last row of ridges, inc 4 <2> sts
evenly across to give 38 (40, 42, 44,
44) <28 (30, 32, 34)> sts.

Change to larger needles and est
Garter ridge at underarm as on
body: Work 4 sts in Garter ridge,
PM, work 30 (32, 34, 36, 36) <20
(22, 24, 26)> sts in St st, PM, work
4 sts in Garter ridge.

At the same time, inc inside the
Garter ridge as follows: Work 4 sts,
inc 1, work across St st, inc 1 before
marker, work 4 rem sts.

Cont inc so that 4 sts in Garter
ridge travel up seam of sweater, as

follows:

Inc 1 st each end:

Every 2nd row 0 (0, 2, 0, 0) <4 (0, 0, 0)> times,

Every 4th row 0 <8 (13, 14, 15)> times

Every 5th row 15 (16, 0, 0, 18) <0> times

Then every 6th row 0 (0, 14, 16, 0) <0> times, to give 70 (74, 76, 78, 82) <54 (58, 62, 66)> sts.

When piece meas 16 (17, 18, 19, 19)" (40.5, 43, 45.5, 48.5, 48.5 cm) <10 (11½, 12, 13)" (25.5, 29, 30.5, 33 cm)>, BO all sts.

FINISHING

Sew shoulder seams.

With circular needle, pu 76 (78, 80, 82, 84) <74 (76, 78, 80)> sts evenly around neckline. Work in Garter ridge as on bottom edge; more ridges for a funnel neck, fewer for crew neck. BO loosely.

Mark underarm points 8½ (9, 9¾, 9½, 10)" (21.5, 23, 25, 24, 25.5 cm) <6½ (7, 7½, 8)" (16.5, 18, 19, 20.5 cm)> down on front and back from shoulder.

Sew sleeve bet points.

Sew underarm and side seams, leaving a slit at the bottom for tunic, if desired.

KEY

☐ = Knit on RS, purl on WS

— = Purl on RS, knit on WS

 = PFC: Sl 2 sts to cn and hold in front, p1, k2 from cn

= PBC: Sl 1 st to cn and hold in back, k2, p1 from cn

= FC: Sl 2 sts to cn and hold in front, k2, k2 from cn

CABLED LADDER PATTERN (multiple of 18 sts)

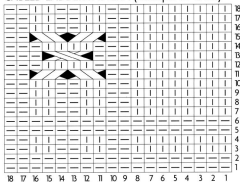

GARTER RIDGE FOR SIDE AND SLEEVE SEAMS

Repeat rows 1 through 4, ending pattern with row 2.

GARTER RIDGE FOR RIBBING

Repeat rows 1 through 10.

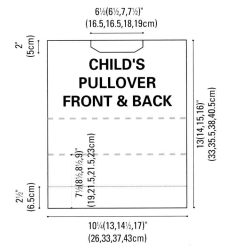

6½(6½,7,7½)"
(16.5,16.5,18,19cm)

2"
(5cm)

CHILD'S PULLOVER FRONT & BACK

13(14,15,16)"
(33,35.5,38,40.5cm)

7½(8½,8½,9)"
(19,21.5,21.5,23cm)

2½"
(6.5cm)

10¼(13,14½,17)"
(26,33,37,43cm)

13½(14½,15½,16½)"
(34,37,39.5,42cm)

CHILD'S SLEEVE

10(11½,12,13)"
(25.5,29,30.5,33cm)

2½"
(6.5cm)

6½(7,7½,8)"
(16.5,18,19,20.5cm)

Wishbone Cable Family

KNITTING RATING
Intermediate

SIZES
Adult: Small (Medium, Large, Extra Large)

Child: <2 (4, 6, 8)>

Finished measurements: 40 (44, 48, 52)" (101.5, 112, 122, 132 cm) <24 (26, 28½, 30½)" (61, 66, 72.5, 77.5 cm)>

Note: Cardigan is sized for adults only.

MATERIALS
Bulky weight yarn for:

Pullover:1200 (1270, 1400, 1525) yds (1097, 1161, 1280, 1394 m) <350 (381, 460, 508) yds (320, 348, 421, 465 m)>

Bulky mohair blend yarn for:

Cardigan: 1080 (1170, 1260, 1350) yds (988, 1070, 1152, 1234 m)

14" knitting needles, sizes 7 and 10 US (4.5 and 6 mm)

16" (40.5 cm) circular needle, size 7 US (4.5 mm)

Cable needle (cn)

Stitch holders

Five ¾" (2 cm) buttons for cardigan

GAUGE
St st on larger needles: 15 sts and 20 rows = 4" (10 cm)

Wishbone cable = 3¾" (9.5 cm)

Twist 5 = ¾" (2 cm)

PATTERN STITCHES
3 x 2 Rib: Multiple of 5 sts plus 2.

Row 1 (RS): p2, ★ k3, p2; rep from ★.

Row 2: k2, ★ p3, k2; rep from ★.

Reverse Stockinette stitch (RSS):

Row 1 (RS): Purl all sts.

Row 2: Knit all sts.

Twist 5: Multiple of 5 sts.

Row 1 (RS): Knit the 5th st from behind the first 4; then k4 and drop all 5 sts off needle.

Row 2: p5.

Wishbone Cable: Multiple of 16 sts.

Rows 1, 3, 7, 9, 11 (RS): k16.

Row 2 and all WS rows: p16.

Row 5: Sl 4 sts to cn and hold in back, k4 , k4 from cn, sl 4 sts to cn

and hold in front, k4, k4 from cn.

BACK
With smaller needles, CO 82 (87, 92, 97) <42 (46, 52, 52)> sts.

Work in 3 x 2 rib for 4" (10 cm) <2" (5 cm)> and inc 10 (13, 14, 17) <10 (10, 8, 12)> sts evenly across last WSR to give 92 (100, 106, 114) <52 (56, 60, 64)> sts.

Change to larger needles and est patt as follows: Work 3 (4, 4, 5) <6 (7, 8, 10)> sts in RSS, ★ Twist 5, work 3 (4, 5, 6) <7 (8, 9, 9)> sts in RSS, work Wishbone Cable over 16 sts, work 3 (4, 5, 6) <7 (8, 9, 9)> sts in RSS ★; rep bet ★s 2 <0> more times, end with Twist 5, work 3 (4, 4, 5) <6 (7, 8, 10)> sts in RSS.

Adult—work as est in patt until piece meas 16½ (17, 18, 18)" (42, 43, 45.5, 45.5 cm) and pm at each

edge to mark for armhole.

When piece meas 25½ (27, 28, 28)" (64.5, 68.5, 71, 71 cm), shape back neck: Work across 30 (32, 34, 37) sts, slip center 32 (36, 38, 38) sts to holder, join another ball of yarn, and work across rem 30 (32, 34, 37) sts.

Working each side sep, BO 1 st at neck edge every other row twice to give 28 (30, 32, 35) sts.

BO rem sts.

Child—work in est patt until piece meas <14 (14½, 16, 16½)" (35.5, 37, 40.5, 42 cm)> and BO all sts.

PULLOVER FRONT
Adult—work as for back.

When piece meas 24½ (26, 27, 27)" (62, 66, 68.5, 68.5 cm), shape neck: Work across 30 (32, 34, 37) sts, sl center 32 (36, 38, 38) sts to holder, join another ball of yarn, and work across rem 30 (32, 34, 37) sts.

Working each side sep, BO 1 st at neck edge every other row twice to give 28 (30, 32, 35) sts at each shoulder.

Work even until piece meas the same length as back; BO all sts.

Child—work as for back until piece meas <12½ (13, 14½, 15)" (31.5, 33, 37, 38 cm)>.

To shape neck, work <13 (14, 15, 17)> sts, sl center <26 (28, 30, 30)> sts to holder, join another ball of yarn, and work rem <13 (14, 15, 17)> sts.

Working each side sep, BO 1 st at neck edge every other row one time to give <12 (13, 14, 16)> sts at shoulder.

When piece meas same as back to shoulder, BO all sts.

CARDIGAN LEFT FRONT
With smaller needles, CO 42 (42, 47, 47) sts and work 3 x 2 rib for 4" (10 cm), inc 2 (4, 3, 5) sts across last WSR of rib to give 44 (46, 50, 52) sts.

Change to larger needles and est

patt as follows: Work 4 (5, 6, 7) sts in RSS, Twist 5, work 5 (5, 6, 6) sts in RSS, work Wishbone Cable over 16 sts, work 5 (5, 6, 6) sts in RSS, Twist 5, and work 4 (5, 6, 7) sts in RSS.

Work as est in patt until piece meas 16½ (17, 18, 18)" (42, 43, 45.5, 45.5 cm); then PM at edge to mark for armhole.

Cont as est until piece meas 24½ (26, 27, 27)" (62, 66, 68.5, 68.5 cm) and shape neck: BO every other row at neck edge 6 sts once, 2 sts 5 (5, 6, 5) times, then 1 st 0 (0, 0, 1) time to give 28 (30, 32, 35) sts. BO rem sts.

CARDIGAN RIGHT FRONT

Work as for left front, reversing neck shaping.

SLEEVES

With smaller needles, CO 42 (42, 47, 47) <27 (32, 37, 37)> sts.

Work in 3 x 2 rib for 4" (10 cm) <2" (5 cm)> and inc 12 (12, 13, 13) <3 (2, 1, 1)> sts across last WSR to give 54 (54, 60, 60) <30 (34, 38, 38)> sts.

Change to larger needles.

Adult—est pattern as follows: Work 6 (6, 9, 9) sts in RSS, Twist 5, work 8 sts in RSS, work Wishbone Cable over 16 sts, work 8 sts in RSS, Twist 5, work 6 (6, 9, 9) sts in RSS.

Cont in est patt, and at the same time, inc 1 st each edge in RSS every 4th row 10 times, then every 7th row 4 times to give 82 (82, 88, 88) sts.

When sleeve meas 18½ (18½, 19½, 19½)" (47, 47, 49.5, 49.5 cm), BO all sts.

Child—work entire sleeve in RSS and inc 1 st each edge every 4th row <5 (5, 5, 7)> times to give <40 (44, 48, 52)> sts.

Work until piece meas 8 (8½, 8¾, 9)" (20.5, 21.5, 22, 23 cm) and BO all sts.

PULLOVER FINISHING

Sew shoulder seams.

With circular needle, pu 75 (80, 80, 85) <60 (65, 70, 70)> sts evenly around neck, including the sts from holders at front and back.

Work 3 x 2 rib for 2" (5 cm) <1½" (4 cm)> and BO all sts loosely.

Sew in sleeves.

Sew underarm and side seams.

CARDIGAN FINISHING

Sew shoulder seams.

Sew in sleeves.

Sew side and underarm seams.

Left band: pu 94 (98, 102, 102) sts evenly along front edge. Work in Single rib (k1, p1) for 1" (2.5 cm) and BO all sts loosely.

Right band: Work as for left band, placing 5 buttonholes (by yo, k2tog) in 3rd row, spacing them evenly and taking into account that you will be placing a buttonhole in the neck band at top.

Neck band: With smaller needles, pu 80 (80, 82, 84) sts. Work Single rib for 1" (2.5 cm), placing buttonhole in neck band.

BO all sts.

Sew on buttons.

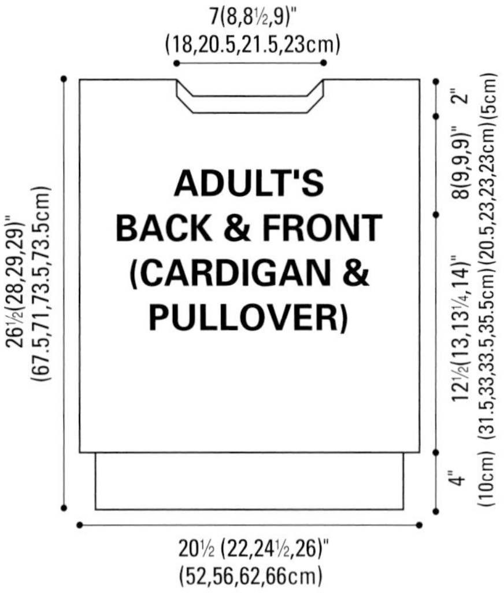

7(8,8½,9)"
(18,20.5,21.5,23cm)
ADULT'S BACK & FRONT (CARDIGAN & PULLOVER)
26½(28,29,29)"
(67.5,71,73.5,73.5cm)
2"
(5cm)
8(9,9,9)"
(20.5,23,23,23cm)
12½(13,13¼,14)"
(31.5,33,33.5,35.5cm)
4"
(10cm)
20½ (22,24½,26)"
(52,56,62,66cm)

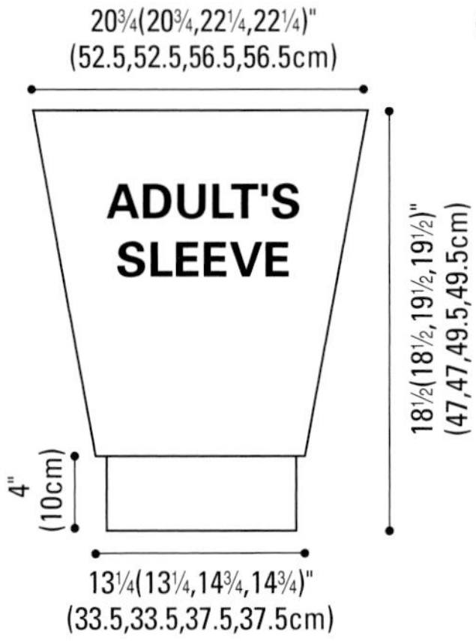

20¾(20¾,22¼,22¼)"
(52.5,52.5,56.5,56.5cm)
ADULT'S SLEEVE
18½(18½,19½,19½)"
(47,47,49.5,49.5cm)
4"
(10cm)
13¼(13¼,14¾,14¾)"
(33.5,33.5,37.5,37.5cm)

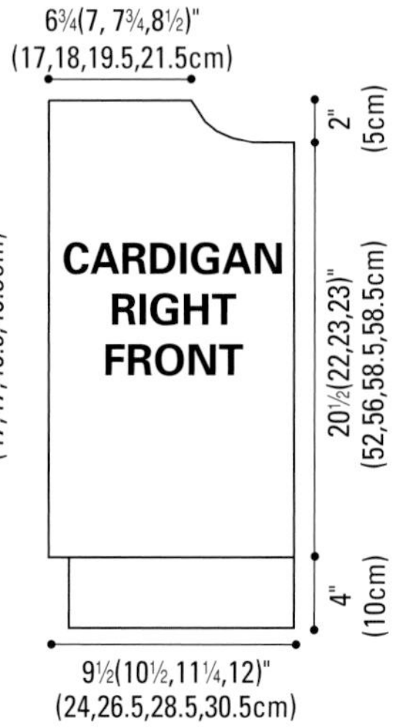

6¾(7, 7¾,8½)"
(17,18,19.5,21.5cm)
CARDIGAN RIGHT FRONT
2"
(5cm)
20½(22,23,23)"
(52,56,58.5,58.5cm)
4"
(10cm)
9½(10½,11¼,12)"
(24,26.5,28.5,30.5cm)

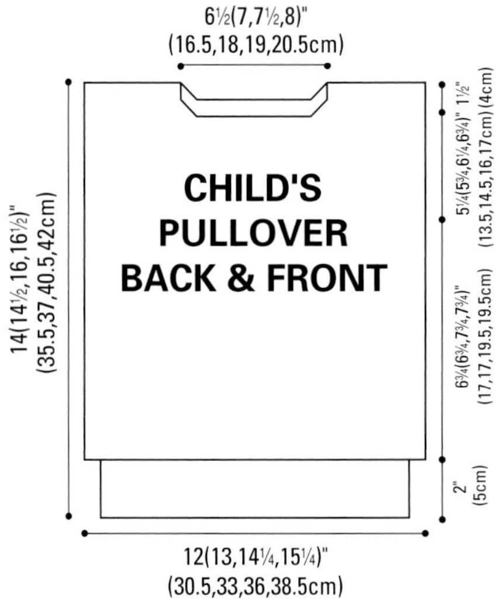

6½(7,7½,8)"
(16.5,18,19,20.5cm)
CHILD'S PULLOVER BACK & FRONT
14(14½,16,16½)"
(35.5,37,40.5,42cm)
5¼(5¾,6¼,6¾)" 1½"
(13.5,14.5,16,17cm) (4cm)
6¾(6¾,7¾,7¾)"
(17,17,19.5,19.5cm)
2"
(5cm)
12(13,14¼,15¼)"
(30.5,33,36,38.5cm)

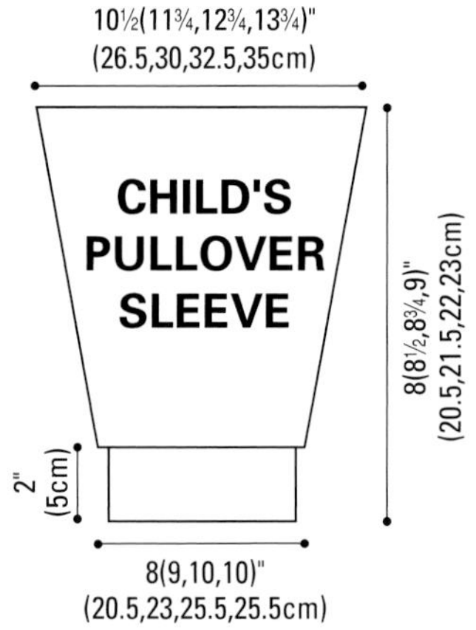

10½(11¾,12¾,13¾)"
(26.5,30,32.5,35cm)
CHILD'S PULLOVER SLEEVE
8(8½,8¾,9)"
(20.5,21.5,22,23cm)
2"
(5cm)
8(9,10,10)"
(20.5,23,25.5,25.5cm)

Ruffles & Lace

KNITTING RATING
Intermediate

SIZES
Small (Medium, Large)

Finished measurements: 38 (42, 46)" (96.5, 106.5, 117 cm)

MATERIALS
Worsted-weight cotton: 1116 (1209, 1302) yds (1020, 1106, 1191 m)

14" knitting needles, size 6 US (4 mm)

24" (61 cm) circular needle in size 4 US (3.25 mm)

Cable needle (cn)

GAUGE
3 x 3 rib with larger needles: 22 sts and 28 rows = 4" (10 cm)

Lacy Cabled T-Shirt

PATTERN STITCHES
See chart below.

BACK
CO 114 (126, 138) sts.

Work in pattern according to chart until piece meas 20 (21, 22)" (51, 53.5, 56 cm).

Shape shoulders and back neck: Keeping in est patt, BO 8 (8, 9) sts, work across 36 (39, 44) sts, join another ball of yarn, BO center 26 (32, 32) sts, and work to end of row.

Next row: BO 8 (8, 9) sts and work to center BO sts.

Working both sides at once, BO at neck edge 5 sts 3 times, and at the same time, BO at shoulder edge 7 (8, 9) sts 3 (3, 1) times, then 0 (0, 10) sts 0 (0, 2) times.

FRONT
Work as for back until piece meas 17 (18, 19)" (43, 45.5,48.5 cm).

Shape front neck: Work 49 (53, 59) sts, join another ball of yarn,

BO center 16 (20, 20) sts, and work to end of row.

Working each side sep, BO at neck edge 4 sts once, 3 sts twice, 2 sts 3 (4, 4) times, then 1 st 4 (3, 3) times. When piece meas the same as back to shoulder, shape shoulders as for back.

SLEEVES
CO 68 (78, 91) sts.

Work in patt according to chart, and at the same time, inc 1 st each side every 4th row 10 times, keeping all inc sts in 3 x 3 rib.

Work even on 88 (98, 111) sts until piece meas 6" (15 cm) from beg. BO all sts.

FINISHING
Sew shoulder seams.

Neck band: With circular needle, pu 132 (144, 144) sts evenly around neck.

Work in 2 x 2 rib (k2, p2 for all rows) for 1½" (4 cm).

BO all sts. Fold top of ribbing to inside of neckline and sew.

Set in sleeves.

Sew sleeve and underarm seams.

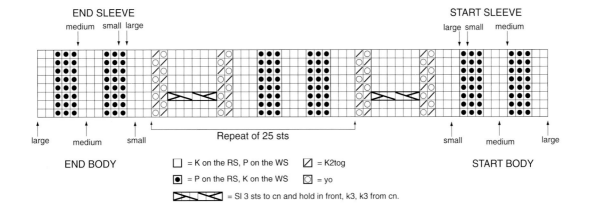

Left: Lacy Cabled T-Shirt; right: Baby's Ruffled Cardigan.

Baby's Ruffled Cardigan

KNITTING RATING

Intermediate

SIZES

6 months (12 months, 18 months)

Finished measurements: 22½ (24½, 26½)" (57, 62, 67.5 cm)

MATERIALS

Fingering-weight 100% cotton yarn: 462 (462, 616) yds (422, 422, 563 m)

14" knitting needles, size 2 US (2.75 mm)

29" circular knitting needle, size 3 US (3 mm)

Crochet hook size B

Five ⅜" (1 cm) buttons

GAUGE

Rib pattern with larger needle: 24 sts and 28 rows = 4" (10 cm)

Twisted rib with smaller needle: 17 sts and 32 rows = 4" (10 cm)

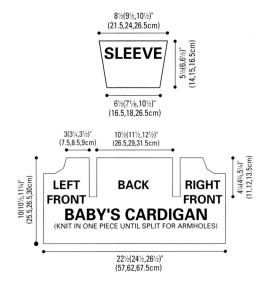

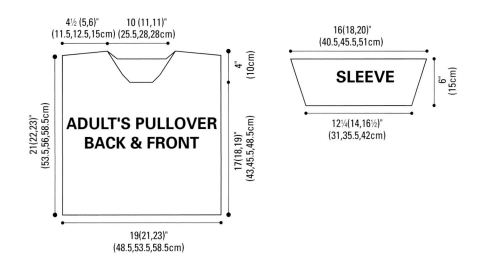

PATTERN STITCHES

Sl 2, k1, p2sso: sl 2 sts as if to knit, k1, pass the 2 slipped sts over.

1 x 3 Rib: Multiple of 4 sts.
Row 1 (RS): (p3, k1) across row.
Row 2 (WS): (p1, k3) across row.

Twisted Rib: Even number of sts.
Row 1 (RS): (p1, k1 tbl) across row.
Row 2 (WS): (p1, k1) across row.

Note: Body is knit in one piece, beg at lower edge, and is divided for fronts and back at armholes. The large number of cast on sts are decreased quickly after row 3. Use contrasting pieces of scrap yarn to mark every 10 or 25 sts, to make counting easier.

BODY

With circular needle, CO 383 (419, 455) sts.

Ruffled edge: Row 1 (WS): k3, p1, (k3, p9) 31 (34, 37) times, k3, p1, k3.

Row 2 : p3, k1, p3, (k9, p3) 31 (34, 37) times, k1 p3.

Row 3: Rep row 1.

Row 4: p3, k1, p3, (k3, sl 2, k1, p2sso, k3, p3) 31 (34, 37) times, k1, p3 to give 321 (351, 381) sts.

Row 5: k3, p1, (k3, p7) 31 (34, 37) times, k3, p1, k3.

Row 6: p3, k1, p3, (k3, sl 2, k1, p2sso, k3, p3) 31 (34, 37) times, k1, p3 to give 259 (283, 307) sts.

Row 7: k3, p1, (k3, p5) 31 (34, 37) times, k3, p1, k3.

Row 8: p3, k1, p3, (k1, sl 2, k1, p2sso, k1, p3) 31 (34, 37) times, k1, p3 to give 197 (215, 233) sts.

Row 9: k3, p1, (k3, p3) 31 (34, 37) times, k3, p1, k3.

Row 10: p3, k1, p3, (sl 2, k1, p2sso, p3) 31 (34, 37) times, k1, p3 to give 135 (147, 159) sts.

Row 11: k3, (p1, k3) 33 (36, 39) times.

Row 12: p3, (k1, p3) 33 (36, 39) times.

Rep rows 11 and 12 for 1 x 3 rib

until body meas 6 (6, 6½)" (15, 15, 16.5 cm), ending with a WSR.

Divide for armholes: Work 30 (33, 36) sts in 1 x 3 rib, BO next 6 sts, work 63 (69, 75) sts in patt, BO next 6 sts, and work across rem 30 (33, 36) sts.

LEFT FRONT

Work on first 30 (33, 36) sts in patt for 1" (2.5 cm), ending with a WSR.

Next row (RS): Change to smaller straight needles (leaving sts for back and right front on circular needle) and beg working in Twisted rib st, centering ribs over those est in 1 x 3 rib.

Work until armhole meas 2½ (3, 3½)" (6.5, 7.5, 9 cm).

Neck shaping: BO 9 (10, 12) sts at neck edge; then dec 1 st at neck edge every other row 3 times. When piece meas 10" (25.5 cm) from beg, BO rem 18 (20, 21) sts.

BACK

With larger straight needles, beg with a WSR, work 63 (69, 75) sts

in patt as est for 1" (2.5 cm), ending with a WSR.

Change to smaller needles and work in Twisted rib until piece meas the same as left front; then BO all sts.

RIGHT FRONT

Beg with a WSR, work 30 (33, 36) sts in patt as est for 1" (2.5 cm), ending with a WSR.

Change to smaller needles and work in Twisted rib until armhole meas 2½ (3, 3½)" (6.5, 7.5, 9 cm).

Shape neck as for left front, reversing shaping.

When piece meas 10" (25.5 cm) from beg, BO rem 18 (20, 21) sts.

SLEEVES

With larger needles, CO 39 (43, 51) sts; purl 1 row (WS).

Next row: p3, work 9 (10, 12) rep of Twisted rib chart.

Cont in 1 x 3 rib and inc 1 st each edge every 6th row 6 (7, 7) times to give 51 (57, 65) sts.

Work even until piece meas 5½ (6, 6½)" (14, 15, 16.5 cm) and BO

all sts.

FINISHING

Sew shoulder seams.

Sew sleeve seams, leaving ½" (1.5 cm) opening at the upper edge.

Sew in sleeves, stitching each side of upper ½" (1.5 cm) of sleeve to half of the BO armhole sts.

Edging: RS, (single crochet [sc] 1, chain [ch] 1) along right front, neck, and left front; at corners, work (sc, ch1, sc); end sc in lower edge; ch 2, turn.

Every other row: work sc, taking care to keep work flat.

Mark position of 5 buttonholes evenly spaced on right front edge.

Next row: (sc in ch1 space, ch1) rep along edge, work (sc, ch1, sc) in corner, dec at curves of neck as necessary. Work (ch 3, skip next ch1 space, sc in following ch1 space) at each buttonhole marker, finish row.

Next row: (sl st into ch1 space, ch1) around and work (sl st, ch1, sl st) in each buttonhole ch 3.

Sew on buttons.

Children's Sweaters

Checker-edged Vest

FINISHED MEASUREMENTS

Chest: 27 (28, 30, 32)" (69, 71, 76, 81 cm)

Length: 14½ (15½, 17½, 19½)" (37, 39, 44.5, 49.5 cm)

MATERIALS

Bulky-weight yarn:

Main color (MC): Approximately 280 (310, 370, 400) yds (252, 279, 333, 360 m)

Black (B) and White (W): Small amounts of yarn

14" knitting needles, sizes 8 and 9 US (5 and 5.5 mm), or size necessary to achieve gauge

GAUGE

St st on larger needles: 16 sts = 4" (10 cm)

Note: When working with two colors, strand the yarn loosely across the back of the work. Refer to page 8.

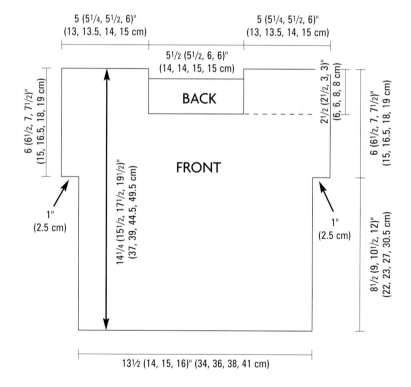

BACK

Using smaller needles and black yarn (B), CO 54 (58, 58, 62) sts, and work 2 rows in Single rib (k1, p1). Join the white yarn (W), and work as follows:

Row 1: (k2W, k2B) to last 2 sts, k2W.

Row 2: (p2W, p2B) to last 2 sts, p2W.

Row 3: (k2B, k2W) to last 2 sts, k2B.

Row 4: (p2B, p2W) to last 2 sts, p2B.

Rows 5 and 6: repeat rows 1 and 2. Cut W.

Using B, k 4 rows (2 Garter st ridges). For the third and fourth sizes only, inc 1 st at each end of the next row (54, 58, 60, 64) sts.

Change to larger needles, attach MC, work in St st until piece meas 8½ (9, 10½, 12)" (22, 23, 27, 30.5 cm) from beg, ending with RS facing.

CO 5 sts at beg of next 2 rows (64, 68, 70, 74) sts.

Cont working in St st, knitting first and last 5 sts of each row, until back meas 13 (14, 16, 18)" (33, 36, 41, 46 cm) from bottom edge, ending with WS facing.

Next row: k5, p13 (15, 15, 17), k28 (28, 30, 30), p13 (15, 15, 17), k5. Knit the following row. Rep these 2 rows once, then the first of these 2 rows again. The RS will now be facing.

Back neck and shoulder shaping: k21 (23, 23, 25), leave these sts on holder, BO 22 (22, 24, 24), k21 (23, 23, 25).

Next row: WS facing, k5, p13 (15, 15, 17), k3. Cont working shoulder sts, maintaining the Garter st edges, until back measures 14½ (15½, 17½, 19½)" (37, 39, 44.5, 49.5 cm) from bottom edge. BO the sts.

Complete other shoulder to match.

FRONT

Work as for back until piece meas 11½ (12½, 14, 16)" (29, 32, 36, 41 cm) from bottom edge, then work front neck and shoulder shaping as given for the back, completing piece to match the back in length.

FINISHING THE VEST

Join shoulder seams. Sew under-arm and side seams, taking care to match checkered borders.

V-Neck Cardigan

FINISHED MEASUREMENTS

Chest: approximately 25 (26, 27, 28, 30)" (63.5, 66, 68.5, 71, 76 cm)

MATERIALS

Worsted weight yarn: 2 (2, 3, 3, 3) 100 g balls

14" knitting needles, sizes 8 and 6 US (5 and 4 mm), or size needed to obtain gauge

Circular needle in size 6 US (4 mm)

5 buttons for front closure

GAUGE

St st with larger needles: 20 sts = 4" (10 cm)

PATTERN STITCH

Rows 1 – 7 in St st

Row 8 (WS facing) knit

BACK

Using smaller needles, CO 62 (66, 68, 72, 76) sts.

Work 1½ (1½, 2, 2, 2)" (4, 4, 5, 5, 5 cm) in Single rib (k1, p1).

Change to larger needles and work in patt st as given until back meas 11 (12, 13, 14, 15)" (28, 30.5, 33, 35.5, 38 cm).

BO 20 (22, 22, 22, 24) sts on each side for shoulders.

Leave remaining 22 (22, 24, 28, 28) sts on holder for back neck.

Place markers for underarm 5 (5½, 6, 6½, 7)" (13, 14, 15, 16.5, 18 cm) from top of shoulder.

LEFT FRONT

With smaller needles, CO 31 (33, 34, 36, 38) sts and work in Single rib as for back.

Change to larger needles and work in patt st until front measures same as back to underarm.

Cont in patt st, beg neck shaping: RS facing, knit to last 3 sts, k2tog, k1.

Cont to dec 1 st at neck edge every 2 rows 8 (6, 11, 9, 8) times, then dec 1 st every 3 rows 3 (5, 3, 5, 7) times until 20 (22, 22, 22, 24) sts remain.

Work until front meas matches back to shoulder.

RIGHT FRONT

Work same as left front, reversing all shaping.

SLEEVES

Using smaller needles, CO 32 (32, 36, 38, 40) sts, work in Single rib for 1½ (1½, 2, 2, 2)" (4, 4, 5, 5, 5 cm).

Change to larger needles and work in patt st, inc 1 st each side every 4 rows until there are 50 (56, 60, 66, 70) sts on needle.

Cont working until sleeve meas 8 (9, 10, 11, 12)" (20.5, 23, 25.5, 28, 30.5 cm).

BO all sts.

NECK BANDS

Mark position of buttons evenly on one side (left for girl, right for boy); bottom button ½" (1.5 cm) up from bottom edge, top button ½" (1.5 cm) below start of neck shaping.

Using circular needle, pu approx 46 (52, 56, 60, 64) sts along right front edge, 22 (22, 24, 28, 28) across back neck, and then approx 46 (52, 56, 60, 64) along left front edge. This is a total of approx 114 (126, 136, 148, 156) sts. Work in Single rib.

Next row, RS facing, work button-holes to correspond to button markers on opposite front.

Work 3 more rows.

BO in rib.

FINISHING

Stitch shoulder seams together.

Sew tops of sleeves in place between markers.

Join sleeve and side seams.

Sew on buttons to correspond with buttonholes.

Embellish as desired.

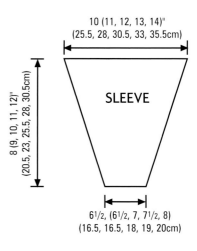

10 (11, 12, 13, 14)"
(25.5, 28, 30.5, 33, 35.5cm)

SLEEVE

8 (9, 10, 11, 12)"
(20.5, 23, 25.5, 28, 30.5cm)

6½, (6½, 7, 7½, 8)
(16.5, 16.5, 18, 19, 20cm)

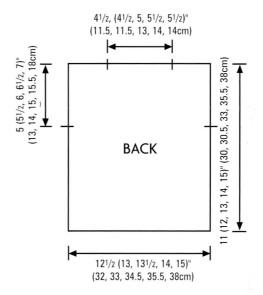

4½, (4½, 5, 5½, 5½)"
(11.5, 11.5, 13, 14, 14cm)

5 (5½, 6, 6½, 7)"
(13, 14, 15, 15.5, 18cm)

BACK

11 (12, 13, 14, 15)" (30, 30.5, 33, 35.5, 38cm)

12½ (13, 13½, 14, 15)"
(32, 33, 34.5, 35.5, 38cm)

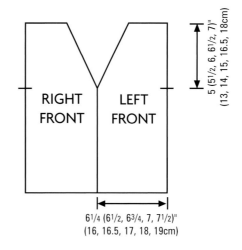

RIGHT FRONT

LEFT FRONT

5 (5½, 6, 6½, 7)"
(13, 14, 15, 16.5, 18cm)

6¼ (6½, 6¾, 7, 7½)"
(16, 16.5, 17, 18, 19cm)

Short Sleeve Crew Neck

FINISHED MEASUREMENTS

Chest: approximately 25 (26, 27, 28, 30)" (63.5, 66, 68.5, 71, 76 cm)

MATERIALS

Worsted weight yarn: 2 (2, 2, 3, 3) 100 g balls

14" knitting needles, sizes 8 and 6 US (5.0 and 4.0 mm) or size needed to obtain correct gauge

Decorative buttons (optional)

GAUGE

St st with larger needles: 20 st = 4" (10 cm)

Note: The short sleeves on this sweater make it work well as part of a twin set under the cardigan on page 120.

BACK

Using smaller needles, CO 62 (66, 68, 72, 76) sts; work in Single rib (k1, p1) for1½ (1½, 2, 2, 2)" (4, 4, 5, 5, 5 cm).

Change to larger needles and work in St st until back meas 11 (12, 13, 14, 15)" (28, 30.5, 33, 35.5, 38 cm).

BO 20 (22, 22, 22, 24) sts on each side for the shoulders.

Leave rem 22 (22, 24, 28, 28) sts on holder for back neck.

Place markers for underarm 5 (5½, 6, 6½, 7)" (13, 14, 15, 16.5, 18 cm) from top of shoulder.

FRONT

Work as for back until the piece meas 8½ (9½, 10½, 11, 12)" (21.5, 24, 27, 28, 30.5 cm).

Begin neck shaping: RS facing, k23 (25, 26, 26, 28) sts; place the rem sts on a holder.

Dec 1 st at neck edge, working the dec 1 st in from the edge, on every alternate row until 20 (22, 22, 22, 24) sts rem.

Cont until the work meas the same as back to the shoulder.

BO shoulder sts.

Return to the sts on the holder; leaving the center 16 (16, 16, 20, 20) sts on holder, knit across rem sts.

Complete neck shaping to match the other side, reversing all shapings.

BO shoulder sts.

SLEEVES

Using smaller needles, CO 40 (46, 50, 56, 60) sts; work in Single rib for 1 (1, 1, 1½ , 1½)" (2.5, 2.5, 2.5, 4, 4 cm).

Change to larger needles and work in St st, inc 10 sts evenly across the first row for all sizes, for a total of 50 (56, 60, 66, 70) sts.

Knit until sleeve meas 4 (4, 4½, 4½, 5)" (10, 10, 11.5, 11.5, 13 cm) from beg.

BO all sts.

NECK BAND

Seam one shoulder.

With smaller needle, pu and knit approx 62 (68, 74, 76, 80) sts.

Work in Single rib for about 1" (2.5 cm).

BO the sts.

FINISHING

Stitch shoulder and neck band seam.

Sew tops of sleeves in place between markers.

Join sleeve and side seams.

Embellish as desired.

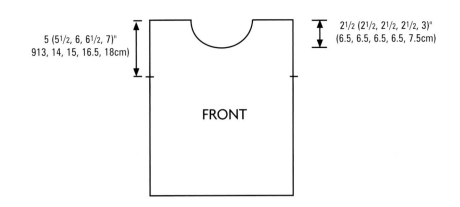

5 (5½, 6, 6½, 7)"
913, 14, 15, 16.5, 18cm)

2½ (2½, 2½, 2½, 3)"
(6.5, 6.5, 6.5, 6.5, 7.5cm)

FRONT

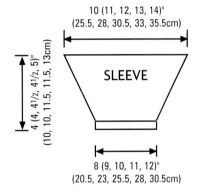

10 (11, 12, 13, 14)"
(25.5, 28, 30.5, 33, 35.5cm)

4 (4, 4½, 4½, 5)"
(10, 10, 11.5, 11.5, 13cm)

SLEEVE

8 (9, 10, 11, 12)"
(20.5, 23, 25.5, 28, 30.5cm)

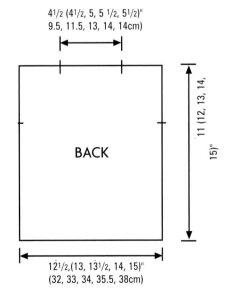

4½ (4½, 5, 5 ½, 5½)"
9.5, 11.5, 13, 14, 14cm)

11 (12, 13, 14, 15)"

BACK

12½,(13, 13½, 14, 15)"
(32, 33, 34, 35.5, 38cm)

Kid's Catch-Stitch Pullover

FINISHED MEASUREMENTS

Chest: 24 (26, 28, 30)" (61, 66, 71, 76 cm)

Length: 10½ (13, 15½, 17½)" (27, 33, 39, 44.5 cm)

MATERIALS

Chunky-weight yarn:

Main color (MC): approx 200 (270, 380, 450) yds (180, 243, 342, 405 m)

Contrast colors (CC1, CC2, CC3): small amounts in at least three colors

14" knitting needles, sizes 10 and 9 US (6 and 5.5 mm), or size necessary to achieve gauge

GAUGE

St st with larger needles: 14 sts = 4" (10 cm)

BACK

Using smaller needles and CC1, CO 43 (45, 52, 54) sts, and work 4 rows in St st. Change to larger needles. With CC2 and RS facing, k 4 rows (2 Garter st ridges). With MC, work 7 rows in St st. Next row: WS facing and CC1, k 2 rows.

With MC, work 4 rows in St st. Next row, with WS facing and CC2, knit 1 row.

Join CC3 and work 6 rows in St st. Next row, with RS facing and MC, purl 1 row.

Next row: WS facing, k3 (4, 2, 3) sts; ★ insert needle into next st as if to knit, then catch into CC2 loop 7 rows below, and knit the 2 sts tog, k5 ★ rep bet ★ across row.

Adjust number of sts in next row as follows:

1st size: dec 1 st (42).

2nd size: inc 1 st (46).

3rd and 4th sizes: dec 2 sts (50, 52).

Cont working in St st until back meas 10½ (13, 15½, 17½)" (27, 33, 39, 44.5 cm) from bottom. BO 14 (15, 15, 15) sts, place center 14 (16, 20, 22) sts on holder, BO rem 14 (15, 15, 15) shoulder sts.

Place markers for underarms 4½ (5½, 6½, 7)" (11, 14, 16.5, 18 cm) from top of shoulders.

FRONT

Work as for back until the piece meas 8½ (10½, 13, 14½)" (22, 27, 33, 37 cm) from bottom.

Neckline shaping: RS facing, k26 (28, 31, 33) sts, place next 16 (18, 19, 19) sts on holder. Dec 1 st at neck edge, working the dec 1 st in from edge on every other row until 14 (15, 15, 15) sts rem. Work straight until piece meas same as back. BO shoulder sts.

Return to sts on holder, leave center 10 (10, 12, 14) sts on holder, replace the rem 16 (18, 19, 19) sts on needle, complete neck shaping to match the first side, reversing all shapings.

SLEEVES

Using smaller needles and color of your choice, CO 24 (26, 28, 30) sts, and work in the color and pattern stitch you like. At the same time, inc 1 stitch at each side every 4 rows until there are 32 (38, 46, 50) sts. Work straight until sleeve meas 7 (8, 9, 11)" (18, 20, 23, 28 cm) (or your required length) from the beg. BO the sts.

NECKBAND

Seam one shoulder. With smaller needles and color of your choice, pu approx 44 (54, 60, 70) sts around neck edge, incl sts on holders. Work 8 rows in St st. BO loosely.

FINISHING

Seam second shoulder and neckband. Sew sleeves in place bet markers. Join side and sleeve seams, carefully matching stripes. Darn in loose ends.

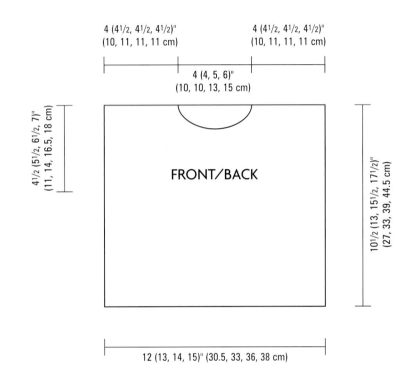

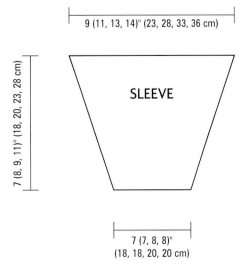

Kid's Pointed Hem Vest

FINISHED MEASUREMENTS
Chest: approximately 24 (26, 28, 30) inches (61, 66, 71, 76 cm)

MATERIALS
Worsted weight yarn:

Main color (MC): 2 (3, 3, 3) balls

Color A (red), B (yellow), C (turquoise), D (purple), or colors of your choice: small amounts of contrasting yarn

14" knitting needles, sizes 8 and 6 US (5 and 4 mm), or size needed to obtain correct gauge

Circular needle in size 6 US (4 mm)

4 buttons

GAUGE
In St st with larger needles: 20 sts = 4" (10 cm)

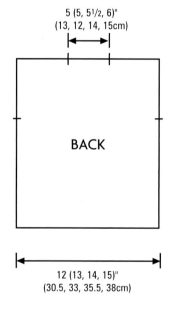

5 (5, 5½, 6)"
(13, 12, 14, 15cm)

BACK

12 (13, 14, 15)"
(30.5, 33, 35.5, 38cm)

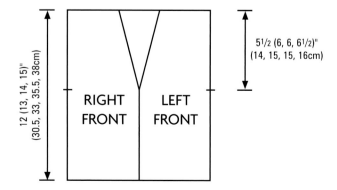

12 (13, 14, 15)"
(30.5, 33, 35.5, 38cm)

RIGHT FRONT

LEFT FRONT

5½ (6, 6, 6½)"
(14, 15, 15, 16cm)

BACK
Make a total of ten knitted triangles.

To make a triangle:

Using larger needles, CO 2 sts; knit 1 row.

Inc 1 st at beg of every row to 12 (13, 14, 15) sts; leave sts on a holder.

Arrange all triangles on needle, k120 (130, 140, 150) sts with Color A

Next row: Knit (1 Garter st ridge).

With RS facing, join Color B and work 6 rows in St st.

With Color A, knit next 2 rows (1 Garter st ridge).

Change to MC and divide sts for back and fronts.

With RS facing, k30 (33, 35, 38) sts, place on holder for right front.

Knit across nxt 60 (64, 70, 74) sts for back; place rem 30 (33, 35, 38) sts on holder for left front.

Working only on sts for back, inc 1 st at each end to form seam allowance, to 62 (66, 72, 76) sts.

Work in St st until piece meas 12 (13, 14, 15)" (30.5, 33, 35.5, 38 cm).

BO 21 (23, 25, 26) sts on each side for shoulders, place rem 20 (20, 22, 24) back neck sts on holder.

Meas 5½ (6, 6, 6½)" (14, 15, 15, 16.5 cm) down from shoulder and PM for underarm.

LEFT FRONT
Replace sts on needle; in MC work in St st, inc 1 st at side seam edge until left front is same length as back to underarm, end RS facing.

Begin neck shaping: Dec 1 st at neck edge every 3 rows until 21 (23, 25, 26) sts rem.

Work until the piece measures same as the back to the shoulder.

BO all sts; PM as on back for underarm.

RIGHT FRONT
Work same as left front, reversing all shaping.

ARM BANDS
Sew shoulder seams together.

RS facing, using smaller needles and Color A, pu and knit approx 50 (56, 56, 60) sts bet markers.

Knit 1 more row (1 Garter st ridge).

Change to Color B and work in Single rib for about 1" (2.5 cm).

BO all sts in rib.

FRONT BANDS
Mark position of buttons on left front, spacing evenly (see photo).

Using circular needle and Color A, pu and knit approx 124 (134, 146, 154) sts evenly along right front edge, across back neck, incl any sts

on holder, and along left front edge.

Knit the next row (1 Garter st ridge).

Using Color C, work 2 rows in Single rib.

Next row, RS facing, make buttonholes to correspond to markers on left front.

Work 3 more rows. BO in rib.

Note: If making garment for a boy, reverse position of buttons and buttonholes.

FINISHING

Stitch underarm and side seams.

Sew on buttons.

Color-Blocked Jacket with Detatchable Hood Choices

SIZES

Small (medium, large, extra large)

FINISHED MEASUREMENTS

Chest: approximately 25 (26, 27, 28, 30) inches (63.5, 66, 68.6, 71, 76 cm)

Note: Two styles of hood are given, both of which button on and off. The buttons serve as decorative trim when the hoods are off.

MATERIALS

Worsted weight yarn:

An assortment of colors that total about 300 (325, 350, 375, 400) grams

14" knitting needles, size 8 and 6 US (5.0 and 4.0 mm) or size needed to obtain gauge

Buttons for front closure

5 buttons to attach hood

Decorative buttons as desired

GAUGE

St st on larger needles: 20 sts = 4 inches (10 cm)

BACK

Using smaller needles, CO 62 (66, 68, 72, 76) sts.

Work 1½ (1½, 2, 2, 2)" (4, 4, 5, 5, 5 cm) in Single rib (k1, p1).

Change to larger needles and work in St st until back meas 12 (13, 14, 15, 16)" (30.5, 33, 35.5, 38, 40.5 cm).

BO 20 (22, 22, 22, 24) sts on each side for shoulders.

Leave rem 22 (22, 24, 28, 28) sts on holder for back neck.

Place markers for underarm 5 (5½, 6, 6½, 7)" (13, 14, 15, 16.5, 18 cm) from top of shoulder.

LEFT FRONT

With smaller needles, CO 31 (33, 34, 36, 38) sts, work in Single rib as for back.

Change to larger needles and work in St st until front meas 9½ (10½, 11½, 12½, 13)" (24, 27, 29, 32, 33 cm).

Beg neck shaping: At neck edge BO 8 (8, 8, 10, 10) sts, then dec 1 st at neck edge every alt row until 20 (22, 22, 22, 24) sts rem.

Work straight until front meas same as the back.

BO all sts.

RIGHT FRONT

Work same as left front, reversing all shaping.

Place markers on the fronts for underarm.

SLEEVES

Using smaller needles, CO 32 (32, 36, 38, 40) sts and work in Single rib for 1½ (1½, 2, 2, 2)" (4, 4, 5, 5, 5 cm).

Change to larger needles and knit in St st, inc 1 st each side every 4 rows until 50 (56, 60, 66, 70) sts rem on needle.

Cont working until sleeve meas 8 (9, 10, 11, 12)" (20.5, 23, 25.5, 28, 30.5 cm).

BO all sts.

NECK BAND

Sew shoulder seams tog.

RS facing, with smaller needles and color of choice, pu approx 60 (62, 70, 74, 80) sts around neck edge incl sts on holder. Single rib for 8 rows.

BO sts in rib.

BUTTON BAND

RS facing, with smaller needles and color of choice, pu approx 42 (46, 50, 54, 56) sts along left front edge from top of neck band to bottom edge of ribbing.

Work in Single rib for 8 rows. BO sts in rib.

Sew on 5 or 6 buttons, spacing evenly.

BUTTONHOLE BAND

Pu sts as for button band. Single rib for 4 rows.

Row 5: Work buttonholes to correspond with buttons.

Single rib 3 more rows; BO sts in rib.

FINISHING

Sew 5 buttons along middle of neckband, placing them as follows:

One at center back, one at each shoulder seam, and one at each first neck shaping decrease.

Sew sleeves in place between markers.

Sew side and sleeve seams.

BOBBLE HOOD

(2 sizes given)

Using smaller needles and color of choice, CO 35 sts for both sizes.

Work 4 rows in Single rib.

Make 3 buttonholes in next row as follows:

Rib 3, yo, k2tog, rib 12, yo, k2tog, rib 11, yo, k2tog, rib 3.

Work 3 more rows in rib.

Next row: Inc 1 in every stitch = 70 sts.

Change to larger needles and 2nd color.

Cont in St st until work meas 7

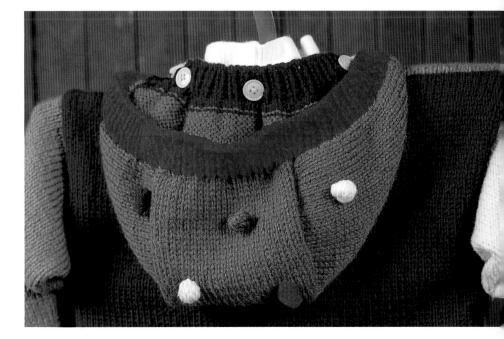

(8)" (18, 20.5 cm) from bottom edge.

RS facing, CO 20 sts, work to end of row.

Next row: CO 20 sts and work to end.

Cont on rem 30 sts until center piece fits along BO edges of sides. BO all sts.

Sew center piece to BO edges.

Using smaller needles and color of choice, pu approx 90 (100) sts along front edge of hood.

Work 6 rows in Single rib.

Next row make 2 more button-holes as follows:

Rib 5, yo, k2tog, rib to last 7 sts, yo, k2tog, rib to end.

Work 3 more rows.

BO all sts.

Making bobbles: CO 1 st, leaving a tail of yarn to secure bobble with; k1, p1, k1, p1 into the st (total of 5 sts).

Work 4 rows St st. Cut yarn, attach tapestry needle and thread tightly through sts.

Thread both tails into tapestry needle and knot bobbles to the hood in desired positions.

SCHOOL HOOD

Work as for basic hood, CO with red yarn for ribbing.

Work St st in 3 rows white, 1 row black until center panel sts remain (30 sts).

Cont panel in black.

Work face ribbing in green.

Decorate with school theme buttons as desired.

Button hood onto sweater.

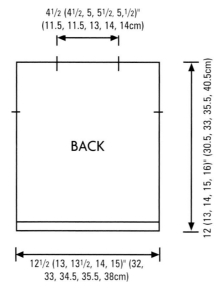

4½ (4½, 5, 5½, 5,½)" (11.5, 11.5, 13, 14, 14cm)

BACK

12 (13, 14, 15, 16)" (30.5, 33, 35.5, 40.5cm)

12½ (13, 13½, 14, 15)" (32, 33, 34.5, 35.5, 38cm)

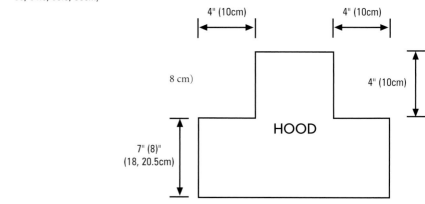

4" (10cm)   4" (10cm)

8 cm)

4" (10cm)

HOOD

7" (8)" (18, 20.5cm)

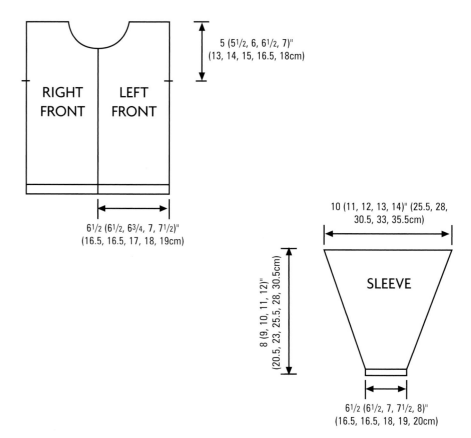

5 (5½, 6, 6½, 7)" (13, 14, 15, 16.5, 18cm)

RIGHT FRONT   LEFT FRONT

6½ (6½, 6¾, 7, 7½)" (16.5, 16.5, 17, 18, 19cm)

10 (11, 12, 13, 14)" (25.5, 28, 30.5, 33, 35.5cm)

SLEEVE

8 (9, 10, 11, 12)" (20.5, 23, 25.5, 28, 30.5cm)

6½ (6½, 7, 7½, 8)" (16.5, 16.5, 18, 19, 20cm)

Long Sleeve Crew-Neck Sweater

FINISHED MEASUREMENTS

Chest: approximately 25 (26, 27, 28, 30)" (63.5, 66, 68.5, 71, 76 cm)

MATERIALS

Worsted weight yarn:

Main color (MC): 2 (3, 3, 3, 3) 100 g balls

Contrasting color (CC): Small amount of yarn

14" knitting needles, sizes 8 and 6 US (5 and 4 mm), or size needed to obtain gauge

Decorative buttons

GAUGE

St st with larger needles: 20 sts = 4 inches (10 cm)

PATTERN STITCH

Rows 1 – 6: MC in St st

Rows 7 and 8: Knit with CC

BACK

Using CC and smaller needles, CO 62 (66, 68, 72, 76) sts.

Change to MC and work 1½ (1½, 2, 2, 2)" (4, 4, 5, 5, 5 cm) in Single rib (k1, p1).

Change to larger needles and work in patt st as given for a total of three repeats. Cont in MC and St st until back meas 11 (12, 13, 14, 15)" (28, 30.5, 33, 35.5, 38 cm).

BO 20 (22, 22, 22, 24) sts on each side for the shoulders.

Leave rem 22 (22, 24, 28, 28) sts on holder for back neck.

Place markers for underarm 5 (5½, 6, 6½, 7)" (13, 14, 15, 16.5, 18 cm) from top of shoulder.

FRONT

Work as given for back until the piece meas 8½ (9½, 10½, 11, 12)" (21.5, 24, 27, 28, 30.5 cm).

Begin neck shaping: RS facing, k23 (25, 26, 26, 28) sts.

Place the rem sts on holder.

Dec 1 st at neck edge, working dec 1 st in from edge on every alt row until 20 (22, 22, 22, 24) sts rem. Cont until piece meas same as Back to shoulder.

BO shoulder sts.

Return to the sts on the holder; leave the center 16 (16, 16, 20, 20) sts on holder and knit across rem sts.

Complete neck shaping to match other side, reversing all shapings.

BO shoulder sts.

SLEEVES

Using CC and smaller needles, CO 32 (32, 36, 38, 40) sts.

Change to MC and work in Single rib for 1½ (1½, 2, 2, 2)" (4, 4, 5, 5, 5 cm)

Change to larger needles and work in patt st for a total of 2 repeats.

Cont in MC and St st, inc 1 st each side every 4 rows until there are 50 (56, 60, 66, 70) sts.

Cont working until sleeve meas 8 (9, 10, 11, 12)" (20.5, 23, 25.4, 28, 30.5 cm).

BO all sts.

NECK BAND

Seam one shoulder.

With smaller needle and MC, pu 62 (68, 74, 76, 80) stitches around neck edge, incl sts on holders.

Work in Single rib for about 1" (2.5 cm). BO in rib.

FINISHING

Stitch shoulder and neck band seam.

Sew tops of sleeves in place between markers.

Join sleeve and side seams.

Embellish as desired.

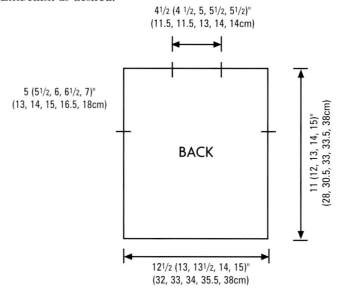

4½ (4 1/2, 5, 5½, 5½)"
(11.5, 11.5, 13, 14, 14cm)

5 (5½, 6, 6½, 7)"
(13, 14, 15, 16.5, 18cm)

BACK

11 (12, 13, 14, 15)"
(28, 30.5, 33, 33.5, 38cm)

12½ (13, 13½, 14, 15)"
(32, 33, 34, 35.5, 38cm)

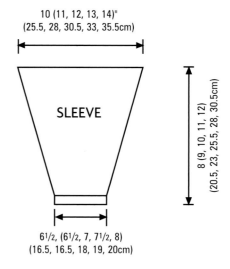

10 (11, 12, 13, 14)"
(25.5, 28, 30.5, 33, 35.5cm)

SLEEVE

8 (9, 10, 11, 12)"
(20.5, 23, 25.5, 28, 30.5cm)

6½, (6½, 7, 7½, 8)
(16.5, 16.5, 18, 19, 20cm)

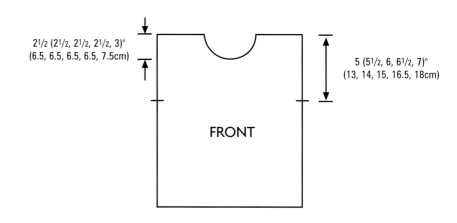

2½ (2½, 2½, 2½, 3)"
(6.5, 6.5, 6.5, 6.5, 7.5cm)

5 (5½, 6, 6½, 7)"
(13, 14, 15, 16.5, 18cm)

FRONT

Accessories

Strappy Little Bag

MATERIALS

Yarns of choice: Approx 1¾ oz (50 g)

Combining highly textured novelty yarn with at least one other yarn to give it body (high cotton content works well) can achieve a stunning effect that will knit up into a fairly firm fabric. Many yarns, threads, and ribbons found in the embroidery department are suitable, as well.

Beads, if desired

Embroidery floss in a coordinating color

Knitting needles of an appropriate size

Crochet hook (to make strap) or purchased cord

GAUGE

Gauge will vary considerably, depending on yarns used.

It is important to knit to a firm gauge, quite a bit tighter than for a garment.

Make at least 2 test swatches to judge comfort of working with needle size and feel of knitted fabric. Measure chosen swatch for number of sts to the inch (cm).

That number x 6 = number of sts to CO.

FINISHED MEASUREMENTS

Bag shown measures 6 x 6" (15 x 15 cm).

BAG

CO required number of sts and knit 4 rows (2 ridges of Garter st). Cont in St st, knitting first and last st of each row, to give firm edge. Work until piece measures about 13" (33 cm) from CO edge. End with purl row.

Knit 4 rows (2 Garter st ridges). BO all sts.

STRAP

4 strands of yarn chain-crocheted to 36" (91 cm) with large crochet hook make a substantial cord, but strap may be as thick or thin as desired. Suitable, ready-made cord can also be found in the drapery department of a fabric store.

FINISHING THE BAG

Choose which side of work will be RS of bag. Fold a rectangle so that bag meas approx 6" (15 cm) deep, with a 3" (8 cm) flap.

Sew side seams firmly together with strong yarn or thread.

Sew strap cord firmly in place just under flap. For novelty, cord may be threaded through beads first.

Flap may be secured with snaps or button and loop closures, or embellished with beads, or embroidery as desired.

Women's Fair Isle Gloves

SIZE:
One size fits most.

FINISHED MEASUREMENTS:
Circumference of hand: Approx 7$\frac{1}{2}$" (17.8 cm)

Top of cuff to knuckle: 4$\frac{1}{4}$" (10.8 cm)

MATERIALS:
100% Shetland Wool, fingering weight

Main Color (MC): 1 oz (56 g) = approx 150 yds (137 m)

Contrasting Colors (CC): small quantities for chosen Pattern

Set of 5 double-pointed needles (dpn), size 1 US (2.25 to 2.5 mm) or size to obtain gauge

GAUGE:
In Fair Isle pattern using size 1 needles:

32 sts and 32 rnds = 4" (10 cm)

Traditional X's and O's

CUFF:
Using MC, CO 42 sts distributed evenly on 4 needles; PM for beg of rnd. Join, being careful not to twist stitches. Work in Single rib (k1, p1) for 3" (7.6 cm). Inc 18 sts (or number for chosen stitch pattern) evenly on last rnd. Total: 60 sts, 15 on each needle.

Note: Stitch pattern repeats vary; it may be necessary to adjust total number of stitches after the cuff to fit the chosen pattern; check number of stitches needed before increasing.

HAND:
Change to Circular St st (knit every rnd) and Fair Isle patt of choice; work even in est patt until piece meas 2$\frac{1}{8}$" (5.4 cm) above cuff.

Thumb Opening, Right Glove: Cont in est patt, work across needles 1 and 2; from needle 3, k9 with waste yarn; return these 9 waste stitches to needle 3 and k9 in est patt; k6 in est patt; work across needle 4 in est patt.

Thumb Opening, Left Glove: Cont in est patt, work across needle 1; from needle 2, k6 in est patt; k9 with waste yarn, return these 9 waste sts to needle 2, and k9 in est patt; work across needles 3 and 4 in est patt.

When piece meas 2$\frac{1}{8}$" (5.4 cm) from waste yarn for thumb, (approx 4$\frac{1}{4}$" [10.8 cm] above cuff edge), place all sts on circular st holder or strand of waste yarn, keeping marker for beg of rnd in place to separate back of glove from palm.

Note: When chosen Chart(s) have been completed, continue with Main Color (or color of choice) for remainder of glove.
Fingers:

Little finger: With MC or color of choice, pu sts from holder with dpn: 8 sts from back of glove, and 8 sts from palm; on inside of finger,

CO 2 sts. Total: 18 sts. Work even until finger meas 1³/4" (4.4 cm) or ¹/4" (6.3 mm) less than desired length. Knitting should reach middle of nail of little finger before shaping. To shape fingertip: for dec rnd, on each needle k2tog, work to last 2 sts, ssk. Total: 8 sts dec. Work 1 rnd even. Rep dec rnd once; cut yarn, leaving a 12" tail (30.5 cm); thread tail through rem sts, going through each st twice; gather sts tog and fasten off. Little finger meas approx 2" (5 cm).

Ring and Middle Fingers:
With MC or color of choice, pu from holder and place on dpns: 7 sts from back of glove, and 7 sts from palm; pu 2 sts from CO sts of previous finger and CO 2 sts at opposite side. Total: 18 sts distributed evenly on 4 needles. Work as for little finger to the middle of nail; shape fingertip as for little finger. Ring finger meas approx 2³/4" (6.9 cm); middle finger meas approx 3¹/4" (8.3 cm).

Index Finger: With MC or color of choice, pu from holder and place on dpns: 8 sts from back of glove, and 8 sts from palm; on inside of finger, pu 2 sts from CO sts of previous finger. Total: 18 sts distributed evenly on 4 needles. Work as for little finger to the middle of nail, shape tip as for little finger. Index finger meas approx 2³/4" (6.9 cm).

Thumb: Remove waste yarn; with MC or color of choice, pu 9 sts from top and 9 sts from bottom of opening, and distribute evenly on dpn; pu 2 sts from glove at each corner. Total: 22 sts. Work as for little finger to the middle of nail, shape tip as for little finger. Thumb meas approx 2¹/2" (6.4 cm).

FINISHING
Weave in ends neatly on reverse side. Steam block to even out stitches and obtain finished measurement desired.

Traditional X's and O's

KEY

■ Main Color—Dark Red
□ White
■ Dark Brown
■ Gold
■ Navy Blue
⊠ Chart B—work with contrasting color used on back of glove
⊡ Chart B—work with background color used on back of glove

After working ribbing, work Chart A, Chart C, then Chart A, [substituting Chart A-1 for center motif of second repeat], while working Chart B on palm in colors indicated. Continue in Main Color to length desired.

CHART A: BACK OF HAND

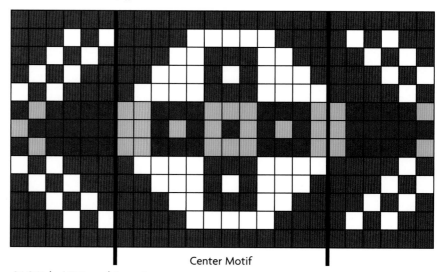

Center Motif

24 Stitch / 13 Round Repeat

CHART A1: ALTERNATE CENTER MOTIF

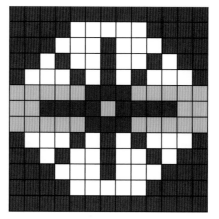

13 Stitch / 13 Round Repeat

CHART C: BORDER

12 Stitch / 7 Round Repeat

Chart B: Palm

2 Stitch / 2 Round Repeat

Traditional Star

CHART A: BACK OF HAND

27 Stitch / 27 Round Repeat

KEY

☐ Main Color—White

■ Dark Brown

■ Lt. Grey

■ Taupe

■ Red

☒ Chart B—work with contrasting color used on back of glove

After working ribbing, work Chart D and first round of Chart A around entire glove; continue Chart A on back of glove while working Chart B on palm; work last round of Chart A around entire glove; work Chart C around entire glove.

CHART B: PALM

4 Stitch / 2 Round Repeat

CHART C: TOP BORDER

4 Stitch / 3 Round Repeat

CHART D: BOTTOM BORDER

4 Stitch / 5 Round Repeat

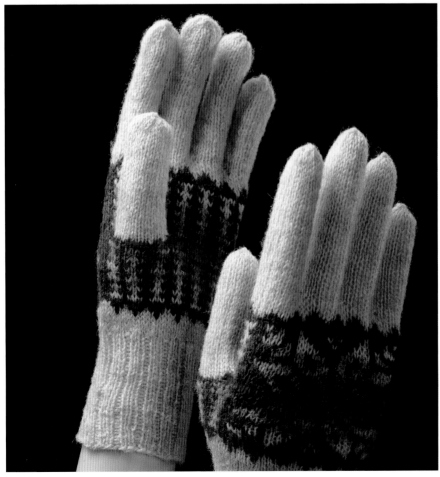

Traditional Star

Women's Fair Isle Fingerless Gloves

SIZE
One size fits most.

FINISHED MEASUREMENTS:
Circumference of hand: Approx. 7" (17.8 cm)

Top of cuff to knuckle: 4½" (11.4 cm)

MATERIALS
100% Shetland Wool, fingering weight

Main Color (MC): 1 oz (56 g) = approx 150 yds (137 m)

Contrasting Colors (CC): small quantities for chosen Pattern

Set of 5 double-pointed needles (dpns), size 0 US (2mm) or size to obtain gauge

GAUGE
In Fair Isle patt using Size 0 needles:

36 sts and 36 rnds = 4" (10 cm)

Tartan: This pattern of interlocking diamonds came from Shetland in the 1950's.

CUFF
Using MC, CO 54 sts, distributed evenly on 4 needles; PM for beg of rnd. Join, being careful not to twist sts. Work in Single rib (k1, p1) for 2¾" (7 cm), inc 8 sts (or number for chosen patt) evenly on last rnd. Total: 62 sts (needles 1 and 3: 15 sts; needles 2 and 4: 16 sts).

Note: Pattern repeats vary. It may be necessary to adjust total number of sts after cuff to fit the chosen Pattern; check number of sts needed before inc.

HAND
Change to Circular St st (knit every rnd) and patt of choice; work even in est patt until piece meas 2½" (6.4 cm) above cuff.

Thumb Opening, Right Glove:
Cont in est patt, work across needles 1 and 2; from needle 3, k2; then k10 with waste yarn; return these 10 sts to needle 3, and knit across them in pattern; k3; work across needle 4 in patt.

Thumb Opening, Left Glove:
Cont in est patt, work across needle 1; from needle 2, k4; then k10 with waste yarn; return these 10 sts to needle 2 and knit across them

in pattern; k2; work across needles 3 and 4 in patt.

When piece meas 2" (5 cm) from waste yarn for thumb, (approx 4½" [11.4 cm] above cuff), place all sts on a circular st holder or strand of waste yarn, keeping marker for beg of rnd in place to separate back of hand from palm.

Note: When chosen Chart(s) have been completed, continue with Main Color (or color of choice) for remainder of glove.

FINGER SECTIONS
Work Single rib (k1, p1) for ½" (1.3 cm) to 1" (2.5 cm) to create finger sections as follows:

Little finger: With MC (or color of choice), pu from holder and place on dpns 7 sts from back of hand and 7 sts from palm. Total: 14 sts. Work Single rib to desired length; BO loosely in rib.

Ring, Middle, and Index Fingers:
Working one finger at a time, pu 8 sts from back of hand and 8 sts from palm for each finger. Work as for little finger.

THUMB
Remove waste yarn; with MC (or color of choice), pu and place on dpns 10 sts from top and 10 sts from bottom of opening and distribute evenly on dpns; pu one st at each corner. Total: 22 sts. Work Single rib to desired length; BO loosely in patt.

FINISHING
Weave in ends neatly on reverse side. Steam block to even out stitches and obtain finished measurements.

Tartan

KEY

☐ White
☐ Pale Yellow
☐ Grey-Green
☐ Purple-Red
☐ Purple Heather
☐ Maroon
☐ Lilac
☐ Loden Green

CHART A: BACK OF HAND AND PALM

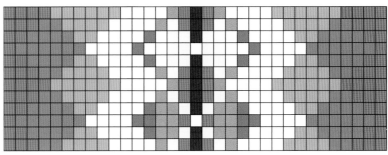

12 Stitch / 33 Round Repeat
Work Chart A around entire glove.

Fishermen of Unst

After working ribbing, work rounds 1-5 of Chart C around entire glove; work Chart A on back of glove while working Chart B on palm in colors indicated; work rounds 5-1 of Chart C around entire glove; work remainder of glove in Main Color.

After picking up sts for fingers, knit 1¼" (1.9 cm) in St st before working Single rib.

CHART B: Palm

6 Stitch / 2 Round Repeat

CHART C: Borders

2 Stitch /5 Round Repeat

CHART A: Back of Hand

KEY

■ Dark Brown—Main color
☐ Salmon
☐ Blue
☐ Yellow
☐ Sky Blue
☐ Pale Blue
☐ White
■ Navy Blue
☒ Chart B—Use contrasting color used on back of glove
Ⓞ Chart B—Use background color used on back of glove

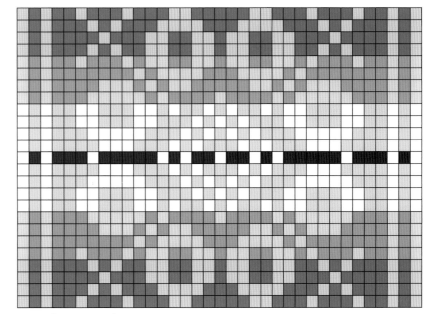

35 Stitch / 25 Round Repeat

Above: Fishermen of Unst: The fingers of these gloves were knit long for warmth, but the fingertips were free to remove fishhooks.

Women's Fair Isle Mittens

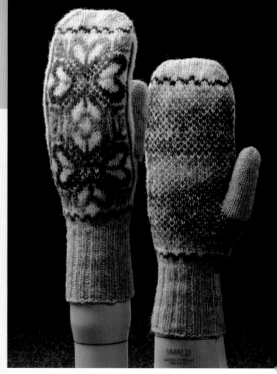

SIZE

One size fits most.

FINISHED MEASUREMENTS:

Circumference of hand: Approx. 7½" (19 cm)

Top of cuff to tip of mitten: 7¾" inches (19.7 cm)

MATERIALS

100% Shetland Wool, fingering weight

Main Color (MC): 1 oz (56 g) = approx. 150 yds (137 m)

Contrasting Colors (CC): small quantities for chosen Pattern.

Set of 5 double-pointed needles (dpns), size 1 US (2.25-2.5 mm), or size to obtain gauge.

GAUGE

In Fair Isle patt with size 1 needles:

32 sts and 32 rows = 4" (10 cm)

Unst Flowers

Unst Flowers

KEY

- ■ Main Color—Natural
- ■ Black
- □ White
- ■ Taupe
- ■ Brown
- ■ Dark Brown
- ■ Charcoal
- ■ Gray
- □ Chart B—use Contrasting Color used on back of mitten

After ribbing, work Rounds 1–4 of Chart C around entire mitten; work Rounds 1–25, then Rounds 2–25 of Chart A on back of hand while working Chart B on palm in colors indicated; work Rounds 4–1 of Chart C around entire mitten; continue with Main Color for length.

CHART A: BACK OF HAND

33 Stitch / 25 Round Repeat

CHART B: PALM

2 Stitch / 2 Round Repeat

CHART C: BORDERS

4 Stitch / 4 Round Repeat

CUFF

Using MC, CO 57 sts, distributed on 4 needles. Total: 14 sts on 3 needles, 15 sts on the fourth. PM for beg of rnd; join, being careful not to twist stitches. Work in 1 by 2 Rib (p1, k2) for 3". Inc for chosen patt, on last rnd, if necessary.

Note: Stitch pattern repeats vary; it may be necessary to adjust total number of sts of the cuff to fit the chosen Stitch Pattern; check number of stitches needed before increasing.

HAND

Change to Circular St st (k every rnd), and beg Fair Isle st patt of choice; work even in est patt until piece meas 2 1/2" (6.4 cm) above cuff.

Thumb Opening, Right Mitten:

Cont in est patt across needles 1 and 2; from needle 3: k2; k10 with waste yarn; return these 10 sts to needle 3 and work across them in patt, k2; work in patt across needle 4.

Thumb Opening, Left Mitten:

Cont in est patt across needle 1; from needle 2: k2; k10 with waste yarn; return these 10 sts to needle 2, and work across them in patt, k2; work in patt across needles 3 and 4.

Shaping: When piece meas approx 4" (10 cm) above waste yarn for thumb, (approx 6 1/2" [16.5 cm] above cuff edge), beg shaping.

Notes: Shaping will add approx 1 1/4" (3.2 cm); adjust length now if needed.

• When chosen Chart(s) have been completed, continue with Main Color only for remainder of mitten.

★ From needles 1 and 3: k1; k2tog (right-slanting dec); k to end. From needles 2 and 4: knit to last 3 sts; ssk (left-slanting dec); k1. Rep from ★ every rnd, 9 times. Total 16 sts (8 sts for palm, and 8 for back of hand).

Cut yarn, leaving a 16" (41 cm) tail; thread tail into tapestry needle and weave rem sts tog.

THUMB

Remove waste yarn; with MC (or color of choice), pu 10 sts from top and 10 sts from bottom of thumb opening and distribute evenly on double-pointed needles; pu 1 st at each corner. Total: 22 stitches.

Work even until thumb meas 2" (5 cm) or 1/4" (6.3 mm) less than desired length (knitting should reach to middle of thumbnail before shaping).

Shape Thumb: work as for hand shaping, rep from ★ 3 times. Cut yarn, leaving a 12" (30.5 cm) tail; thread tail into tapestry needle and through rem sts, going through each st twice; gather sts together, BO. Thumb meas approx 2 1/4" (5.7 cm).

FINISHING

Weave in ends neatly on reverse side. Steam block to even out sts and obtain finished measurements.

Fishermen of Yell

KEY

- ▨ Olive Green
- ☐ White

CHART A: Back of Hand and Palm

6 Stitch / 4 Round Repeat

CHART B: Thumb gusset

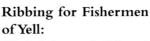

Edge of Mitten

Palm

Ribbing for Fishermen of Yell:

Work ★ 4 rounds Olive, 4 rounds White; repeat from ★ twice, then work 4 rounds Olive. Begin Chart A with 5 White stripes/6 Olive stripes on back of mitten and 6 White/5 Olive on palm. Work thumb gusset as shown, inserting gusset in 2nd dark stripe on palm.

Fishermen of Yell: Originally meant for men, these mittens were traditionally knit in black and white.

Children's Fair Isle Mittens

SIZE:

One size fits most.

FINISHED MEASUREMENT:

Circumference of hand: Approx 7½" (19 cm)

Bottom of cuff to tip of mitten: 6" (15.2 cm)

MATERIALS:

100% Shetland Wool, fingering weight

Main Color (MC): 1 oz (56 g) = approx 150 yds (137 m)

Contrasting Colors (CC): Small quantities for chosen Pattern.

Set of 5 double-pointed needles (dpns), size 0 US (2 mm) or size to obtain gauge.

GAUGE:

In Fair Isle knitting using size 0 needles:

36 sts and 36 rnds = 4" (10 cm)

X and Cross

X and Cross

KEY

- ▨ Main Color
- ■ Blue
- ▦ Medium Brown
- ▢ Pale Yellow
- ▢ White
- ■ Cranberry
- ■ Black

Stripe Sequence: Work Chart B, Chart A, Chart C, Chart A; work Chart B using Medium Brown as Contrasting Color; then repeat Chart A.

CHART A: BACK OF HAND AND PALM

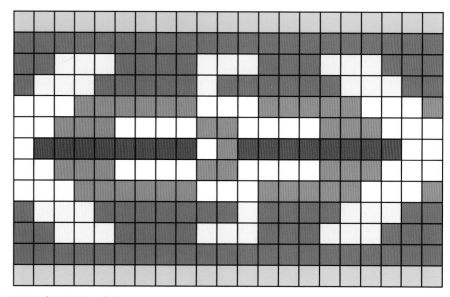

21 Stitch / 13 Round Repeat

CHART B: TOP AND BOTTOM BORDERS

6 Stitch / 6 Round Repeat

CHART C: MIDDLE BORDERS

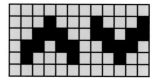

12 Stitch / 6 Round Repeat

CUFF

Using MC, CO 50 sts, distributed as follows: needles 1 and 3: 12 stitches; needles 2 and 4: 13 stitches. PM for beg of rnd. Join, being careful not to twist sts. Work in Single rib for 2¼" (5.7 cm), inc 10 sts (or number for chosen patt), evenly on last rnd. Total: 60 sts, 15 on each needle.

Note: Stitch Pattern repeats vary. It may be necessary to adjust total number of stitches after the cuff to fit the chosen Stitch Pattern; check number of stitches needed before increasing.

HAND

Change to Circular St st (k every rnd) and Fair Isle patt of choice; work even in est patt until piece meas 1¾" (4.4 cm) above cuff.

Thumb Opening, Right Mitten: Cont in est patt, work across needles 1 and 2; from needle 3, k9 with waste yarn; ret these 9 sts to needle 3 and knit across them in pattern; k6; work across needle 4 in pattern.

Thumb Opening, Left Mitten: Cont in est patt, work across needle 1; from needle 2, k6; then k9 with waste yarn, ret these 9 sts to needle 2 and knit across them in est patt; work across needles 3 and 4 in est patt.

Shaping: When piece meas 3" (7.6 cm) above waste yarn for thumb, (approx 4¾" [12.1 cm] above cuff edge), beg shaping.

Notes: Shaping will add approx 1¼" (3.2 cm); adjust length now if needed.

• When chosen Chart(s) have been completed, continue with Main Color only for remainder of mitten.

★ From needles 1 and 3: k1, k2tog (right-slant decrease); knit to end. From needles 2 and 4: Knit to last 3 sts; ssk (left-slant decrease); k1. Rep from ★ every rnd 10 times. Total: 16 sts (8 sts for palm, and 8 for back of hand). Cut yarn, leaving a 16" (40.6 cm) tail; using tap-estry needle and tail, weave rem sts tog.

THUMB

Remove waste yarn; with MC (or color of choice), pu 9 sts from top and 9 sts from bottom of thumb opening, distribute evenly on dpns; pu one st at each corner. Total: 20 sts for thumb. Work even until thumb meas 2" (5 cm), or ¼" (6.35 mm) less than desired length. Knitting should reach middle of thumbnail before shaping.

Shape thumb: (k2tog around) twice. Total: 5 sts rem. Cut yarn, leaving 12" (30.5 cm) tail; thread tail through tapestry needle and rem sts, going through each st twice; gather sts tog and fasten off. Thumb meas approx 2¼" (5.7 cm).

FINISHING

Weave in ends neatly on reverse side. Steam block to even out stitches and obtain finished measurements.

Small Diamonds

KEY

- ☐ Main color
- ■ Mahogany
- ☐ Peach
- ■ Black
- ☐ Lt. Yellow
- ☐ White
- ■ Grey

CHART A: Back of Hand and Palm

12 Stitch / 15 Round Repeat

Work Chart A 3 times.

Small Diamonds

Toddlers' Fair Isle Mittens

SIZE:

One size fits most.

FINISHED MEASUREMENT:

Circumference of hand: Approx 5" (12.7 cm)

Bottom of cuff to tip of mitten: 4½" (11.4 cm)

MATERIALS:

100% Shetland Wool, fingering weight

Main Color (MC): 1 oz (56 g) = approx 150 yards (137 m)

Contrasting Colors (CC): Small quantities for chosen Pattern.

Set of 5 double-pointed needles (dpns), size 0 US (2 mm) or size to obtain gauge.

GAUGE:

in Fair Isle knitting using size 0 needles:

36 sts and 36 rnds = 4 inches (10 cm)

Butterflies

Butterflies

KEY

- ⬛ Main Color—Red
- ⬜ Aqua
- ☐ White
- ⬛ Jade Green
- ☐ Off-White (50 g)
- ⬜ Orange (50 g)
- ⬛ Brown
- ☐ Butter Yellow

Chart B: Border

2 Stitch / 4 Round Repeat

Stripe sequence: Work 15 rounds Chart A; 4 rounds Chart B; 15 rounds Chart A.

CHART A: BACK OF HAND AND PALM

12 Stitch / 15 Round Repeat

CUFF

Using MC, CO 52 sts, distributed evenly on 4 needles. Total: 13 sts on each needle. PM for beg of rnd. Join, being careful not to twist sts. Work in 2 by 2 Rib (k2, p2) for 2¼" (5.7 cm), inc for chosen patt on last rnd, if necessary.

Note: Stitch Pattern repeats vary. It may be necessary to adjust total number of stitches after the cuff to fit the chosen Stitch Pattern; check number of stitches needed before increasing.

HAND

Change to Circular St st (k every rnd). Establish patt and work even until piece meas 1¾" (6.4 cm) above cuff.

Thumb Opening, Right Mitten: Cont in est patt, work across needles 1 and 2; from needle 3, k8 with waste yarn; ret these 8 sts to needle 3 and knit across them in patt; k5; work across needle 4 in patt.

Thumb Opening, Left Mitten:
Cont in est patt across needle 1; from needle 2, k5; k8 with waste yarn; ret these 8 sts to needle 2 and knit across them in patt; work across needles 3 and 4 in patt.

Shaping: When piece meas 1¾" (6.4 cm) from waste yarn for thumb (approx 3½" [8 to 9 cm] above cuff edge), beg shaping.

Note: Shaping will add approximately 1¼" (3.2 cm); adjust length if desired. When chosen Chart(s) are completed, cont with MC only for remainder of mitten.

★ From needles 1 and 3: k1; k2tog; knit to end. From needles 2 and 4: Knit to last 3 sts; ssk; k1. Rep from ★ every rnd 9 times. Total: 12 sts (6 sts for palm, and 6 for back of hand). Cut yarn, leaving a 16" (40.6 cm) tail; using tapestry needle and tail, weave rem sts tog.

THUMB

Remove waste yarn; using MC (or color of choice), pu 8 sts from top and 8 sts from bottom of thumb opening and distribute evenly on dpns; pu 1 st at each corner. Total: 18 sts for thumb. Work even until thumb meas 1¹/4" (3.2 cm) or ¹/4" (6.35 mm) less than desired length. Thumb should reach middle of thumbnail before shaping.

Shape thumb: k2tog around twice. Cut yarn, leaving a 12" (30.5 cm) tail; thread tail through tapestry needle and rem sts, going through each st twice; gather sts tog and fasten off. Thumb meas approx 1¹/2" (3.8 cm).

FINISHING

Weave in ends neatly on reverse side. Steam block to even out stitches and obtain finished measurements.

Nursery Rhyme Mittens

MATERIALS

Fingering or sport weight yarn (See pattern charts for quantities. Amounts given will make set of mittens, hat, and scarf.)

Double-pointed needles, size 0 or 1 US (2 – 2.25 mm)

Soft knit fabric for lining

GAUGE

9 stitches and 11 rows = 1" (2.5 cm)

SIZING

Ages 4 to 6

Note: Items may be made smaller or larger by using a different weight yarn and/or smaller or larger needle(s). Test gauge to determine measurements.

"Sailing, Sailing"

INSTRUCTIONS

Knit each mitten in one piece by working in a round. All stitches are knit unless purl stitch is specifically mentioned.

Sailing, Sailing

FACING

With double-pointed needles (dpns) and color at the bottom of Chart A, CO number of sts specified. Join in a round, place marker (pm) at beg of row. Knit in St st for number of rows indicated on Chart A, plus 2 rows. This forms a facing that will be hemmed inside the cuff.

Note: The 2 extra rows compensate for difference in gauge between solid-color facing and multi-color band.

CUFF

Purl 1 row. Knit cuff following Chart A patt.

RIGHT HAND

Work Chart B for Right Hand: on first row, inc by number of sts indicated.

Transfer 10 thumb sts as marked to a holder; CO 10 sts and continue with Chart B.

Finger shaping: at beg of row, ★ k1, sl 1, psso; at the next dec point, k2tog. Rep from ★ for second half of row. When only 6 to 8 stitches rem, cut yarn, attach tapestry needle and pull thread through rem sts; fasten off.

THUMB

Transfer sts from holder to dpn; pu same number of sts on opposite side of thumb hole, plus 1 st on each end. Follow Chart C, making sure to keep patt on thumb in line with patt on mitten. Work dec using same method as for hand (Chart B). When 2 to 4 sts rem, cut yarn, attach tapestry needle and thread through rem sts; fasten off.

LEFT HAND

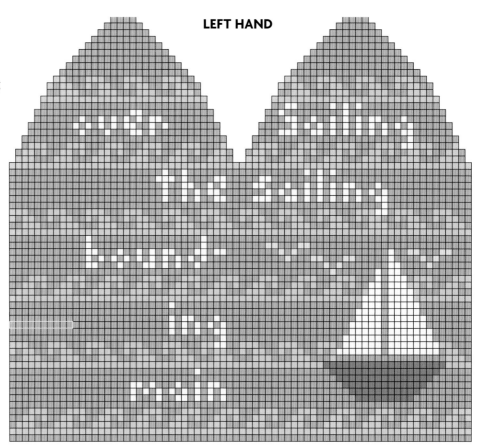

CHART B: Left Hand/Increase 24 (72)

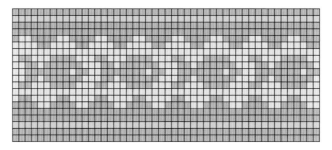

CHART A: Left Cuff/20 rows + 2 for facing/Cast on 48

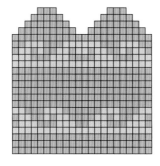

CHART C: Left Thumb/22 stitches

☐ Med. Blue (200 g)
☐ Aqua (50 g)
☐ Dk. Blue (50 g)
☐ Lt. Blue (50 g)
☐ Off-White (50 g)
☐ Orange (50 g)

RIGHT HAND

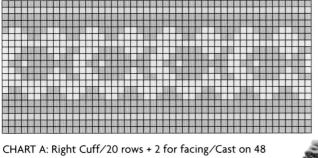

CHART B: Right Hand/Increase 24 (72)

CHART A: Right Cuff/20 rows + 2 for facing/Cast on 48

CHART C: Right Thumb/22 stitches

FINISHING

Weave loose threads from top of mitten and thumb, as well as any other threads, through inside of mitten. Slipstitch facing inside cuff.

Following the same instructions, complete Charts A through C for the left mitten.

LINING THE MITTENS

A lining adds warmth and prevents little fingers from getting tangled in the carried threads. Stretchy, light cotton knit is easy to work with and comfortable inside the mitten.

Make a Pattern: Trace around the mitten, including the cuff. Mark where thumb emerges from the hand, then reposition the mitten so thumb extends from the side and trace around it. You should end up with a drawing the shape of a hand as shown. Cut out pattern; position pattern on doubled fabric; cut 4 pieces.

Sew: With two pieces RS tog, sew a seam around hand and thumb. Turn mitten inside out. Place lining over mitten, WS together. Fold in lining edge along cuff, slipstitch lining to cuff.

Repeat process for second mitten.

"Hickory, Dickory, Dock"

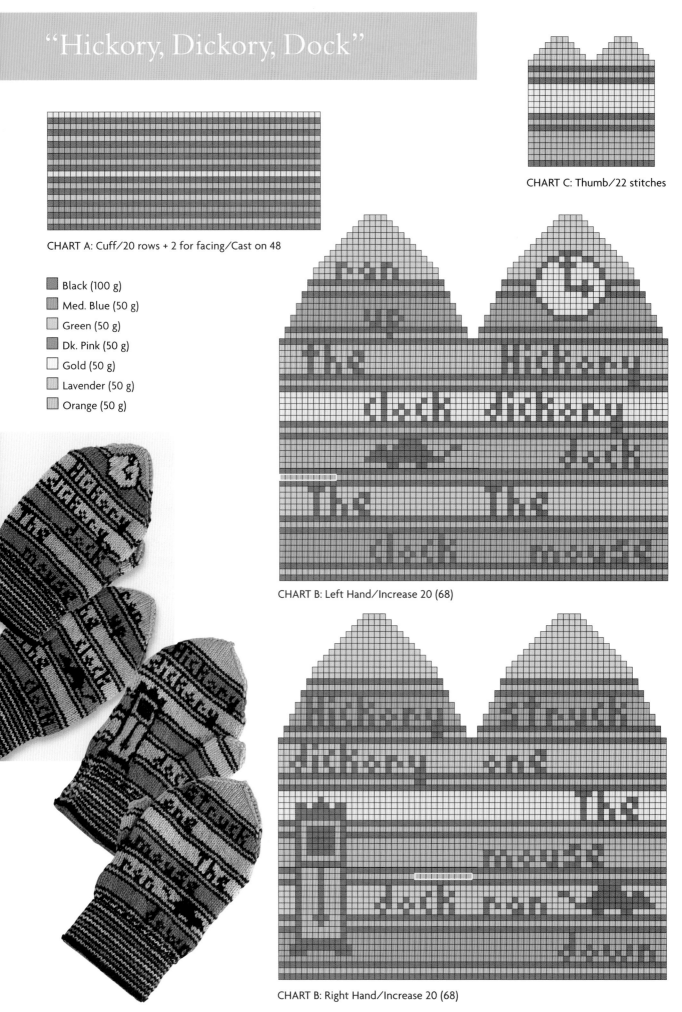

CHART C: Thumb/22 stitches

CHART A: Cuff/20 rows + 2 for facing/Cast on 48

- Black (100 g)
- Med. Blue (50 g)
- Green (50 g)
- Dk. Pink (50 g)
- Gold (50 g)
- Lavender (50 g)
- Orange (50 g)

CHART B: Left Hand/Increase 20 (68)

CHART B: Right Hand/Increase 20 (68)

"Itsy Bitsy Spider"

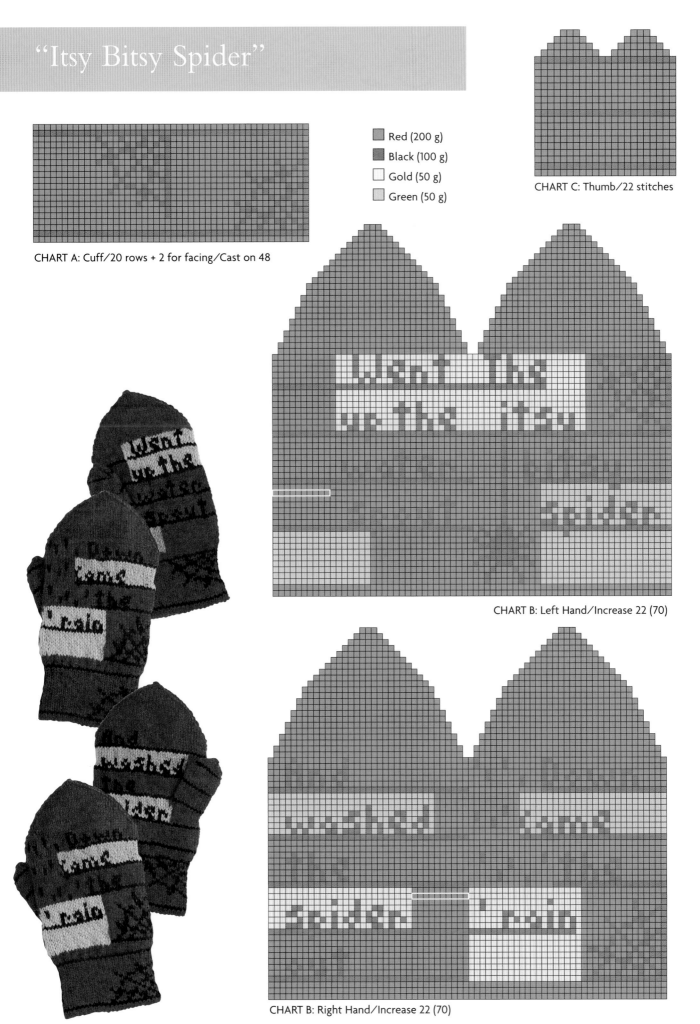

CHART A: Cuff/20 rows + 2 for facing/Cast on 48

- ▨ Red (200 g)
- ▨ Black (100 g)
- ☐ Gold (50 g)
- ▨ Green (50 g)

CHART C: Thumb/22 stitches

CHART B: Left Hand/Increase 22 (70)

CHART B: Right Hand/Increase 22 (70)

Nursery Rhyme Scarves

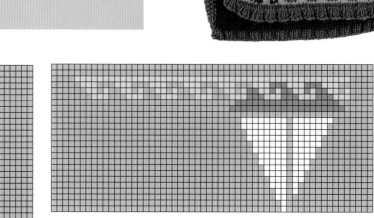

SIZE

Ages 4 to 6

MATERIALS

Fingering or sport weight yarn

14" knitting needles, size 0 or 1 US (2 – 2.25mm)

Fabric for lining

GAUGE

9 stitches and 11 rows = 1" (2.5 cm)

Note: Items may be made smaller or larger by using a different weight yarn and/or smaller or larger needle(s). Test gauge to determine measurements.

"Sailing, Sailing"

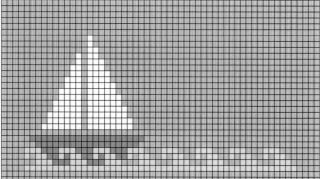

CHART D: Scarf/Cast on 56

Chart F: Scarf

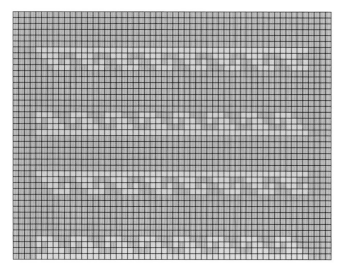

Chart E: Scarf

INSTRUCTIONS

Knit the scarf in one piece on straight or circular needle(s), working back and forth (RS knit, WS purl).

RIBBING

With MC, CO number of sts indicated in Chart D. Work 6 rows of 2/2 ribbing (k2, p2, repeat across).

BODY

Work Chart D, keeping first and last 4 sts of each row in Seed st (k1, p1 across, purl the knit stitches, and knit the purl stitches on subsequent rows).

Work Chart E, keeping first and last 4 sts of each row in Seed st. Rep until approx 35" (89 cm) from beg.

Work Chart F, keeping first and last 4 sts of each row in Seed stitch.

RIBBING

Work last 6 rows as follows.

Row 1: St st, keeping first and last 4 sts in Seed st.

Rows 2-6: 2/2 Ribbing. BO all sts.

FINISHING

Weave in any loose ends on reverse side of scarf.

To block: Lay scarf out flat, steam and press it, using pressing cloth.

LINING THE SCARF

Lining is recommended to cover carried threads on back of scarf and prevent snagging and pulling. Polar fleece comes in a variety of colors, doesn't fray, and adds warmth.

Cut a piece of fabric the size of the scarf. Place RS out over back side of the scarf, pin in place. Working within Seed st and ribbing borders, fold edges under and slipstitch lining in place.

"Itsy Bitsy Spider"

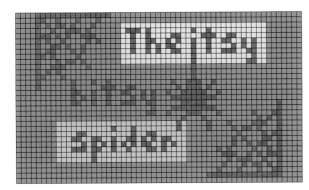

CHART D: Scarf/Cast on 57

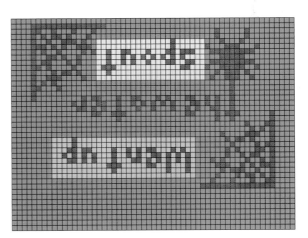

CHART F: Scarf

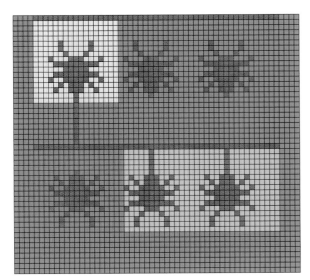

CHART E: Scarf

Alphabet Rebus

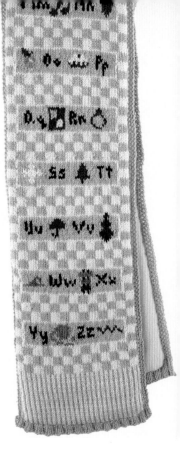

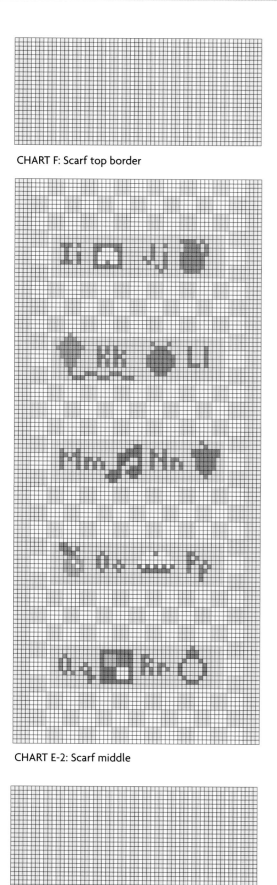

CHART F: Scarf top border

CHART E-2: Scarf middle

CHART D: Scarf bottom border/cast on 58

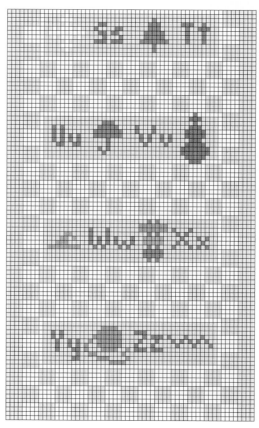

CHART E-1: Scarf bottom

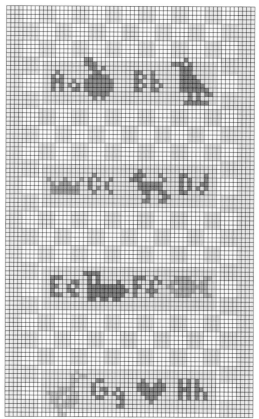

CHART E-3: Scarf top

- ◻ Gold (100 g)
- ◻ Lt. Yellow (100 g)
- ◼ Red (50 g)
- ◼ Dk. Green (50 g)
- ◻ Purple (50 g)
- ◼ Brown (50 g)
- ◼ Dk. Blue (50 g)
- ◻ Dk. Pink (50 g)
- ◻ Off-White (50 g)
- ◻ Orange (50 g)
- ◻ Lavender (50 g)
- ◻ Med. Blue (50 g)
- ◼ Black (50 g)

Nursery Rhyme Hats

MATERIALS

Use a fingering or sport weight yarn

16" (40.6 cm) circular or double-pointed needle(s) size 0 or 1 US
(2–2.25 mm)

Fabric for linings

GAUGE

9 stitches and 11 rows = 1" (2.5 cm) for mittens, scarf, and hat

$8^{1}/_{2}$" stitches and 10 rows = 1" (2.5 cm) for blankets

SIZE

Ages 4 to 6

Note: Items may be made smaller or larger by using a different
weight yarn and/or smaller or larger needle(s). Test gauge to determine
measurements.

"Sailing, Sailing"

INSTRUCTIONS

Knit the hat in one piece by
working in a round. Knit all stitches unless a purl stitch is specifically
mentioned.

FACING

With color at bottom of Chart G,
CO number of sts indicated. Join
in a round, place marker at beg of
row. In St st, work number of rows
called for in Chart G plus 2 rows,
to form facing that will be
hemmed inside the band.

Note: 2 extra rows compensate
for the difference in gauge
between solid–color facing and
multi–color band.

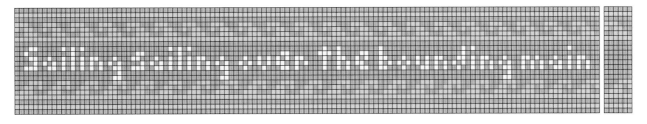

CHART G: BAND

22 rows + 2 for facing

Cast on 174 stitches

(Note: Repeat the small section of the
chart (above far right) 4 times before and
after the longer section.)

CHART H: HAT
Increase 6 (180)

BAND

Purl 1 row. Work band according to Chart G.

BODY

Inc to number of sts needed for Chart H (see chart). Work Chart H, rep patt until hat is approx 7" (18 cm) from purl row.

CROWN

Choose one of the two following options to finish crown of the hat:

Traditional Stocking Cap with a pompom
Four-pointed Hat with tassels

FOUR-POINTED HAT

★Transfer one-fourth of the sts to 2 double-pointed needles (dpns). (For example, if there are 120 stitches, transfer the first 15 stitches to one needle and the next 15 stitches on to the second needle. It is possible that 1 needle will end up with 1 more st than the second

needle.) Thread the tapestry needle with same color yarn that is on dpns, hold dpns parallel and work Kitchener stitch: (Pass tapestry needle through first st on front dpn as if to knit, sl st off dpn, pass tapestry needle through next st on front dpn as if to purl, leave st on dpn. Pass tapestry needle through first st on back dpn as if to purl, sl st off dpn; pass tapestry needle through next st on back dpn as if to knit, leave st on dpn.) cont until all sts have been woven, forming a seam to center of hat. Repeat from ★ until all sts have been worked, forming points with seams that meet in the middle. Fasten off.

Following the instructions below, make four tassels out of coordinating yarn and fasten 1 to each point. Slipstitch facing inside band. Steam and press the body of the hat.

MAKING TASSELS

To make a tassel, wind yarn around a piece of cardboard (or any flat object) that is 3 or 4" (7.5 or 10 cm) wide. Wind until desired thickness (approx 30 times). Slip a 6" (18 cm) piece of yarn in same color between loops and cardboard, work to one edge, tie tightly around the strands. Slip scissors between loops and card-

"Hickory, Dickory, Dock"

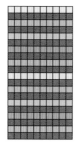

CHART G: BAND
20 rows + 2 for facing
Cast on 180

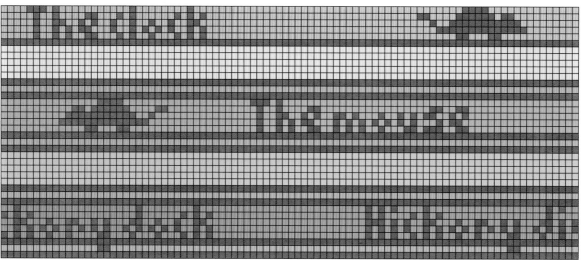

CHART H: HAT/No increase (180)/(Note: Repeat the chart to get 180 stitches.)

board; work to opposite edge and cut across all strands. Bind around and tie off about 1/2" (1.5 cm) from the tied top to form head of tassel. Trim.

STOCKING CAP

Dec as follows, keeping with the patt on chart as you go:

Row 1: Knit 1, knit 2 together across.

Row 2: Knit all stitches.

Row 3: Knit 1, knit 2 together across.

Row 4: Knit all stitches.

Row 5: Knit 2 together across.

Row 6: Knit all stitches.

Row 7: Knit 2 together across.

Cut yarn, attach tapestry needle and thread through rem sts; fasten off.

Make pompom out of coordinating yarn and fasten to top of hat.

Slipstitch facing inside band. Steam and press the body of the hat.

MAKING POMPOMS

Cut two cardboard circles the desired size of pompom. Cut out a 1/4" (6 mm) hole in the center of both. Place the circles together and wind yarn around both through the center holes. The result will look like a doughnut. Cover the disk three times making three layers. Slip the scissors between the two disks and cut the yarn along the outside edge. Draw a strand of yarn down between the two disks, wind several times very tightly and knot. Remove disks. Fluff out and trim.

"Itsy Bitsy Spider"

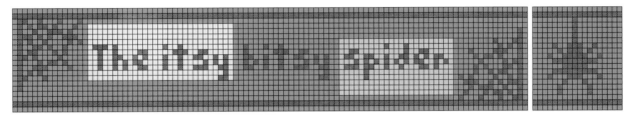

CHART G: BAND/20 rows + 2 for facing/Cast on 175
(Note: Repeat the small section of the chart with the spider (above far right) 2 times before and after the longer section.)

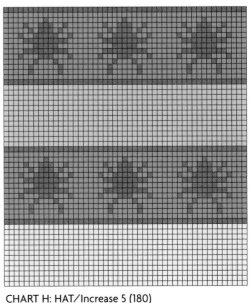

CHART H: HAT/Increase 5 (180)

Classic Man's Hat

SIZE

Fits average adult head

MATERIALS

Bulky yarn: 3½ oz (100 g) = 110 yds (99 m)

16" [40 cm] or 24" (60 cm) circular needle, sizes 9 and 10½ US (5 and 7 mm)

Set of double-pointed needles (dpns), size 10½ US (7 mm)

GAUGE

In Stockinette st on larger needles:

3 sts = 1" (2.5 cm)

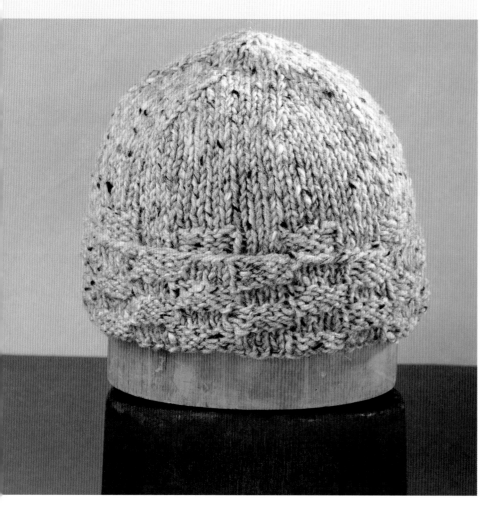

HAT

Using smaller needle(s), CO 72 sts, place marker, join into a round, careful not to twist stitches.

Work pattern stitch as follows:

Rounds 1-4: (k4, p4), rep to end of round.

Rounds 4-8: (p4, k4), rep to end of round.

Rep rounds 1-8 for approx 6" (15 cm), ending on a round 4 or 8.

Next row: k2tog, k34, k2tog, k34 (70 sts). Change to the larger needle(s) and cont in patt rounds for 2" (5 cm).

CROWN DECREASES:

Change to dpns when you have too few sts for circular needle.

Round 1: (k8, k2tog) to end of round.

Round 2 and all even-numbered rounds: knit.

Round 3: (k7, k2tog) to end of round.

Round 5: (k6, k2tog) to end of round.

Round 7: (k5, k2tog) to end of round.

Round 9: (k4, k2tog) to end of round.

Round 11: (k3, k2tog) to end of round.

Round 13: (k2, k2tog) to end of round.

Round 15: (k1, k2tog) to end of round.

Round 17: k2tog to end of round.

Cut yarn, thread into tapestry needle and through rem sts; fasten off.

FINISHING

Darn in yarn ends.

Classic Man's Scarf

MATERIALS

Bulky yarn: 3½ oz (100 g) = 110 yds (99 m)

Note: If making the hat that matches (see page 156), make it first. You should have yarn left over, which may be used to make scarf longer if you wish.

14" knitting needles, size 10½ US (7 mm), or size necessary to achieve gauge

GAUGE

In Stockinette stitch:

3 sts = 1" (2.5 cm)

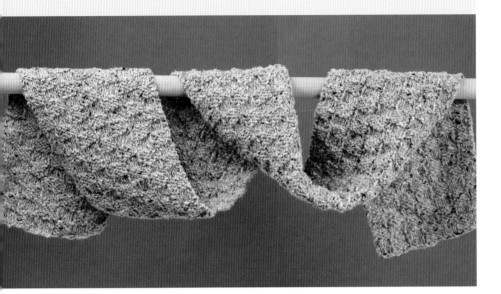

SCARF

CO 28 sts loosely, work the 8-row patt st, below:

Note: Knit first and last st of every row for uniform edge.

Row 1: (k4, p4) to last 4 sts, k4.

Row 2: (p4, k4) to last 4 sts, p4.

Rows 3 and 4: rep rows 1 and 2.

Row 5: (p4, k4) to last 4 sts, p4.

Row 6: (k4, p4) to last 4 sts, k4.

Rows 7 and 8: rep rows 5 and 6.

Rep patt st until there is just sufficient yarn left to BO loosely, ending on row 4 or 8 of patt st.

FINISHING

Darn in the yarn ends.

Button-Up Hat

SIZES

Small (medium, large)

14, (16, 18)" [36, (41, 46) cm]

MATERIALS

Worsted-weight yarn (all sizes): total of 1¾ oz (50 g)

14" knitting needles, size 8 US (5 mm), or size necessary to achieve gauge

Buttons for trim

GAUGE

In Stockinette stitch:

5 sts = 1 inch (2.5 cm)

HAT

CO 72 (82, 92) sts, and work 1½" (4 cm) in St st.

Next row: (WS facing) knit.

Rows 1–7: work in St st.

Row 8: (WS facing) knit.

Rep rows 1–8 once more. Cont in St st until piece meas 4 (4½, 5)" (10, 11, 13 cm) from cast on edge, changing colors/textures at beg of rows, as desired.

SHAPE CROWN

Row 1: k1, ★ k5 (6, 7), k2tog ★, rep to last st, k1.

Row 2 and every alt row: purl.

Row 3: k1, ★ k4 (5, 6), k2tog ★, repeat to last st, k1.

Cont dec 10 sts every knit row until there are 20 sts on needle. Purl 1 row.

Next row: RS facing, k2tog across row. 10 sts remain.

Cut yarn, thread tapestry needle, draw up sts tightly, fasten off securely.

FINISHING

Sew center back seam, reversing seam on rolled edge. Darn in yarn ends. Sew buttons on as desired.

Cravat-Style Scarf

SIZE

Approximately 38 x 6" (96.5 x 15 cm)

MATERIALS

Medium weight brushed or mohair type yarn: 130 yards (117 m)

14" knitting needles, size 10 US (6 mm)

GAUGE

In Stockinette stitch:

3½ sts = 1" (2.5 cm)

CO 24 sts loosely, and work in k2, p2 Rib for 8" (20 cm).

Note: Knit first and last st of every row for uniform edge.

Pass-through hole: Rib 12 sts, put rem 12 sts on a holder. Work 2" (5 cm) on sts on needle, place on another holder, cut the yarn. Return to sts on first holder; rejoin yarn, work to match first side of pass-through hole; add sts from second holder and work across to close pass-through. Cont until scarf is about 38" (96.5 cm) long, or length desired. BO in rib.

FINISHING

Darn in yarn ends neatly. To wear scarf, loop one end through pass-through.

VARIATION

Showcase an antique button or handsomely carved object. Adjust finished scarf around neck, mark button placement with a pin and sew on button. Button scarf around neck, instead of passing end through hole.

Beret or Tam-o'-shanter

SIZE

Fits average adult head

MATERIALS

Bulky weight novelty yarn (MC): Approx 65 yards (58.5 m)

Worsted-weight yarn (for band): Small amount

Double-pointed needles (dpns), sizes 7 and 10 US (4.5 and 6 mm) or sizes needed to achieve gauge.

GAUGE

In St st:

Band: Approx 5 sts = 1" (2.5 cm)

Hat: Approx 3 sts = 1" (2.5 cm)

HATBAND

With smaller dpns and worsted-weight yarn, CO 100 sts.

Join into rnd, being careful not to twist the sts. PM for beg the rnd; work in Single Rib (k1, p1) for 1½" (4 cm); Knit one rnd.

HAT

Change to novelty yarn and larger dpns, knit rnds till work meas 2" (5 cm) from top of band.

Shaping the crown: 1st dec rnd: (k2, k2tog) to the end of the round (75 sts).

Work a further 2" (5 cm).

2nd dec round: (k2, k2tog) to last three sts, k1, k2tog (56 sts).

Work a further 1" (2.5 cm).

3rd dec round: (k1, k2tog) to the last two sts, k2tog (37 sts).

★ Knit 1 rnd.

4th dec round: k1 (k2tog) to end ★ (19 sts).

Repeat between ★s once (10 sts).

Cut yarn; thread it through a tapestry needle and draw up rem sts tightly. Fasten off; darn in any loose ends.

Freestyle Shawl

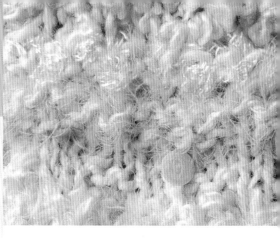

MATERIALS

Assorted yarns, incl several novelty yarns: Approx 1 lb total

36" circular needle, size 10 or 10½ US (6 or 6.5 mm)

Note: Since you will be mixing yarns of different weights and textures, choose a needle size quite a lot bigger than you might ordinarily use.

GAUGE

Determine gauge by knitting a 6" (15 cm) square swatch from the Main Color (MC). Measure swatch carefully to establish number of stitches per inch.

Alternate colorway embellished with rows of small buttons

PATTERN STITCH

CO 3 sts in MC

Row 1: k3

Row 2: k1, inc 1 st, k1, inc 1 st, k1. You now have 5 sts. PM at center st.

Row 3: Knit

Row 4: Inc 1 st, knit to marked st, inc 1 st, knit the marked st, make next inc, knit to last st, inc 1 = 9 sts.

Row 5: Knit

Repeat rows 4 and 5 throughout. Total inc of 4 sts, each alt row.

Join in new yarns at either end of row, or even in the middle, as desired. Alternate several rows of St st, with purl st ridges. Improvise, maintaining an odd number of total sts (or, an equal number of sts either side of the marked st.)

Note on Increases: If a decorative row of holes in the center of shawl is desired, knit to marked st, pu and knit the thread lying between last knitted st and marked st; knit marked st; pu and knit next st in same way. If no holes are preferred, place lifted thread onto left needle and knit tbl (through back of loop). Make increases one stitch in from the edge for a neater edge.

To determine size of shawl: With large tapestry needle and strong, smooth scrap yarn of contrasting color, thread through all sts and remove from needle. Try on shawl for length, estimating additional length from any fringe planned. Replace sts on needle to add length, or BO loosely.

Fringe: Refer to p. 186. Start by placing a fringe tassel at each corner, then space the rest evenly along the two sides.

Embellish shawl with bobbles, beads, tiny buttons, tying in bits of other yarn, or by threading tapestry needle with contrasting color and working running or duplicate stitches.

Lacy Scarf or Wrap

FINISHED MEASUREMENTS

Scarf (Wrap): Approx 10 x 60" [25 x 152 cm] (Approx 22 x 72" [56 x 183 cm])

MATERIALS

Brushed or mohair type yarn:

Scarf (Wrap): 3 balls of 1¾ oz [50 g] = 90 yds [81 m] (7 balls of 1¾ oz (50 g) = 90 yds [81 m])

14" knitting needles, size 11 US (8 mm), or size necessary to achieve correct gauge

GAUGE

In St st:

9 sts = 4 inches (10 cm)

Note: Gauge for this project is not crucial to fit; gauge can vary widely depending on the knitter and the yarn because of the lacy pattern and fluid drape.

PATTERN STITCH

Rows 1–6: p1 (yo, p2tog) to last st, p1.

Rows 7–12: knit (3 Garter st ridges).

SCARF (WRAP)

CO 22 (50) sts, and knit 6 rows (3 Garter st ridges).

Work the 12-row patt st for the required length, ending with a 12th row. BO loosely.

Note: For ease in darning in ends, join new balls of yarn on Garter st rows.

FINISHING

Darn in yarn ends.

Afghans

"Sleep Baby Sleep" Blanket

FINISHED MEASUREMENT
24 x 24" (61 x 61 cm) square

MATERIALS
Fingering or sport weight yarn
36" circular or 14" straight knitting needles, size 2 US (2.75 mm)
Knitting markers
Stitch holders
Tapestry needle
Soft fabric for lining (prewashed)

GAUGE
In Stockinette stitch:
8½ stitches and 10 rows = 1" (2.5 cm)

Blanket is knit in one piece on straight or circular needle(s), working back and forth (RS knit, WS purl).

To lengthen the blanket: Add a row or two of yellow above and below each row of words, and/or add Chart B sheep pattern to bottom and top of blanket as well as to sides. To do this, deduct 11 sts from Chart B (omit 1 sheep, add 2 sts of blue at each end of patt row).
Note: If adding length to blanket, increase stitches for side borders accordingly.

BOTTOM FACING
With green yarn, CO 170 sts (or, if adding sheep border to top and bottom, use blue yarn).

In St st, work 12 rows in green (or 26 rows in blue). This forms a facing that will be hemmed inside the band.

Note: 2 rows more are called for in band to compensate for difference in gauge between the solid-color facing and the multicolor band.

BODY
Purl 1 row. Work according to Charts A-1 and A-2; Blanket Body (Bottom and Top).

TOP FACING
When Chart A (or—if added— Chart B) is completed, knit 1 extra row, purl 1 row, knit same number of rows as for bottom facing. BO all sts. Block.

SIDE BORDER
With blue yarn, pu 182 sts along side of blanket as indicated for Chart B.

Note: If you have lengthened the blanket, pu approx 2 more sts for every 3 rows added, and adjust pattern accordingly. Chart B has a 15 st repeat.
Work Chart B in St st.

SIDE FACING
Purl 1 row. Work 24 rows in St st (for facing). BO all sts.

Repeat for the opposite side of the blanket.

FINISHING
To block: Lay blanket flat, steam and lightly press it using pressing cloth.
Stitch facings into place along bottom and sides of blanket. Weave in loose ends on reverse side of blanket.

Lining: Cut a piece of lining fabric slightly larger than the dimensions of blanket back not covered by the facings. Place fabric, RS out, over the area and pin in place. Working within facing borders, tuck raw edges under and slip stitch lining to back of blanket.

- ▨ Med. Blue (150 g)
- ☐ Lt. Yellow (100 g)
- ▧ Green (50 g)
- ▨ Dk. Pink (50 g)
- ☐ Off-White (50 g)
- ▨ Black (50 g)

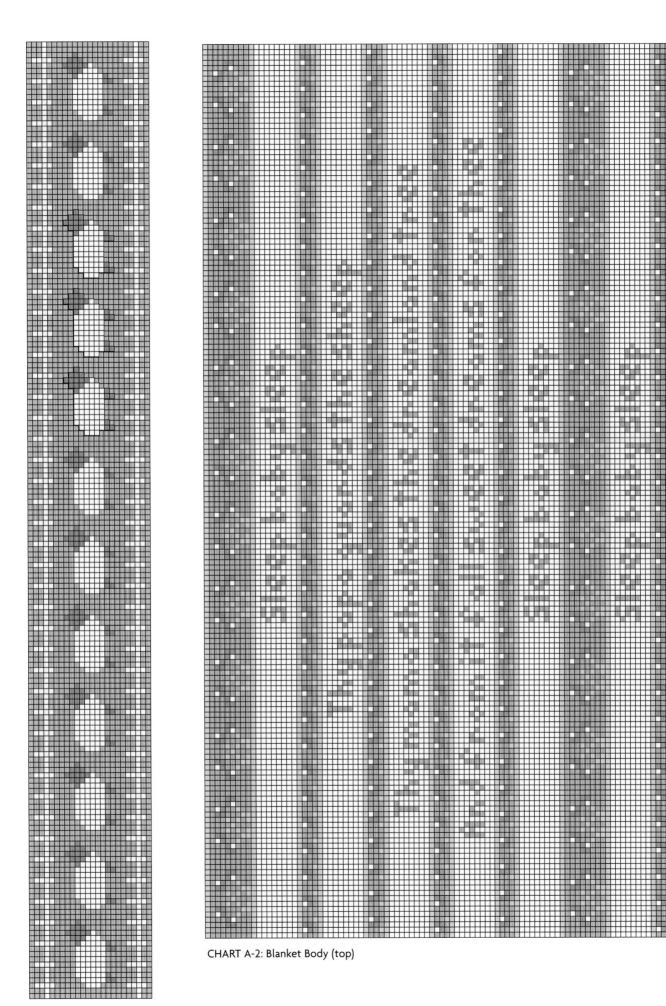

CHART B: Side Border

CHART A-2: Blanket Body (top)

CHART A-1: Blanket Body (bottom)

"Wee Willie Winkie" Blanket

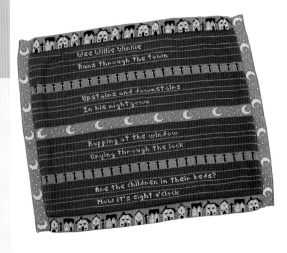

FINISHED MEASUREMENT

24 x 24" (61 x 61 cm) square

MATERIALS

Fingering or sport weight yarn

36" circular or 14" straight knitting needles, size 2 US (2.75mm)

Knitting markers

Stitch holders

Tapestry needle

Soft fabric for lining (prewashed)

GAUGE

In Stockinette stitch:

8½ stitches x 10 rows = 1" (2.5 cm) square

Blanket is knit in one piece on straight or circular needle(s), working back and forth (RS knit, WS purl).

To lengthen the blanket: Add a row or two of dk. blue above and below each row of words, and/or add Chart B moon pattern to bottom and top of blanket just inside the house border with 4 to 8 rows of dk. blue between them.

Note: If adding length to blanket, increase stitches for side borders accordingly.

BOTTOM FACING

With teal yarn, CO 186 sts; work 17 rows in St st. This forms a facing that will be hemmed inside the band.

Note: 2 extra rows compensate for difference in gauge between the solid-color facing and the multicolor band.

BODY

Purl 1 row. Work patt according to Chart A: Blanket Body (Bottom and Top). Because there are so many colors of yarn used for houses border, it is easier to cut 10" (25.5 cm) lengths of yarn for main color of each house, rather than carry them across. Black and white yarn, used for accents on all houses, should be carried across. (Refer to p. 000 for review of techniques.)

TOP FACING

When Chart A is completed, knit 1 extra row, purl 1 row, knit same number of rows for top facing as for bottom facing. BO all sts.

SIDE BORDER

With teal yarn, pu 186 sts as indicated for Chart B.

Note: If you have lengthened the blanket, pu approx 2 more sts for every 3 rows added, and adjust pattern accordingly. Chart B has a 25 st repeat.

Work Chart B in St st.

SIDE FACING

Purl 1 row. Work 15 rows in St st (for facing). BO all sts.

Repeat for the opposite side of the blanket.

FINISHING

To block: Lay blanket flat, steam and lightly press it using pressing cloth.

Stitch facings into place along bottom and sides of blanket. Weave in loose ends on reverse side of blanket.

Lining: Cut a piece of lining fabric slightly larger than the dimensions of blanket back not covered by the facings. Place fabric, RS out, over the area and pin in place. Working within facing borders, tuck raw edges under and slip stitch lining to back of blanket.

- ■ Dk. Blue (100 g)
- ▨ Teal (100 g)
- □ Lt. Yellow (50 g)
- ▤ Lt. Blue (50 g)
- ▨ Lavender (50 g)
- ▫ Aqua (50 g)
- ■ Black (50 g)

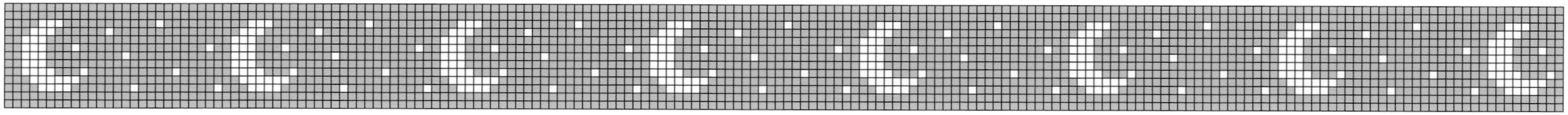

CHART B: Side Border

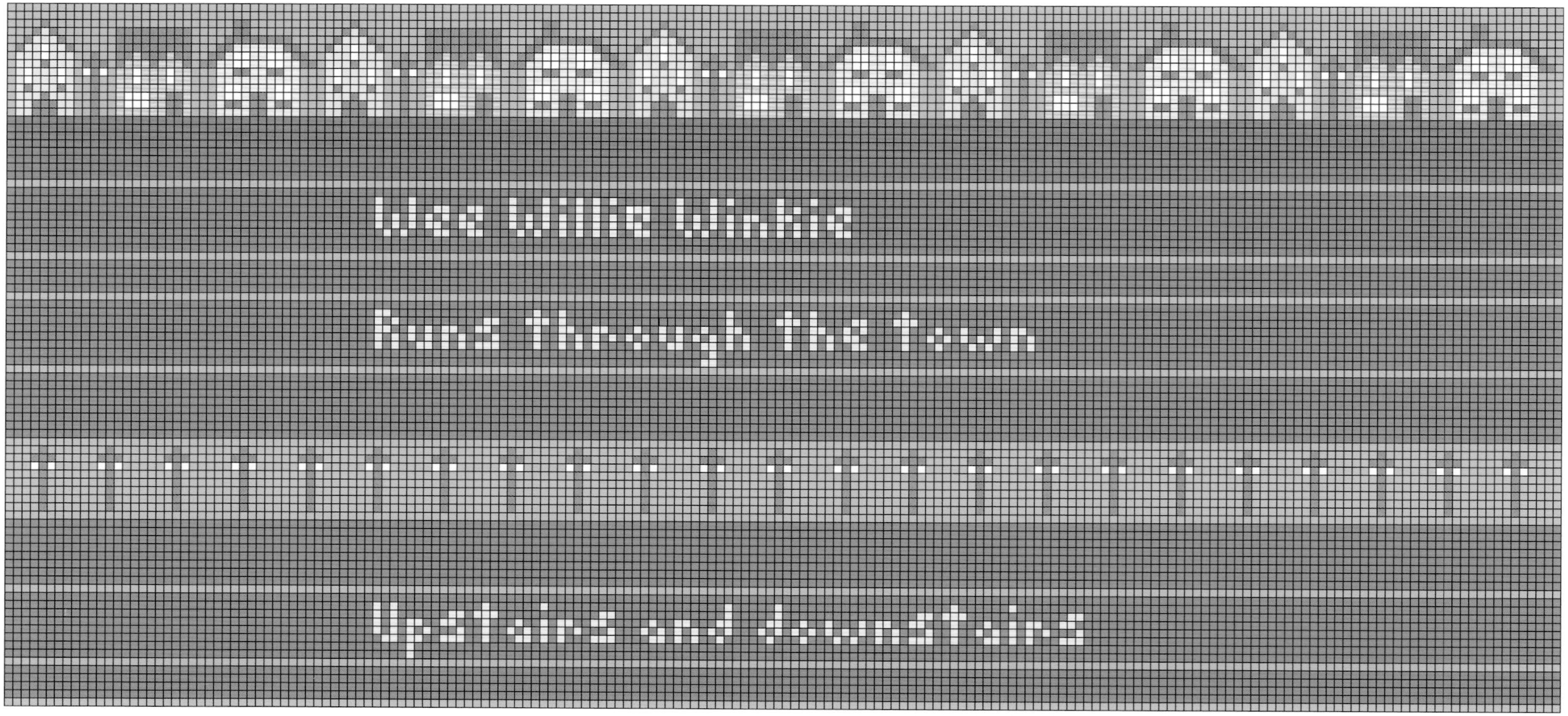

CHART A-2: Blanket Body (top)

168

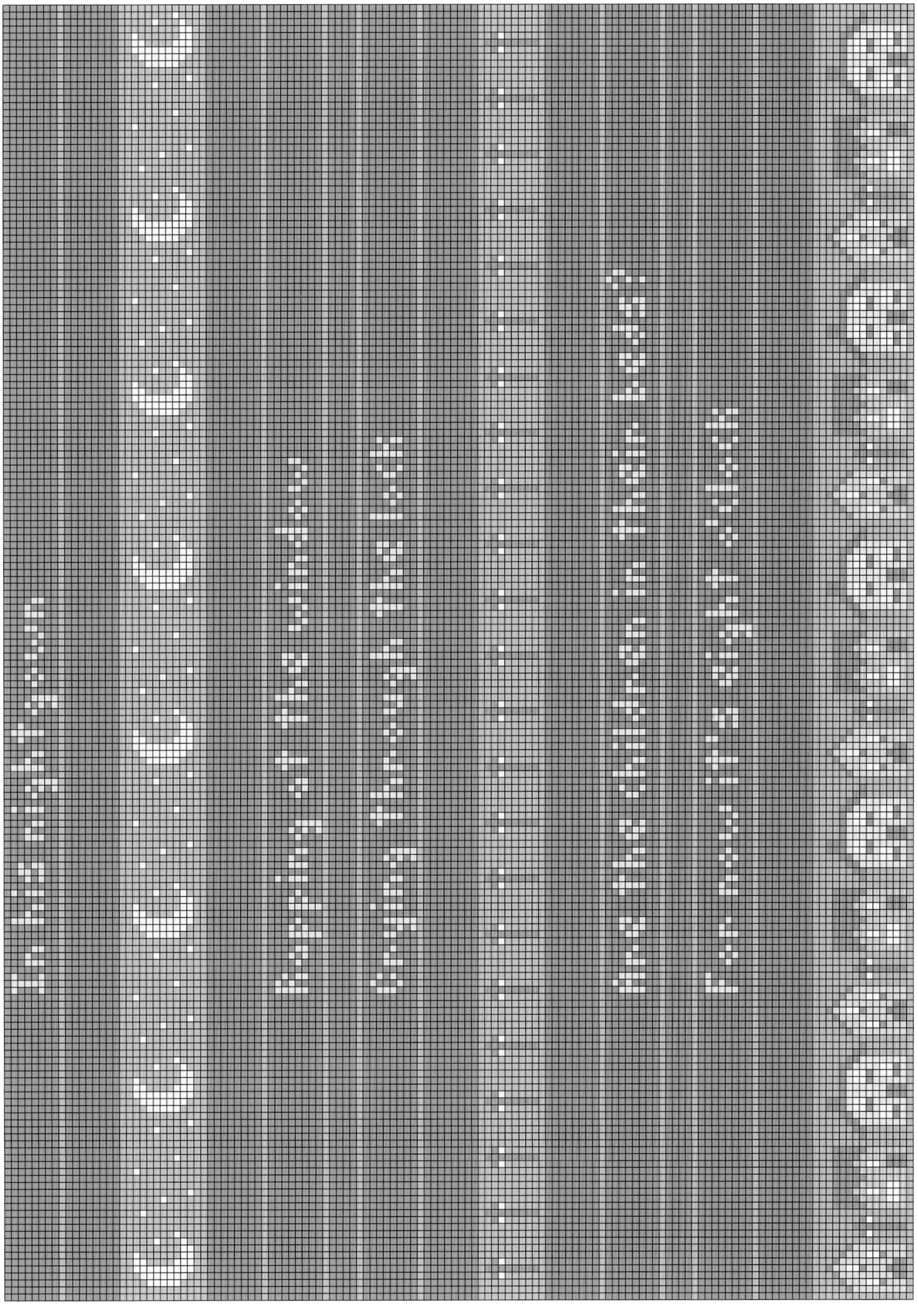

CHART A-1: Blanket Body (bottom)

Mock-Cable Crib Throw

FINISHED MEASUREMENT

35" x 38" (88.9 x 96.5 cm)

MATERIALS

Mohair type worsted weight yarn:

9 oz Color A

6 oz Color B

29" circular needle, size 11 (or size required for gauge)

2 stitch markers

GAUGE

In Garter stitch (knit every row): 12 sts = 3" (7.6 cm)

INSTRUCTIONS

With color A, CO 116 sts loosely; work 12 rows of Garter st. Cut Color A, join Color B.

Note: There are 12 sts of Garter stitch border on each side of afghan; markers are suggested after the first 8 Garter sts and before the last 8 Garter sts for ease in working pattern; slip markers on each row.

PATTERN STITCH

Row 1 (WS): k8, place marker on needle; k1, ★ p2, k2; rep from ★ across, to last 11 sts, p2, k1; place marker on needle, k8.

Row 2: k8; p1, ★ k1, yo, k1; p2; rep from ★ to last 11 sts, k1, yo, k1, p1; k8.

Row 3: k8; k1, ★ p3, k2; rep from ★ to last 12 sts, p3, k1; k8.

Row 4: k8; p1, ★ k3, pass first k st over the next 2 k sts; p2; rep from ★ to last 12 sts, k3, pass first k st over next 2 k sts, p1; k8.

Repeat Rows 1–4, 3 times more (but sl markers rather than place them as on Row 1); drop (do not cut) Color B, join Color A.

Note: For following sequence, carry color not in use loosely up the side when working the 4-row intervals; cut the inactive color before working the 16-row interval, rejoining it for the next series of 4-row stripes.

Repeating Rows 1–4 for pattern, work in following color sequence:

4 rows Color A

4 rows Color B

4 rows Color A

4 rows Color B

16 rows Color A

4 rows Color B

4 rows Color A

4 rows Color B

4 rows Color A

16 rows Color B

4 rows Color A

4 rows Color B

4 rows Color A

4 rows Color B

16 rows Color A

4 rows Color B

4 rows Color A

4 rows Color B

Cut Color B, join Color A; work 12 rows Garter st. BO loosely; weave in all loose ends.

Checkered Crib Blanket

FINISHED MEASUREMENT
32" x 36" (81.3 x 91.4 cm)

MATERIALS
Mohair type worsted weight yarn:

9 oz Color A

6 oz Color B

2 stitch markers

14" straight needles, size 11 (or size required for gauge)

GAUGE
In Seed stitch:

7 sts = 2" (5.1 cm)

9 rows = 2" (5.1 cm)

INSTRUCTIONS
With Color A, CO 113 sts loosely.

BOTTOM BORDER
Row 1: ★ k1, p1; rep from ★ across row, ending k1.

Repeat this row (Seed stitch) until border measures 2" (5.1 cm); do not cut Color A.

Note: Afghan has a 7-st Seed stitch border on each side. Markers are placed on Row 1 after the first 7 sts and before the last 7 sts for ease in following pattern. Slip markers on all following rows. Pattern is worked alternately in two rows of each color; do not cut yarn not in use; carry loosely up side of work.

PATTERN ROWS
Row 1: With Color B, (k1, p1) 3 times, k1, place a marker on right needle to indicate end of Seed stitch side border; k2, ★ with yarn in back of work, sl 1 as to purl, k2; rep from ★ to last 9 sts, k2; place a marker on right needle to indicate beginning of Seed st side border; work in Seed st across last 7 sts.

Row 2: Seed st over 7 sts; p2, ★ with yarn in front, sl 1 st as to purl, p2; rep from ★ to marker, Seed st over last 7 sts; drop Color B.

Row 3: Pick up Color A, Seed st over 7 sts; knit to last 7 sts, Seed st over last 7 sts.

Row 4: Seed st over 7 sts, purl to last 7 sts, Seed st over last 7 sts.

Repeat Rows 1–4 until piece measures about 34" (86.4 cm) from cast-on row, ending by working Row 2; cut off Color B.

TOP BORDER
Pick up Color A, rep Bottom Border Row 1 for 2" (5.1 cm); BO loosely in Seed st.

Weave in all loose ends.

Baby Fisherman Afghan

FINISHED MEASUREMENT

32" x 36" (81.3 x 91.4 cm) before fringing

MATERIALS

18 oz mohair type worsted weight yarn (2 strands of yarn held together throughout)

29" circular needle, size 15 (or size required for gauge)

8 stitch markers

GAUGE

18 sts = 7½" (19.1 cm); 8 rows = 2½" (6.4 cm)

STITCH PATTERNS

Seed Stitch Pattern: (worked over 7 sts):

(k1, p1) 3 times; k1.

Chevron Panel Pattern: (worked over 11 sts):

Patt Rows 1, 3, 5, 7: Purl (WS).

Patt Row 2: k1, yo, sl 1, k1, psso, k5, k2tog, yo, k1.

Patt Row 4: k2, yo, sl 1, k1, psso, k3, k2tog, yo, k2.

Patt Row 6: k3, yo, sl 1, k1, psso, k1, k2tog, yo, k3.

Patt Row 8: k4, yo, sl 1, k2tog, psso, yo, k4.

INSTRUCTIONS

With 2 strands of yarn CO 79 sts; do not join; work back and forth in rows.

Row 1 (WS): Work in Seed st for 7 sts, ★ place marker on right needle; p11 (Chevron Panel), place marker on right needle; work Seed st for 7 sts; rep from ★ across row.

Row 2: Seed st to marker; ★ sl marker, work Chevron Patt Row 2, sl marker, Seed st to marker; rep from ★ across row.

Row 3: rep Row 1.

Row 4: Seed st to marker; ★ sl marker, work Chevron Patt Row 4, sl marker, Seed st to marker; rep from ★ across row.

Row 5: rep Row 1.

Row 6: Seed st to marker; ★ sl marker, work Chevron Patt Row 6, sl marker, Seed st to marker; rep from ★ across row.

Row 7: rep Row 1.

Row 8: Seed st to marker; ★ sl marker, work Chevron Patt Row 8, sl marker, Seed st to marker; rep from ★ across row.

Repeat these 8 rows until afghan measures approx 36" (91.4 cm); finishing with a Row 8.

BO loosely on a Row 1.

FRINGE

Follow Single Knot Fringe Instructions on page 186. Cut strands 16" (40.6 cm) long and use two strands doubled for each knot. Tie knot through every other CO or BO stitch across each short end of afghan.

Herringbone Lace

FINISHED MEASUREMENT

41" x 53" (104.1 x 134.6 cm) before fringing

MATERIALS

21 oz worsted weight yarn

36" circular needle, size 10½ (or size required for gauge)

14 stitch markers

GAUGE

In Lace Pattern, 16 sts = 4½" (11.4 cm)

INSTRUCTIONS

CO 152 sts; do not join, work back and forth in rows. Knit 2 rows for border.

Note: For ease in establishing the Lace panels and the Garter stitch panels, placing markers on the first row of each is suggested. Slip markers as you work each following row. Markers may be removed when pattern is clearly established.

Row 1: k8, place marker; ★ k2tog, k2; yo, k5, yo; k2, sl 1 as if to knit, k1, psso; k3, place marker, k4, place marker; rep from ★ across to last 8 sts, place marker, k8.

Row 2: k8, slip marker, ★ p16, slip marker, k4; rep from ★ to last marker, k8.

Continue to slip markers on following rows.

Row 3: k8, ★ k5, k2tog, k2; yo, k1, yo, k2; sl 1, k1, psso, k2, k4; rep from ★ to last marker, k8.

Row 4: Repeat Row 2.

Row 5: k8, ★ k4, k2tog; k2, yo, k3, yo, k2; sl 1, k1, psso; k1, k4; rep from ★ to last marker, k8.

Row 6: Repeat Row 2.

Row 7: k8, ★ k3, k2tog; k2, yo, k5, yo, k2; sl 1, k1, psso; k4; rep from ★ to last marker, k8.

Row 8: Repeat Row 2.

Row 9: k8, ★ k2, k2tog, k2; yo, k1, yo, k2; sl 1, k1, psso; k5, k4; rep from ★ to last marker, k8.

Row 10: Repeat Row 2.

Row 11: k8, ★ k1, k2tog, k2; yo, k3, yo, k2; sl 1, k1, psso; k8; rep from ★ to last marker, k8.

Row 12: Repeat Row 2.

Repeat these 12 rows for pattern. Work until piece measures approx 53" (134.6 cm), ending by working Row 11. Knit 2 more rows. BO loosely in knit.

FRINGE

Follow Single Knot Fringe Instructions on page 186. Cut strands 16" (40.6 cm) long, and use 2 strands folded in half for each knot. Tie knot through each stitch across each short end of afghan.

Braid yarn from first 3 knots together loosely, knot firmly to fasten, leaving 1" ends. Continue braiding across. Trim ends.

Fisherman Cables and Lattice

FINISHED MEASUREMENT

50" x 66" (127 x 167.6 cm) before fringing

MATERIALS

64 oz of worsted weight yarn (2 strands of yarn held together throughout).
36" circular needle, size 11 (or size required for gauge)
Cable stitch holder or double-point needle

GAUGE

With 2 strands of yarn held together:
4 sts = 1" (2.5 cm)
4 rows = 1" (2.5 cm)

INSTRUCTIONS

Side Panel (make 2)

Starting at narrow edge, with 2 strands held together, CO 64 sts loosely. Do not join; work back and forth in rows.

Row 1: p2, k6, p2, place marker on needle; k44, place marker on needle; p2, k6, p2.

Row 2: k2, p6, k2, slip marker; purl to next marker, slip marker, k2, p6, k2. Always slip markers.

Row 3: p2, k6, p2; ★ skip next st; with yarn in front of left-hand point of needle, knit in front of next st but do not slip off needle, knit the skipped st, slip both sts off left-hand point of needle: Right Twist made. Skip next st, knit in back of next st, knit the skipped st, slip both sts off left-hand point of needle: Left Twist made. Repeat from ★ to next marker, p2, k6, p2.

Row 4: Repeat Row 2.

Row 5: p2, slip next 3 sts onto dpn and hold in front of work; knit next 3 sts, knit the 3 sts from dpn: Cable Twist made; p2, ★ make a Left Twist, make a Right Twist. Rep from ★ to next marker, p2, Cable Twist as before, p2.

Row 6: Repeat Row 2.

Repeat last 4 rows (Rows 3–6) for pattern. Work in pattern until length is 66" (167.6 cm), ending

by working a wrong-side row. BO loosely.

Center Panel: Starting at narrow edge, with 2 strands held together, CO 72 sts.

Row 1: p3, k6, (p4, k6) 6 times; p3.

Row 2: k3, p6, ★ k4, p6; rep from ★ to last 3 sts, k3.

Row 3: p3, sl next 3 sts onto dpn or cable needle and hold in back of work, knit next 3 sts, knit the 3 sts from dpn: Right Cable Twist made; (p4, Right Cable Twist) 6 times; p3.

Row 4: Repeat Row 2.

Row 5: p2, ★ sl next sts onto dpn and hold in back of work, knit next 3 sts, purl the st from dpn: Cable moved to the right; sl next 3 sts onto dpn and hold in front of work, purl next st, knit the 3 sts from dpn: Cable moved to the left; p2; rep from ★ across.

Row 6: k2, ★ p3, k2, rep from ★ across.

Row 7: p1, ★ move Cable to the right, p2, move Cable to left; rep from ★ to last st, p1.

Row 8: k1, p3, k4, ★ p6, k4; rep from ★ to last 4 sts, p3, k1.

Row 9: p1, k3, p4, sl next 3 sts onto dpn and hold in front of work, k next 3 sts, k3 sts from dpn: Left Cable Twist made; (p4, Left Cable Twist) 5 times; p4, k3, p1.

Row 10: Repeat Row 8.

Row 11: p1, ★ move Cable to left, p2, move Cable to right; repeat from ★ to last st, p1.

Row 12: Repeat Row 6.

Row 13: p2, move Cable to left; ★move Cable to right, p2, move Cable to left; repeat from ★ to last 6 sts, move Cable to right, p2.

Row 14: Repeat Row 2.

Repeat last 12 rows (Rows 3–14) for pattern. Work in pattern until length is same as side panel, ending by working a wrong-side row. BO loosely.

FINISHING

Pin panels out to measurements, dampen and let dry. Then sew panels together lengthwise, taking care to match rows. For fringe, follow Double Knot Fringe instructions on page 186. Cut strands each 26" (66 cm) long, and use 6 strands in each knot. On each narrow edge of afghan, for Row 1 of fringe, make a knot at corner of each end; then make 49 more knots evenly spaced along same edge. Complete fringe as per instructions.

Lacy Ripples

FINISHED MEASUREMENT

40" x 54" (101.6 x 137.2 cm) before fringing

MATERIALS

24 oz mohair type worsted weight yarn

36" circular needle, size 11 (or size required for gauge)

GAUGE

11 sts = 3½" (8.9 cm); 8 rows = 2½" (6.4 cm)

INSTRUCTIONS

CO 143 sts; do not join; work back and forth in rows.

Row 1: Knit.

Row 2: Purl.

Row 3: ★ (p2tog) twice; (inc 1, k1) 3 times [to inc, pick up bar before next st]; inc 1, (p2tog) twice; repeat from ★ across.

Row 4: Purl.

Repeat these 4 rows for pattern until afghan measures 54" (137.2 cm), ending by working row 4.

BO in p.

FRINGE

Follow Single Knot Fringe Instructions on page 186. Cut strands 16" (40.6 cm) and use one strand for each knot. Tie knot through every other stitch across each short end of afghan.

Cable Stripes

FINISHED MEASUREMENT

41" x 54" (104.1 x 137.2 cm) before fringing

MATERIALS

Mohair type worsted weight yarn:

12 oz color A for side cable stripes

6 oz color B for center cable stripe

18 oz color C for ombre stripes

14" straight needles, size 10 (or size required for gauge)

Size G aluminum crochet hook for joining panels

Cable stitch holder or double point needle

GAUGE

For ombre panel, knit in pattern:

20 sts = 3¾" (9.5 cm) wide before assembling

INSTRUCTIONS

Ombre Panel (make 4)

CO 20 sts.

Row 1: yo, k7, k2tog, k11.

Repeat Row 1 until there are 150 yo loops on each side of the panel. BO loosely.

Note: A yo loop begins every row; for ease in counting loops and assembling panels, tie a marker of contrasting yarn every 25th loop on each side of panel. Mark CO row of each panel as panel bottom.

Cable Panel: (make 2 in Color A; make 1 in Color B)

CO 41 sts.

Row 1 (cable twist row): yo, k7, k2tog, k3; sl next 4 sts onto cable needle and hold in back of work; k4, k4 sts from cable needle, k3, sl 4 sts onto cable needle and hold in back of work; k4, k4 sts from cable needle, k11.

Row 2: yo, k7, k2 tog; k2, p8, k3; p8, k11.

Row 3: yo, k7, k2 tog, k30.

Rows 4–9: rep Rows 2 and 3, 3 more times.

Row 10: rep Row 2.

Repeat Rows 1–10 until there are 150 yo loops on each side of the panel, ending by working Row 10.

BO Row: BO 7 sts; k2tog, BO the k2tog; ★ place next 4 sts on cable needle, BO 4 sts; BO 4 sts on cable needle; BO 3 sts; rep from ★ to last 11 sts, BO.

JOINING

Join panels with crochet hook, as follows: WS of Color B Cable panel facing WS of an Ombre panel (with bottom CO ends aligned); join Color B yarn with SC, working through both bottom yo loops; continue working SC to join yo loops, adjusting tension to keep work flat. Work on top of panels, finish off. Join another Ombre panel to other side of Color B cable panel in same manner. Using Color A yarn, join a Color A Cable panel to each of the joined Ombre panels in same manner. Then, using Color A yarn, join remaining Ombre panels, one to each outer edge of Color A panels. Weave in all loose ends.

FRINGE

Single Knot Fringe instructions on page 186. Cut strands 16" (40.6 cm) long in all colors. Working across each short end of afghan, knot 1 strand in each st across, matching fringe color to panel color.

Feather and Fan

FINISHED MEASUREMENT

48" x 64" (121.9 x 162.6 cm) before fringing.

MATERIALS

21 oz mohair type worsted weight yarn.

36" circular needle, size 10 (or size required for gauge)

Crochet hook for fringe

GAUGE

Each fan point = 4½" (11.4 cm) wide

INSTRUCTIONS

CO 192 sts loosely; do not join; work back and forth in rows.

Row 1: Knit.

Row 2: (k2tog) 4 times; (yo, k1) 8 times; ★ (k2tog) 8 times; (yo, k1) 8 times; rep from ★ 6 times; then (k2tog) 4 times.

Row 3: Knit.

Row 4: Purl.

Repeat these four rows for pattern; work until piece measures about 64" (162.6 cm), ending by working Row 4. BO loosely.

FRINGE

Follow Single Knot Fringe instructions on page 186. Cut strands 16" (40.6 cm) long and use 2 strands for each knot. Tie 4 knots in yos at center of fan point and 2 knots in outer corner points along short ends.

Top: Lacy Ripples; left: Cable Stripes; right: Feather and Fan

Diagonal Lace

FINISHED MEASUREMENT

46" x 58" (116.8 x 147.3 cm) before fringing

MATERIALS

Mohair type worsted weight yarn:

12 oz Color A

12 oz Color B

36" circular needle, size 11 (or size required for gauge)

GAUGE

In Stockinette stitch (knit 1 row, purl 1 row): 3 sts = 1" (2.5 cm)

INSTRUCTIONS

With Color A, CO 158 sts loosely, do not join; work back and forth in rows.

Row 1 (RS): ★ k1, p1; rep from ★ across row.

Row 2: ★ p1, k1; rep from ★ across row.

These two rows create a Seed stitch pattern.

Row 3–10: Repeat Rows 1 and 2, 4 times.

STOCKINETTE STRIPE

★★ Row 11: Knit.

Row 12: Purl.

These two rows create a Stockinette stitch pattern.

Rows 13–26, rep Rows 11 and 12.

Row 27: Knit. Fasten off Color A.

LACE PATTERN STRIPE

Join Color B.

Row 28 (WS): Purl.

Row 29: k1, ★ yo, sl 1, k1, psso, p2; rep from ★ across, ending with k1.

Row 30: k3, ★ p1, k3; rep from ★ across, ending with p1, k2.

Row 31: k1, p1; ★ yo, sl 1, k1, psso, p2; rep from ★ across, ending last repeat with p1, k1.

Row 32: k2, ★ p1, k3; repeat from ★ across.

Row 33: k1, p2; ★ yo, sl 1, k1, psso, p2; repeat from ★ across, ending with yo, sl 1, k1, psso, k1.

Row 34: k1, ★ p1, k3; repeat from ★ across, ending with k1.

Row 35: k1, p3, ★ yo, sl 1, k1, psso, p2; repeat from ★ across, ending yo, sl 1, k1, psso.

Row 36: k4, ★ p1, k3; repeat from ★ across, ending p1, k5.

Repeat Rows 28–36 twice more for Lace Pattern stripe. Fasten off Color B.★★

Repeat between ★★s 3 more times.

Join Color A. Work in St st for 17 rows.

Left: Textured Stripes; right: Diagonal Lace

Work in Seed stitch for 10 rows.
BO loosely in Seed stitch.

FRINGE

Follow Single Knot Fringe
Instructions on page 186. Cut
strands, in both colors, 16" (40.6
cm) long, and use 2 strands folded
in half for each knot. Knot
through EVERY OTHER stitch
across each short end of afghan. (9
knots for Color A panel and 10
knots for Color B panel.) Repeat
for other side.

Textured Stripes

FINISHED MEASUREMENT

40" x 54" (101.6 x 137.2 cm)

MATERIALS

Mohair type worsted weight yarn (2 strands of yarn held together
throughout).

15 oz Color A

30 oz Color B

36" circular needles, size 17 (or size required for gauge)

Two stitch markers

GAUGE

With 2 strands of yarn: 6½ sts = 2" (5.1 cm)

PATTERN STITCH

Row 1 (RS): k1, ★ with yarn in
back, sl 1 as to purl, k1; rep from ★
across, ending k1.

Row 2: k1; ★ with yarn in front, sl
1 as to purl, k1; rep from ★ across,
ending k1.

Rows 3 and 4: Knit.

These four rows comprise one
pattern.

INSTRUCTIONS

With Color B, CO 129 sts; do not
join; work back and forth in rows.

Work 5 patterns of Color B.

3 patterns of Color A

4 patterns of Color B

3 patterns of Color A

Repeat above sequence 2 more
times.

End 5 patterns of Color B.

BO loosely.

FRINGE

Follow Single Knot Fringe
Instructions on page 186. Using
Color B, cut strands 16" (40.6 cm)
long, and use 2 strands folded in
half for each knot. Tie knot
through every other stitch across
each short end of afghan.

Quick Lace

FINISHED MEASUREMENT

47" x 75" (119.4 x 190.5 cm)

MATERIALS

52 oz worsted weight yarn (2 strands are used throughout).

36" circular needle, size 15 (or size required for gauge)

GAUGE

With 2 strands of yarn held together, in St st (k1 row, p1 row):

5 sts = 2" (5.1 cm)

4 rows = 1½" (3.8 cm)

INSTRUCTIONS

Starting at narrow edge, with 2 strands held together, CO 116 sts. Do not join; work back and forth in rows.

Row 1: yo, sl 1, k2tog, psso; ★ yo, k1, yo, sl 1, k2tog, psso; rep from ★ across to within last st, yo, k1.

Note: Be careful not to drop the yo at beg of rows.

Row 2: yo, purl across: 117 sts.

Row 3: yo, k2tog; ★ yo, sl 1, k2tog, psso, yo, k1; repeat from ★ across, end with yo, sl 1, k2tog, psso: 116 sts.

Row 4: Purl.

Rows 5–36: Repeat Rows 1–4, eight times.

Row 37: Work first and last 12 sts as on Row 1, knit center 92 sts.

Row 38: yo, purl across.

Row 39: yo, k2tog; (yo, sl 1, k2tog, psso, yo, k1) twice; yo, k2tog, k to last 12 sts, work in pattern across last 12 sts.

Row 40: Purl across.

Rows 41–52: Repeat Rows 37–40, three more times.

Row 53: Work in pattern across first 12 sts, k16; work in pattern across next 60 sts, k16; work in pattern across last 12 sts.

Row 54: yo, purl across.

Row 55: Repeat Row 53.

Row 56: Purl.

Rows 57–76: Repeat Rows 53–56, five more times.

Row 77: Work in pattern across first 12 sts, k16; work in pattern across next 16 sts, k28; work in pattern across next 16 sts, k16; work in pattern across last 12 sts.

Row 78: yo, purl across.

Row 79: Repeat Row 77.

Row 80: Purl.

Rows 81–124: Repeat Rows 77–80, eleven more times.

Rows 125–148: Repeat Rows 53–76.

Rows 149–164: Repeat Rows 37–52.

Rows 165–200: Repeat Rows 1–36. BO loosely.

Horseshoe Cables

FINISHED MEASUREMENT
59" x 64" (149.9 x 162.6 cm)

MATERIALS
44 oz worsted weight yarn (2 strands of yarn are used throughout)

36" circular needle, size 15 (or size required for gauge)

Cable stitch holder or double-point needle

GAUGE
In Cellular stitch (see Pattern Row 1) with two strands of yarn:

5 sts = 2½" (6.4 cm)

13 rows = 4" (10.2 cm)

INSTRUCTIONS

With 2 strands held together, CO 120 sts. Do not join; work back and forth in rows.

Row 1 (WS): yo, sl 1, k2tog, psso; (yo, k1, yo, sl 1, k2tog, psso) 6 times; yo, k1, yo: Cellular Panel started; ★ place a marker on needle, p1, place another marker on needle, k2, p12, k2: Horseshoe Panel started; place a marker, p1, place another marker, yo, sl 1, k2tog, psso; (yo, k1, yo, sl 1, k2tog, psso) 6 times; yo, k1, yo. rep from ★ once more.

Three Cellular Panels and two Horseshoe Panels have been started.

Note: Be careful not to drop the yo at beg or end of row; each yo is worked as a st. Always slip markers.

Row 2: ★ p to next marker, sl marker, k1, sl marker, p2, k12, p2, sl marker, k1, sl marker; rep from ★ once more; p remaining sts.

Row 3: yo, k2tog; (yo, sl 1, k2tog, psso; yo, k1) 6 times; yo, sl 1, k2tog, psso; ★ p1, k2, p12, k2, p1, yo, k2 tog; (yo, sl 1, k2tog, psso, yo, k1) 6 times; yo, sl 1, k2tog, psso; rep from ★ once more.

Row 4: Repeat Row 2.

Row 5: yo, sl 1, k2tog, psso; (yo, k1, yo, sl 1, k2tog, psso) 6 times; yo, k1, yo, ★ p1, k2, p12, k2, p1, yo, sl 1, k2tog, psso; (yo, k1, yo, sl 1, k2tog, psso) 6 times; yo, k1, yo; rep from ★ once more.

Row 6: ★ p to next marker, k1, p2; sl next 3 sts onto dpn and hold in back of work; k next 3 sts, k the 3 sts from dpn, sl next 3 sts onto dpn and hold in front of work; k next 3 sts, k the 3 sts from dpn, p2, k1; rep from ★ once more, p remaining sts.

Row 7: Repeat Row 3.

Row 8: Repeat Row 2.

Row 9: Repeat Row 5.

Repeat last 8 rows (Rows 2–9) for pattern. Work in pattern until afghan measures about 59" (149.9 cm), ending with Row 9; BO.

Pin to measurements, dampen and allow to dry.

Layer Cake Afghan

FINISHED MEASUREMENT

40" x 54" (101.6 x 137.2 cm)

MATERIALS

Mohair type, worsted weight yarn:

12 oz Color A (ombre)

18 oz Color B (solid)

36" circular needle, size 10^1/$_2$ (or size required for gauge)

Two stitch markers

Safety pin

GAUGE

In Garter stitch (knit every row):

3 sts = 1" (2.5 cm)

INSTRUCTIONS

With Color A, CO 120 sts; do not join; work back and forth in rows.

Knit 12 rows (Garter stitch). Mark last row with safety pin to indicate WS of afghan. Fasten off Color A; join Color B.

Row 1: k6, place marker on right needle to set off Garter st border; k across to last 6 sts, place marker on right needle, k6.

Row 2: k6, sl marker; p across to marker, sl marker, k6.

Note: Slip markers on every row following; this will not be mentioned again.

Row 3 (RS): k6, purl to last 6 sts, k6.

Row 4: k6; ★ k1; (k1, p1, k1) all in next st; rep from ★ across to last 6 sts, k6.

Row 5: k6; ★ k3, p1; rep from ★ across to last 6 sts, k6.

Row 6: k6; ★ k1, p3 tog; rep from ★ across to last 6 sts, k6.

Row 7: k6; purl to last 6 sts, k6.

Row 8: k6; ★(k1, p1, k1) all in next st, k1; rep from ★ to last 6 sts, k6.

Row 9: k6; ★ p1, k3; rep from ★ across to last 6 sts, k6.

Row 10: k6; ★ p3 tog, k1; rep from ★ across to last 6 sts, k6.

Rows 11–14: rep Rows 3–6, ending on RS.

★★ rep rows 3–14 one more time; rep Rows 3–10 once (total: 30 rows of Color B). Fasten off Color B.

Join Color A, work in Garter st for 11 rows, ending on WS. Fasten off Color A.

Join Color B, rep Rows 3–14 twice; rep Rows 3–10 once. Fasten off Color B.

Join Color A, work in Garter st for 11 rows, ending on WS.★★ Fasten off Color A.

Left: Layer Cake Afghan; right: Bright Waves

Join Color B, rep Rows 3–10, twice. Fasten off Color B.

Join Color A, work in Garter st for 11 rows, ending on WS. Fasten off Color A.

Join Color B, rep from ★★ to ★★ once; k one more row; BO loosely.

Bright Waves

FINISHED MEASUREMENT

48" x 54" (121.9 x 137.2 cm) before fringing

MATERIALS

18 oz mohair type worsted weight yarn, ombre or solid

36" circular needle, size 10½ (or size required for gauge)

GAUGE

In pattern (Rows 1–8):

21 sts = 7" (17.8 cm)

8 rows = 3" (7.6 cm)

INSTRUCTIONS

CO 143 sts; do not join; work back and forth in rows.

Row 1: Knit.

Row 2: Knit.

Row 3: k3, ★ wind yarn twice around needle (abbreviated: y2rn); k1, y2rn; k1, y2rn; k5; repeat from ★ to end.

Row 4: k1, ★ k4; (drop yarn wound around needle, k1) 3 times; repeat from ★ to last 2 sts, k2.

Row 5: Knit.

Row 6: Knit.

Row 7: k1, y2rn; ★ k5, y2rn; k1, y2rn; k1, y2rn; repeat from ★ to last 2 sts, k2.

Row 8: k2; ★ (drop yarn wound around needle, k1) 3 times, k4; repeat from ★ to last st. drop yarn wound around needle, k1.

Repeat these 8 rows for pattern until afghan measures approx 54" (137.2 cm), ending with a Row 2. BO loosely.

FRINGE

Follow Single Knot Fringe Instructions on page 186. Cut strands 16" (40.6 cm) long, and use 2 strands doubled for each knot. Tie knot in every other stitch at the short ends of afghan.

Sampler Stripes

FINISHED MEASUREMENT
46" x 64" (116.8 x 162.6 cm)

MATERIALS
Worsted weight yarn, 12 oz each of:

Color A

Color B

Color C

Color D

36" circular needle, size 10 (or size required for gauge)

10" size 10 straight needles (or size required for gauge)

2 small stitch holders (or large safety pins)

GAUGE
In Stockinette stitch:

4 sts = 1" (2.5 cm)

6 rows = 1" (2.5 cm)

INSTRUCTIONS
With circular needle and Color A, CO 208 sts loosely; do not join, work back and forth in rows. Knit 18 rows in Garter stitch (k every row); fasten off Color A. Place first 8 sts and last 8 sts on stitch holders to be worked later for borders.

First Pattern Stripe
Join Color B.

Row 1: ★ p1, k15; repeat from ★ across.

Row 2: ★ p14, k2; repeat from ★ across.

Note: Hereafter always repeat from ★ across row.

Row 3: ★ p3, k13.

Row 4: ★ p12, k4.

Row 5: ★ p5, k11.

Row 6: ★ p10, k6.

Row 7: ★ p7, k9.

Row 8: ★ p8, k8.

Row 9: ★ p9, k7.

Row 10: ★ p6, k10.

Row 11: ★ p11, k5.

Row 12: ★ p4, k12.

Row 13: ★ p13, k3.

Row 14: ★ p2, k14.

Row 15: ★ p15, k1.

Row 16: Purl across; fasten off Color B.

Second Pattern Stripe
Join Color C.

Row 1: Knit.

Rows 2–8: ★ k8, p8.

Rows 9–16: ★ p8, k8.

Rows 17–24: ★ k8, p8; fasten off Color C.

Third Pattern Stripe
Join Color D.

Row 1: Knit.

Row 2: k2, ★ p12, k4; end k2.

Row 3: p2, ★ k12, p4; end p2.

Row 4: p1, ★ k2, p10; k2, p2; end p1.

Row 5: k1, ★ p2, k10; p2, k2; end k1.

Row 6: p2, ★ k2, p8; k2, p4; end p2.

Row 7: k2, ★ p2, k8, p2, k4; end k2.

Row 8: p3, ★ k2, p6; end p3.

Row 9: k3, ★ p2, k6; end k3.

Row 10: p4, ★ k2, p4, k2, p8; end p4.

Row 11: k4, ★ p2, k4, p2, k8; end k4.

Row 12: p5, ★ k2, p2, k2, p10; end p5.

Row 13: k5, ★ p2, k2, p2, k10; end k5.

Row 14: p6, ★ k4, p12; end p6.

Row 15: k6, ★ p4, k12; end k6.

Row 16: rep Row 14.

Rows 17–29: Work back from Row 13 through Row 1 to complete the Diamond Pattern; fasten off Color D.

Fourth Pattern Stripe

Join Color A; Purl one row.

Rows 1–4: ★ k4, p4.

Rows 5–8: ★ p4, k4.

Rows 9–32: rep Rows 1–8 three times; fasten off Color A.

Fifth Pattern Stripe

Join Color B.

Row 1: Knit.

Row 2: ★ k2, p6.

Row 3: ★ k6, p2.

Row 4: p1, ★ k2, p6; end p5.

Row 5: k5, ★ p2, k6; end k1.

Row 6: p2, ★ p2, p6; end p4.

Row 7: k4, ★ p2, k6; end k2.

Row 8: p3, ★ k2, p6; end p3.

Row 9: k3, ★ p2, k6; end k3.

Row 10: p4, ★ k2, p6; end p2.

Row 11: k2, ★ p2, k6; end k4.

Row 12: p5, ★ k2, p6; end p1.

Row 13: k1, ★ p2, k6; end k5.

Row 14: ★ p6, k2.

Row 15: ★ p2, k6.

Row 16: k1, ★ p6, k2; end k1.

Row 17: p1, ★ k6, p2; end p1.

Rows 18–31: rep Rows 2–15; fasten off Color B.

Sixth Pattern Stripe

Join Color C.

Row 1: Purl.

Row 2: K2, ★ P8, K4; end K2.

Row 3: P2, ★ K8, P4; end P2.

Rows 4–9: Repeat Rows 2 and 3 alternately.

Row 10: Knit.

Row 11: Purl.

Row 12: P4, ★ K4, P8; end P4.

Row 13: K4, ★ P4, K8; end K4.

Rows 14–19: Repeat Rows 12 and 13 alternately.

Row 20: Knit.

Rows 21–40: Repeat Rows 1–20; fasten off Color C.

Seventh Pattern Stripe

Join Color D.

Row 1: Purl.

Row 2: p11, ★ k2, p22; end k2, p11.

Row 3: k11, ★ p2, k22; end p2, k11.

Row 4: p10, ★ k4, p20; end k4, p10.

Row 5: k10, ★ p4, k20; end p4, k10.

Row 6: p9, ★ k6, p18; end k6, p9.

Row 7: k9, ★ p6, k18; end p6, k9.

Row 8: p8, ★ k8, p16; end k8, p8.

Row 9: k8, ★ p8, k16; end p8, k8.

Row 10: p7, ★ k10, p14; end k10, p7.

Row 11: k7, ★ p10, k14; end p10, k7.

Row 12: p6, ★ k12, p12; end k12, p6.

Row 13: k6, ★ p12, k12; end p12, k6.

Row 14: p5, ★ k14, p10; end k14, p5.

Row 15: k5, ★ p14, k10; end p14, k5.

Row 16: p4, ★ k16, p8; end k16, p4.

Row 17: k4, ★ p16, k8; end p16, k4.

Row 18: p3, ★ k18, p6; end k18, p3.

Row 19: k3, ★ p18, k6; end p18, k3.

Row 20: p2, ★ k20, p4; end k20, p2.

Row 21: k2, ★ p20, k4; end p20, k2.

Row 22: p1, ★ k22, p2; end k22, p1.

Row 23: k1, ★ p22, k2; end p22, k1.

Row 24: rep Row 22.

Rows 25–44: Work back from Row 21 through Row 2 to complete Diamond Patterns; fasten off Color D.

Eighth through Thirteenth Pattern Stripes

Join Color C, work Sixth Pattern Stripe (Rows 1–39); fasten off Color C.

Join Color B, work Fifth Pattern Stripe; fasten off Color B.

Join Color A, work Fourth Pattern Stripe; fasten off Color A.

Join Color D, work Third Pattern Stripe (Rows 1–28); fasten off Color D.

Join Color C, work Second Pattern Stripe; fasten off Color C.

Join Color B, work First Pattern Stripe; fasten off Color B. Leave sts on needle to be worked for border.

Left Border

Move 8 border sts from holder to a straight needle, attach Color A. Work in garter stitch until border measures same length as center section, ending at inner edge. Break off Color A. Place sts on stitch holder.

Right Border

Work as for Left Border, ending at outer edge. Do not break off Color A.

Top Border

With Color A of Right Border, k across sts of Right Border, pick up sts of center Pattern Stripes and Left Border. Work in Garter st for 17 rows. BO loosely.

Sew inner edges of Right and Left Border in place.

Fringing

BASIC INSTRUCTIONS

Cut a piece of cardboard about 6"
(15.2 cm) wide and half as long as
specified in instructions for strands
plus ½" (1.3 cm) for trimming
allowance. Wind yarn loosely and
evenly lengthwise around cardboard. When card is filled, cut yarn
across one end. Do this several
times, then begin fringing; you can
wind additional strands as you need
them.

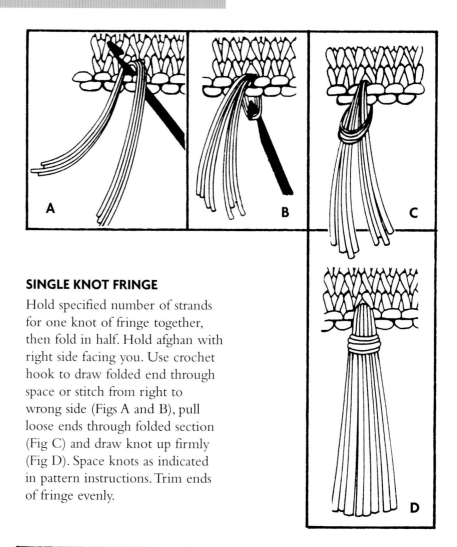

SINGLE KNOT FRINGE

Hold specified number of strands
for one knot of fringe together,
then fold in half. Hold afghan with
right side facing you. Use crochet
hook to draw folded end through
space or stitch from right to
wrong side (Figs A and B), pull
loose ends through folded section
(Fig C) and draw knot up firmly
(Fig D). Space knots as indicated
in pattern instructions. Trim ends
of fringe evenly.

DOUBLE KNOT FRINGE

Begin by working Single Knot
Fringe completely across one end
of afghan. With right side facing
you and working from left to
right, take half the strands of one
knot and half the strands in the
knot next to it, and knot them
together (Fig E).

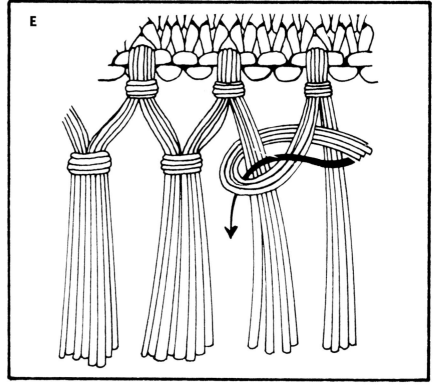

INDEX

Credits and Rights Information

(continued from p. 4)

The publishers of *The Pattern Companion: Knitting* gratefully acknowledges permission for the use of material designated below from the following previously published works: